THE RISE OF
MODERN YIDDISH
CULTURE

PITT SERIES IN RUSSIAN
AND EAST EUROPEAN STUDIES

Jonathan Harris, Editor

THE RISE OF
MODERN
YIDDISH
CULTURE

David E. Fishman

UNIVERSITY OF PITTSBURGH PRESS

Published by the University of Pittsburgh Press, Pittsburgh, PA 15260

Copyright © 2005, University of Pittsburgh Press

Manufactured in the United States of America

Printed on acid-free paper

10 9 8 7 6 5 4 3 2 1

Library of Congress Cataloging-in-Publication Data

Fishman, David E., 1957—

   The rise of modern Yiddish culture / David E. Fishman.

      p. cm.— (Pitt series in Russian and East European studies)

   Includes bibliographical references and index.

   ISBN 0-8229-4272 -0 (hardcover : alk. paper)

   1. Yiddish language—Europe, Eastern—History— 19th century.   2. Yiddish language—

Europe, Eastern—History—20th century.   3. Yiddish language—Social aspects—Europe,

Eastern.   4. Yiddish language—Political aspects—Europe, Eastern.   5. Jews—Europe,

Eastern—Intellectual life.   6. Jews—Europe, Eastern—Politics and government.

7. Yiddishists—Europe, Eastern.   I. Title.   II. Series.

   PJ5 113.F562005

   439'.10947'09034—dc22

                                                                   2005013314

Contents

Preface

This book examines the development of Yiddish culture in its east European context. It is an attempt to view Yiddish culture historically, that is, to connect its development to social and political conditions and to broader intellectual currents among east European Jews. It also evaluates the position of Yiddish in east European Jewish culture as a whole, which was, from the second half of the nineteenth century on, trilingual—written, performed, and lived in Hebrew, Yiddish, and either Russian or Polish.

While modern Yiddish literature has received extensive scholarly attention, this book's point of departure is the view that Yiddish culture did not consist of poetry and artistic prose alone, but embraced all forms of writing, including political and philosophic discourse, journalism, and scholarship. It also examines the institutional infrastructure that modern Yiddish culture, like all modern cultures, developed in order to sustain itself and flourish: the daily and periodical press, publishing houses, libraries, theaters, literary and cultural associations, schools and academies. It pays special attention to the relationship between Yiddish culture and the Jewish national and social movements in east European Jewry, including Zionism and Bundism, and the "language question" that arose in the Russian Jewish intelligentsia at the turn of the century.

In considering the rise of modern Yiddish culture, this book gives sociology priority over ideology. Many scholars have presented the changing attitude toward Yiddish among the Jewish literary and intellectual elite as the paramount development leading to the rise of Yiddish. I consider the shifts in ideas and attitudes on Yiddish to be one factor among many. The dramatic emergence of a new, large Yiddish readership, with new intellectual needs and expectations, was no less important a factor. The new readership/audience was itself an impetus for the intelligentsia to reevaluate its attitude toward Yiddish.

Many have assumed that modern Yiddish culture was proletarian based and Socialist oriented. This view is challenged in several chapters. The rise of Yiddish cut across socioeconomic classes, and much of the Jewish middle class (especially those who would be classified by Marxists as petit bourgeois) actively partook of Yiddish books, newspapers, theater performances, and concerts. Yiddish became a major vehicle for Zionist journalism. And, to complicate matters even further, the commitment of the Jewish Workers' Bund to Yiddish emerged gradually, and its relationship toward modern Yiddish literature was complexly ambivalent.

The rise of Yiddish culture was not a smooth social process but one that was highly contested and debated by the Jewish intelligentsia. Contempt for Yiddish as a jargon or corrupted German was as old as the Haskalah (Jewish enlightenment) movement. What was new at the turn of the twentieth century was the emergence of a pro-Yiddish intelligentsia, which embraced the language, its literature, and its culture as values. Several chapters explore the varieties of this pro-Yiddish orientation, and the Yiddishist movement, in eastern Europe.

Yiddishism was predicated on certain Jewish nationalist and populist ideas: the Jews needed to preserve their linguistic distinctiveness as part of their struggle for national survival in the diaspora. On the other hand, the linguistic chasm that had separated the Jewish intelligentsia from the Jewish masses needed to be eliminated. The intelligentsia needed to draw near to the masses and learn from the latter's accumulated wisdom, as embodied in their language and folklore. This common core of Yiddishism was embraced by a large part of the Jewish intelligentsia from 1905 on: Bundists, non-Bundist socialists, socialist Zionists, liberal Diaspora Nationalists, and even a few general Zionists.

Whether the rise of Yiddish signaled a radical shift in the content and direction of Jewish culture was a subject of debate among Yiddishists. For Chaim Zhitlovsky, the rise of Yiddish and anticipated decline of Hebrew marked a shift from a religious-dominated culture to a thoroughly secular and European one. Language would be the glue of Jewish group cohesiveness, not content. Modern Yiddish culture did not need to have particularly Jewish content, any more than French culture needed to be uniquely French, let alone Catholic, in its content. But for I. L. Peretz, it was imperative that the new Yiddish culture inherit the riches of the old, Jewish religious culture, from the Bible through Hasidic thought, which had been created primarily in Hebrew, and that modern Yiddish culture perpetuate its spirit. For Peretz, Yiddish could only legitimately claim to be a Jewish national language once all great Jewish cultural treasures, such as the Bible and Midrash, would be available in it. Modern Yiddish culture arose in tension between the positions of Zhitlovsky and Peretz.

The tension is best illustrated in the curricula and textbooks of modern Yiddish schools. While it is commonly assumed that Yiddish schools were staunchly secularist, much traditional Jewish content was integrated into Yiddish schools under new, transformed rubrics. Bible could be recast as ancient Jewish history, Midrash and Agadah could be considered folk literature, the holidays and their rituals were national customs, Hasidic tales were folklore. Even the Vilna Gaon, an ascetic and elitist and an arch opponent of Hasidism, could be appropriated by some Yiddishists as a folk hero. Furthermore, Yiddish literature could itself be used as a source to teach children about the Sabbath and holidays. Thus the break between traditional Judaism and secular Yiddish nationalism was far from total and was often less dramatic in practice than in theory.

One of Yiddishism's most daunting tasks was the creation of an intelligentsia, which would speak Yiddish at home and in its own circles and would satisfy its cultural needs and aspirations not in Russian or Polish but in the language of the Jewish masses. The pinnacle of this effort was the establishment of the Yiddish Scientific Institute, YIVO, in Vilna in 1925, as an institution dedicated to historical, philological, and sociological scholarship in Yiddish.

This book is divided into two sections, on tsarist Russia and on Poland between the wars. Each section begins with an overview essay on Yiddish culture in the period under consideration, laying out general trends and placing the chapters that follow in their context. The concluding chapter tells the dramatic story of the fate of YIVO's library and archive, and other Judaic collections in Vilna, during the years of

annihilation and postwar Soviet rule. The efforts of Abraham Sutzkever, Shmerke Kaczerginski, and others to rescue Jewish books and
papers from destruction and oblivion are an inspiring model of Jews'
commitment to preserve the east European Jewish cultural heritage
for posterity. This book is a much more mundane attempt to do the
same. Several of the chapters were originally published as articles and
have been substantively revised and expanded.

I thank the following libraries and institutions for their assistance
and support of my research: first of all my home institution, the Jewish
Theological Seminary of America, whose chancellor, Ismar Schorsch,
has always shown a sincere and intense interest in my work; the YIVO
Institute for Jewish Research, where I was a research fellow for many
years; the Institute for Advanced Studies of the Hebrew University in
Jerusalem and the Center for Advanced Judaic Studies at the University of Pennsylvania, where I spent fruitful time as a visiting fellow;
and the National Library of Lithuania, where the head of the Judaica
Department, Esfir Bramson, provided access to some rare periodicals.
Work on the manuscript was concluded in Jerusalem, thanks to a fellowship from the Lady Davis Fellowship Trust.

PART I

TSARIST
RUSSIA

1

THE RISE OF
MODERN YIDDISH CULTURE

AN OVERVIEW

The use of Yiddish has been a feature of Ashkenazic Jewish life for approximately a millennium. The first known Yiddish sentence, written in Hebrew letters and containing both Germanic and Hebraic words, is found in a manuscript holiday prayer book from 1272; the first known literary document in Yiddish, a codex consisting of seven narrative poems, was composed in 1382; and the first known printed Yiddish book, a Hebrew-Yiddish dictionary of biblical terms, was issued in 1534. During the sixteenth and seventeenth centuries, numerous belletristic, homiletical, moralistic, and ritual works were published in Yiddish, and this period was the heyday of what is now referred to as Old Yiddish literature. The most popular book of all was Jacob ben Isaac Ashkenazi's *Tse'enah u-re'enah*, a collection of rabbinic homilies and exegesis on the Pentateuch, first issued in the 1590s, which went through 175 editions by 1900.

Despite this millennial history, one can speak of a new, modern Yiddish culture that began to arise in the 1860s and continued its upward trajectory for the next half century, until the outbreak of the First World War, and, in many respects (but not all), during the interwar period as well. The new culture bore the imprint of European modes of expression and of secular thinking. The processes involved in its ascendancy were numerous and intertwined.[1]

TRADITIONAL AND HASKALAH LEGACIES

Before the appearance of the Haskalah (the Jewish enlightenment), in the late eighteenth century, Yiddish occupied a legitimate, but clearly subordinate, position vis-à-vis Hebrew in the culture of Ashkenazic Jews. While Yiddish was the language of everyday speech, the most culturally valued activities in the eyes of nearly all Jews were conducted in Hebrew—communal prayer in the synagogue, the reading of the Torah scroll, and the performance of the religious rituals. The revered texts of the Jewish tradition, whose study was considered a religious commandment—the Torah, the Talmud, and the medieval commentaries of Rashi and the Tosafists—were in Hebrew and Aramaic, and mastery of those texts in the original bestowed upon their student a high social status. Yiddish translations and explications of the prayer book, Bible, and the narrative parts of the Talmud abounded, but they were by definition intended for those Jews who could not achieve the desired cultural ideal of studying the originals.

After the introduction of Hebrew printing in central and eastern Europe in the early sixteenth century, printed Yiddish literature grew consistently, both in the number of imprints and in the range of genres, paralleling the rise of vernacular literatures throughout Europe. By the mid-eighteenth century, the Yiddish literature available throughout the Ashkenazic Diaspora, from Holland in the west to Lithuania and Ukraine in the east, included original storybooks *(mayse bikhlekh)*, narrative poems, historical chronicles, moralistic treatises, homiletical works on the Torah, ritual manuals, and collections of nonobligatory prayers for women *(tkhines)*. The readership of Yiddish books certainly included, by then, not only women and unlettered men but also men who were fully literate in Hebrew, who satisfied some of their reading interests in Yiddish. Nonetheless, the most socially valued and respected types of Jewish literature were still produced exclusively in Hebrew and never in Yiddish: rabbinic literature (legal responsa, commentaries on the Talmud and on subsequent codes), as well as theological and kabbalistic literature.

This situation changed only slightly with the rise of the Hasidic movement in the second half of the eighteenth century. Storytelling occupied an important position in Hasidic culture, and collections of Hasidic tales, which were told in praise of the movement's masters, or told by the masters themselves, and which appeared in Yiddish (or in both Hebrew and Yiddish), were considered holy books by the movement's adherents. But these books were never viewed as equal in sanctity to the homiletical and theological works by the Hasidic masters (called rebbes) that were written in Hebrew. Similarly, a few Hasidic rebbes composed original religious songs and prayers in Yiddish, but the focal point of the Hasidic communities' religious life remained their enraptured prayer in Hebrew. In short, Yiddish existed for many centuries in Hebrew's shadow: always present but always in a secondary role—as seen from the perspective of the community's own value system.[2]

This Hebrew-Yiddish symbiosis was shattered by the Haskalah, inaugurated by the German Jewish philosopher Moses Mendelssohn (1729–1786), which was the dominant ideological trend among modernized Jews in eastern Europe for most of the nineteenth century. For the Haskalah, the adoption of modernity (reason/science, moderate secularization, European culture, education, and habits) went hand in hand with the rejection and dismissal of Yiddish, which was derided as a corrupt German Jewish jargon *(zhargon)*. In place of the traditional Hebrew-Yiddish bilingualism, the Maskilim (adherents of the Haskalah) championed a new Hebrew-German, or Hebrew-Russian, bilingualism. Thus, the Maskilim in imperial Russia spoke among themselves in German during the first half of the nineteenth century and, from the 1850s on, in Russian. They wrote the vast majority of their works in Hebrew—poetry, prose, biblical studies, historical scholarship, philosophy, popular science, and so on—and, from the 1860s on, they and other modernized Jews wrote increasingly in Russian. The Jewish schools established by the Maskilim, which featured a broad secular curriculum, used German, and from the 1850s on, Russian, as the language of instruction, with Hebrew language and the Bible in the original as subjects in the curriculum. In their modernized synagogues, the prayers were in Hebrew, but the sermons were delivered in German, and later on in Russian.

Many Maskilim dabbled in Yiddish writing, but it was not their primary medium. As a rule, they did not publish these pieces, which either languished in the authors' desk drawers or circulated in limited copies in manuscript—a sign that they did not ascribe importance to their Yiddish writings and may have been embarrassed by them. The only Maskilic author to devote himself mainly to Yiddish writing in the 1840s and 1850s, Isaac Meir Dik, was held in very low regard by his fellow Maskilim, as a scribbler and dilettante. In all, the Haskalah created a modern Jewish subculture of literature, schools, synagogues, and salons in which Yiddish was cast aside to the margins. The Haskalah's negative attitude toward Yiddish as a *zhargon* became the norm among Jews who considered themselves modern and enlightened.[5]

The Russian Maskilim did not succeed in effecting the radical linguistic transformation of east European Jewry at large that they themselves pursued. As late as 1897, 97 percent of the 5.3 million Jews in the Russian Empire claimed Yiddish as their mother tongue, and only 26 percent of them claimed to be literate in Russian. In no other country in Europe was Jewish linguistic acculturation so modest. The persistence of Yiddish was a consequence of Russian Jewry's basic social features: its size (in 1897, more than five times the size of any other European Jewry); its compact concentration in the cities and towns of the western provinces designated as the Jewish Pale of Settlement, where Jews constituted 36.9 percent of the total urban population; the Jews' separate legal status and the tight restrictions on their obtaining a Russian higher education and government employment; and the climate of growing national consciousness, national tensions, and anti-Semitism in Russia and Russian Poland, which reinforced Jewish social cohesion. Full linguistic Russification (with the dropping of Yiddish) was the exception rather than the rule among Russian Jews and could be found mainly in communities outside the Pale of Settlement, such as St. Petersburg, or among exceptional groups, such as Jewish university students.[4]

THE BEGINNINGS OF YIDDISH PRESS AND THEATER

The first modern Yiddish cultural institution in Russia was the periodical press, which came into being, alongside the Hebrew and Russian Jewish press, during the 1860s, the era of the great reforms of Tsar Alexander II. The first modern Yiddish newspaper, the weekly *Kol Mevaser* (Hebrew for "The Heralding Voice"), was established in 1862 by the Maskil Alexander Zederbaum. Since the modern newspaper was itself an institution that migrated from European and Russian culture to Jewish culture, it comes as no surprise that the founder and editor of *Kol Mevaser* was a Maskil, someone who advocated the Jews' modernization.

Many of the characteristics of *Kol Mevaser,* which was published in Odessa between 1862 and 1873, would become mainstays of the Yiddish press. Each issue opened with a news section consisting of a mix of world news, items about Jewish communities across the globe, Russian news, and governmental decrees from St. Petersburg. The section exposed Yiddish readers in the Pale of Settlement to the goings-on in the wide world beyond their immediate horizons. But news actually occupied a minority of the weekly's space. Most of its pages were taken up with biographies of famous Russian, European, and Jewish historical figures; articles on science, technology, medicine, and health; and Maskilic feuilletons with social criticism of Russian Jewry for its ignorance, superstition, and backwardness.

Two types of nonnews material stood out in *Kol Mevaser.* First, it published Yiddish stories and the first Yiddish novels in serialization. S. J. Abramovitch, better known by his pen name, Mendele Moykher Seforim, and by the title of grandfather of Yiddish literature, published his first Yiddish novel, *Dos kleyne mentshele* (The little man), in *Kol Mevaser.* Abraham Goldfaden, the father of Yiddish theater, published poems in *Kol Mevaser.* The close association between the press and literature would become a basic feature of modern Yiddish culture. The press gave an impetus to the spread of Yiddish literature and provided a measure of financial security for writers. But it also created limitations on the kinds of works that could be published, given that Yiddish newspapers were directed at a broad general readership.

The second type of nonnews material published in *Kol Mevaser* was reports on Jewish life in the cities and towns of the Pale of Settlement, sent in not by professional journalists or regular correspondents but by local inhabitants, unsolicited and free of charge. These reports often

took the form of exposés or simple gossip about Jewish communal
conflicts and the shortcomings of local institutions and leaders. The
material transformed *Kol Mevaser* (and subsequent newspapers) into
a folk institution, where the boundary between reader and writer was
porous—and sometimes nonexistent. Popular participation in the Yiddish press (far beyond the confines of a letters to the editor column)
created an informal and familial atmosphere in its pages.

In *Kol Mevaser*, as in many later Yiddish newspapers, the voice of
the editor was ubiquitous and his role domineering. Zederbaum did
not merely compose much of the newspaper himself. He frequently
penned responses to the feuilletons and reports he published by others; he freely edited his contributors' language and content, including
the belle lettres submitted by writers such as Mendele Moykher Seforim; and he used the newspaper as a forum to settle personal accounts.

While Zederbaum's attitude toward Yiddish was ambivalent at best
—he urged the readers of *Kol Mevaser* to give their children a Russian
education—the newspaper he founded thrust Yiddish writing into the
modern world. It provided the opportunity for a significant Maskil,
Abramovitsh, to launch his career as a Yiddish novelist. The paper also
helped create a modern Yiddish style, as it vacillated between the me-
andering loquaciousness of a traditional storyteller and the highfalutin
German of a Maskil, to present the problems of the modern world in
Yiddish.

Zederbaum maintained the basic features of *Kol Mevaser* in his
subsequent weekly newspaper, *Yidishes Folksblat* (Jewish People's Paper; St. Petersburg, 1881–1890), where the most famous Yiddish writer
of all, Sholem Rabinovitch, better known by his pen name, Sholem Aleichem, debuted in 1883. The only shift was in the newspaper's editorial orientation. Whereas *Kol Mevaser* was enthusiastically patriotic
and supportive of the regime of Alexander II, *Yidishes Folksblat*, published after the pogroms of 1881–1882, was reserved in its treatment of
Russian affairs, while devoting considerable attention to the new Jewish colonies in Palestine.[5]

The second institution of modern Yiddish culture to arise, Yiddish
theater, was, like the press, established by westernized Jews who were

proponents of Haskalah ideas. Its forerunners, Wolf Ehrenkrantz (popularly known as Velvl Zbarzher) and Berl Broder, performed Yiddish songs and rhymes in taverns and wine cellars across Besarabia, Galicia, and Romania during the 1850s and 1860s. They drew upon Yiddish folk songs and poems by traditional Jewish wedding bards, to which they added their own material. Many of Zbarzher's songs were humorous spoofs on Hasidic beliefs and practices. Broder went several artistic steps further by dressing up in costume and performing monologue character songs and later by enlisting a group of singers ("the Broder singers") to perform musical dialogues and skits along with him. The Broder singers reached the peak of their success in the 1870s, when they performed in the Jewish metropolis of Odessa (Jewish population in 1897: 138,915) to audiences sipping wine and eating knishes. A secular Yiddish leisure culture was in the making.

The bona fide father of the Yiddish theater was Abraham Goldfaden (1840–1907). Goldfaden spent his formative young adulthood in Zhitomir as a student in the Haskalah-orientated Rabbinical Seminary, and there he was exposed to the city's thriving Polish theater culture. Goldfaden launched his one-man performing career in the wine cellars of Odessa in the early 1870s, but then moved to Romania, where he produced and directed the first modern Yiddish theater production, in Jassy in 1876. He proceeded to compose the classical repertoire of Yiddish theater during the next nine years.

Goldfaden's repertoire consisted at first of musical melodramas and later of historical operettas. Songs were the core of his plays and were often inserted with little connection to the plot. The music was highly eclectic: opera, classical and cantorial music, and all sorts of folk music (Yiddish, Ukrainian, Rumanian). Regardless of a play's genre, it always included a comic character and many sentimental moments that elicited tears.

In the 1870s, Goldfaden's plays had Maskilic messages. Thus, *Di tsvey kuni-leml* (The two Kuni-Lemls) is a story of love overcoming social conventions. A loving couple, thwarted by the institution of arranged marriage, devise a plan to subvert the girl's forthcoming arranged marriage to a stuttering, limping yeshiva student named Kuni-Leml. Her true love disguises himself as Kuni-Leml and presents himself to the parents as her groom. In the comic climax, the two grooms confront each other on the wedding day, leading to a happy ending.

In the 1880s, Goldfaden's plays had a national-romantic bent. In *Bar Kokhba*, Goldfaden staged the Jews' final revolt against the Roman Empire, using declamatory rhetoric. The play ends with Bar Kokhba's death in battle, preceded by a soliloquy in which he swears victory for the Jewish people in the future. The play mirrored the proto-Zionist sentiments in Russian Jewry during the 1880s.

In 1878, Goldfaden moved his company to Russia. In Odessa, it performed frequently in the Marinsky theater, with 1,500 seats, and generated "theater mania" in the city. It toured locales as diverse as Berdichev, Minsk, Warsaw, and St. Petersburg. The new phenomenon of Yiddish theater elicited opposition: rabbis and Hasidim were offended by the "frivolity" of theater and by the mingling of men and women; the Russified and Polonized Jewish intelligentsia was scandalized by its "coarseness" and by the use of *zhargon* in a public arena. But Yiddish theater was a stunning popular success, and a whole generation of Yiddish actors began their careers under Goldfaden's tutelage.[6]

The development of the Yiddish press and theater was severely hampered by tsarist bans—on the press in the 1870s and 1890s and on the theater from 1883 to 1905.[7] Nonetheless, the press and the theater became the strongest, most popular, and most financially viable institutions of modern Yiddish culture.

LITERARY ALMANACS AND POLITICAL LITERATURE

A landmark event in the development of Yiddish literature (and of Yiddish culture at large) was the publication in Kiev in 1888 and 1889 of the literary almanac *Di Yidishe Folksbibliotek* (The Jewish people's library), published and edited by Sholem Aleichem. The handsome volumes were modeled after the Russian "thick journals" of the time in the diversity and scope of their material. Besides prose by Mendele and Sholem Aleichem, they featured lyric poetry—a genre that had been virtually nonexistent in modern Yiddish writing—and works by Hebrew and Russian Jewish authors who had not published in Yiddish before, such as I. L. Peretz and Shimon Frug. Also included were literary criticism, bibliography, historical documents, and essays on current affairs. *Di Yidishe Folksbibliotek* emitted a message: Yiddish could be the language of a literature of artistic value, while remaining at the same time accessible to "the people." Similar almanacs were issued by I. L. Peretz and other writers in its aftermath, during the 1890s.

Di Yidishe Folksbibliotek and its offshoots reflected—and stimulated—a more positive view of Yiddish, its role in Jewish life, and its cultural possibilities. The young Simon Dubnov, then the literary critic of the main Russian Jewish journal *Voskhod* (The Dawn) and later the preeminent Russian Jewish historian, applauded the emergence of literature in the folk tongue, which would elevate the cultural level of the Jewish masses. The Hebrew writer Y. H. Ravnitsky commented that Yiddish embodied the "spirit of the people," its humor and moral strength, and should be treasured rather than denigrated. During the 1890s, writers began to refer to the language as Yiddish (in Russian, Novo-evreiskii; in Hebrew, Yehudit or Yudit), rather than by the Maskilic term of contempt, *zhargon*. The new positive attitude toward the language was a by-product of the rising Jewish national sentiments in Russia in the aftermath of the wave of anti-Jewish pogroms in 1881–1882. Rather than denigrate their own victimized community for its shortcomings, former Maskilim now looked more favorably upon its cultural and moral resources, including Yiddish. After the pogroms and state measures against the Jews during the 1880s, Jewish cultural and linguistic Russification seemed both impossible and inappropriate.[8]

In the 1890s, mass political movements arose in Russian Jewry: Zionism and Jewish Socialism. Since Jewish politics were no longer conducted by small elite groups behind closed doors, both Zionism and Jewish Socialism considered the mobilization of popular support to be essential to their success and produced literature in Yiddish to spread their ideas. Jewish socialist propaganda was produced almost exclusively in Yiddish, since the Jewish working class knew no other language. More than thirty underground socialist pamphlets and six underground newspapers, the most prominent of which was *Di Arbeter Shtime* (The Workers' Voice; 1897–1902), were printed in tsarist

Russia during the 1890s. The Zionist movement published more material in Russian and Hebrew than in Yiddish, first because much of its constituency belonged to the Jewish middle class, which read Hebrew and Russian, and second because cultural Zionists were ideologically committed to the revival of Hebrew. But the Zionists also established a weekly organ in Yiddish, called *Der Yid* (The Jew; Cracow/Warsaw, 1899–1903), which was succeeded by the first Yiddish daily in the Russian Empire, *Der Fraynd* (The Friend; St. Petersburg/Warsaw, 1903–1913). The writings of Theodore Herzl and Max Nordau were also published in Yiddish translation, and Sholem Aleichem himself penned Zionist pamphlets in Yiddish.[9]

The attitude of both the Jewish socialist Bund and the Russian Zionist organization toward Yiddish was basically pragmatic and utilitarian until 1905. In fact, the Zionist *Der Yid* and *Der Fraynd* served as the most important forums for the publication of Yiddish fiction in Russia from 1899 to 1905.

EXPANSION, GROWTH, DIFFERENTIATION

To speak of an explosion of modern Yiddish culture in the early twentieth century, and especially after the revolution of 1905, is more than a rhetorical flourish. It is an apt characterization of a series of developments in the position of Yiddish in Jewish life in Russia.

Publication of Yiddish books and periodicals increased dramatically. When Sholem Aleichem compiled a list of Yiddish books printed in the Russian Empire in 1888, he recorded 78 titles. Twenty-four years later, in 1912, an analogous list prepared by Moshe Shalit consisted of 407 titles. In 1888, there was only one Yiddish periodical in all of Russia; in 1912 there were forty periodicals, including seven daily newspapers. Yiddish theater troupes jumped from one or two in 1888 to more than a dozen in 1912.[10]

While the growth in the number of books, publications, and theaters can be attributed in part to the loosening of state censorship after the revolution of 1905, the exponential growth of the Yiddish readership cannot. In the 1880s, the only Yiddish newspaper in the empire, the weekly *Yidishes Folksblat*, attained a peak circulation of 7,000 copies (according to its editor, Alexander Zederbaum). In early 1905, the only Yiddish daily in the empire at the time, *Der Fraynd*, was distributed in close to 50,000 copies (according to one of its editors). By 1912, the combined circulation of the two most popular Yiddish dailies in Warsaw, *Haynt* (Today) and *Moment*, was 175,000.[11]

The explosion in readership (and, analogously, in the theater audience) should be seen against the backdrop of the rapid modernization of east European Jewry. During the period between 1888 and 1912, Russian Jewry experienced massive urbanization, industrialization, increased literacy, secularization, and political mobilization. Consequently, the community had new cultural needs—for secular books, newspapers, and magazines and for modern literature, theater, and music. At the same time, the Jews' overall acculturation to Russian and Polish proceeded at a much slower pace than the other modernization trends, for reasons mentioned above. The disparity between the pace of Jewish modernization and Jewish acculturation caused modern Yiddish literature and culture to flourish.

In the absence of modern Yiddish-language schools (which were banned by the tsarist authorities and were a negligible phenomenon until World War I), the most influential Yiddish cultural institution was the daily newspaper. The mass-circulation Yiddish dailies that came into being after 1905, *Haynt* and *Moment*, were run by businessmen, not by intellectuals or political movements. They attracted readers by printing sensational headlines and "thrilling romances," whose first chapters were distributed free of charge on the streets of Warsaw. Ideologically, the newspapers gravitated toward a Jewish center: Jewish nationalist (but not stridently Zionist), liberal (but not openly socialist), sympathetic toward the Jewish religion (but not so pious as to stop printing the romances). During this decade of tumultuous political events (1905–1915), Yiddish columnists such as Yitzhak Grünbaum (in *Der Fraynd* and elsewhere) and Noyekh Prilutski (in *Moment*) were among the most influential figures in Russian-Polish Jewry and used their journalistic fame to advance their political careers, as leaders of the Zionist and Folkspartei movements.[12]

With the expansion of Yiddish cultural output, there arose simultaneously a modern Yiddish-speaking and Yiddish-writing intelligentsia: a social class of writers, artists, political activists, small businessmen,

workers, and professionals, with either a higher education or expo-
sure to Western culture, who spoke, wrote, and read in Yiddish. This
intelligentsia began to use Yiddish not only to communicate with the
uneducated "masses" but also for communication among itself, to satisfy its own intellectual and artistic needs. In other words, a process of
differentiation took place within the Yiddish readership and audience,
leading to the rise of a Yiddish high culture. The *Literarishe Monatshriftn* (Literary Monthlies; Vilna, 1908), the first Yiddish journal dedicated exclusively to belle lettres, proclaimed in its opening editorial,
"Literature which is intentionally directed at readers with a low level
of development cannot be artistic literature. . . . It is our goal to become a focal point for that which will enrich Jewish spiritual life, aug-
ment our cultural treasures, refine the taste of veteran readers, and
enlist new ones."

In a sign of the consolidation of Yiddish high culture, one of the
best Russian-language Jewish periodicals, *Evreiskii Mir* (The Jewish
World), closed down and was reincarnated as the Yiddish-language *Di
Yidishe Velt* (1912–1915), with essentially the same editors and con-
tributing writers. Such high-brow Yiddish journals challenged, or at
least counterbalanced, the dominance of the daily press in Yiddish culture and created space for more sophisticated discourse.[13]

An analogous process of differentiation between popular culture
and high culture took place in the theater. A new repertoire of serious
Yiddish drama appeared, pioneered by an emigrant playwright in
America, Jacob Gordin. His *Mirele Efros*, a realistic drama without music, on the clash between the generations in a well-to-do Jewish family
in Grodno, became an instant classic of serious Yiddish theater and
was dubbed the Yiddish Queen Lear. The role of Mirele Efros, the
materfamilias, catapulted and sustained the career of Esther-Rokhl
Kaminska, "the mother of Yiddish theatre." The Kaminski theater in
Warsaw, founded by her husband in 1905, with Kaminska in the lead
roles, became the first standing Yiddish theater in the empire and a
model of better Yiddish theater. Other highbrow troupes, usually referred to as art theaters or literary theaters, followed in its wake, performing dramas by Yiddish writers such as Sholem Aleichem, I. L.
Peretz, Sholem Asch, and others.[14]

A refined Yiddish musical culture also arose, independent from the theater. Concerts of Yiddish folk songs were now performed by opera singers, using arrangements by composers such as Joel Engel and M. Milner, who in 1908 formed the Society for Jewish Folk-Music in St. Petersburg.[15]

THE LANGUAGE QUESTION, YIDDISHISM

The dramatic transformation of *zhargon* into Yiddish, and the expansion and diversification of its cultural output, put the language question squarely on the agenda of Russian Jewry. What was to be the language of the Jewish future: Hebrew, Russian, or Yiddish? When the oldest Hebrew daily newspaper in Russia, *Ha-melitz* (The Advocate), closed down in 1904, it seemed to confirm that Yiddish was surpassing Hebrew as the primary language of Jewish discourse. A combination of Jewish-nationalist and "democratic" sentiments led many in the Jewish intelligentsia to embrace Yiddish as a value during the revolution of 1905.[16]

Yiddishists, the most prominent of whom was Dr. Chaim Zhitlovsky, considered Yiddish language and culture to be important Jewish national values and advocated the cultivation of Yiddish into the primary linguistic medium of Jewish life in the Diaspora. Yiddishists demanded recognition of Yiddish by the state, within the framework of its granting Jews national autonomy. They also pressed for Yiddish, rather than Russian (or Polish), to be the language of instruction in modern Jewish schools and of public discourse in communal bodies and organizations. The major event marking the upswing of Yiddishism was the conference for the Yiddish language held in Czernovitz, Bukovina, in 1908, led by Nathan Birnbaum, Zhitlovsky, and Peretz, which proclaimed Yiddish to be a national language of the Jewish people.[17]

On the other hand, antipathy toward Yiddish persisted, and even grew, among the Hebrew writing intelligentsia and cultural Zionists, who warned of the *zhargon* peril *(ha-sakanah ha-zhargonit)* and complained of "the maid-servant seeking to inherit her mistress" (Proverbs 30:23). The leading Hebrew essayist, Ahad Ha'am (the pseudonym of Asher Ginsberg), referred to the embrace of Yiddish by the Jewish intelligentsia as "a cultural Uganda," an allusion to Herzl's much-disparaged 1903 attempt to create a Jewish republic in East Africa, rather than in the land of Israel.

The newly ascendant Socialist Zionist movement was divided on the language issue. The Palestino-centric wing, whose sole goal was to build a Jewish socialist society in the land of Israel, led by Nahman Syrkin, was Hebraist, and considered Yiddish to be a passing linguistic instrument, doomed for extinction—like Diaspora Jewry itself. The revolutionary wing of Socialist Zionism, led by Ber Borochov, struggled not only for socialism and Jewish sovereignty in Palestine but also for socialism and Jewish national autonomy in Russia. It consequently favored Hebrew as the primary language in Palestine (with a secondary role for Yiddish) and Yiddish as the primary language in the Diaspora (with a secondary role for Hebrew). Borochov was himself a pioneering scholar of Yiddish philology whose original tombstone in Kiev bore an inscription from one of his studies: "The first task of an awakening people is to become the master over its own language."[18]

Meanwhile, Diaspora Nationalists, who strove for a liberal democracy in Russia and the granting of Jewish national autonomy, led by Simon Dubnov, advocated Russian-Hebrew-Yiddish trilingualism, with an equal status to be granted within the Jewish community to all three languages. But the various Jewish socialist parties—ranging from the Marxist Bund to the non-Marxist Jewish Socialist Workers' Party (SERP, popularly known as the Sejmists) and the Socialist Territorialists, all of which combined socialism with Diaspora Nationalism—were Yiddishist. Language thus became emblematic of the various movements' positions on the broader issues facing Russian Jewry at the time.[19]

Most of the readers of the Yiddish press, or viewers of the Yiddish theater, were not Yiddishists in any sense of the term, but simply Jews who satisfied their modern cultural needs and intellectual interests in the language they knew best. The Yiddishists formed the self-conscious and activist core of the culture, and they created a cultural movement. Especially after the collapse of the 1905 revolution, and the onset of political reaction, Yiddish cultural associations became extremely numerous, as the political intelligentsia shifted its focus to cultural activity. The strongest of these associations was the Jewish Literary Society, founded in St. Petersburg in 1908. By mid-1910, the society had fifty-five branches in Russia and sponsored literary programs, lectures, and concerts. While some of its founders, including Dubnov and S. An-sky, had initially intended for the society to support Jewish literature in all three languages, it quickly became an association for the spread of Yiddish literature.[20]

The half century prior to World War I was a period of great dynamism in the position and roles of Yiddish in Jewish life. While it makes little sense to speak of a distinct Yiddish culture before 1860, by 1914 a full-fledged Yiddish culture not only existed but seemed to be the wave of the future in east European Jewish life.

2

THE POLITICS
OF YIDDISH

In 1897, tsarist Russia conducted a census that recorded the religion and language of the populace. Of the 5,215,000 Jews living in the empire, 97 percent declared Yiddish as their native tongue. Only 26 percent claimed to be able to read Russian. Given this impressive degree of Jewish linguistic cohesion on the threshold of the twentieth century, a lively and developed modern Yiddish culture could have been expected in Russia at the time, comprising literature, the press, periodicals, theater, and education, as well as social and cultural organizations. In fact, however, there was not a single Yiddish newspaper, daily or weekly, and not a single Yiddish literary journal in all of tsarist Russia in 1897. Nor were there any established, well-known Yiddish theater ensembles, any modern Jewish schools with instruction in Yiddish, or any social or cultural organizations operating in Yiddish. Few other languages in central or eastern Europe possessed such a paucity of cultural institutions.[1]

Whereas Yiddish fiction, published in book or pamphlet form, was a substantial force in Russian Jewish life from the 1860s on, the other institutions of modern Yiddish culture lagged far behind it in their historical development. The Yiddish short story and novel were important vehicles by which Jewish intellectuals expressed themselves and communicated with the Jewish public. Between the 1860s and 1880s, tens of thousands of Russian Jews flocked to their local book peddlers and bookshops to obtain the belletristic writings of Isaac Meyer Dik,

Mendele Moykher Seforim, Isaac Joel Linetski, Nokhem Meyer Shay-
kevitch (Shomer), and the young Sholem Aleichem. The spread of
Yiddish belle lettres altered the reading habits, leisure activity, and
thinking patterns of a considerable segment of the Russian Jewish
community. But in the areas of the press, periodicals, theater, and
schooling, Yiddish activity was sparse, sporadic, and flimsy at best.
During the 1890s it was virtually nonexistent. Not until the first decade
of the twentieth century did a strong multidimensional modern Yiddish cultural system (i.e., not only belle lettres but also other spheres
of cultural endeavor) establish itself. This fact has often gone unno-
ticed because of the remarkable literary achievements of Mendele,
Sholem Aleichem, and I. L. Peretz during that very period. Indeed the
very term "Yiddish culture" did not gain currency until the early years
of the twentieth century.[2]

The delayed development of modern Yiddish culture demands a
historical explanation. The nineteenth century was a period when the
languages of many nationalities in eastern and central Europe came
into their own: Polish-language theater, Russian-language education,
and a strong and diverse Czech and Hungarian periodical press all
flourished. Yiddish would have all of this too, but considerably later.

Those who have addressed the question directly or indirectly have
offered two complementary explanations. The first maintains that Russian Jewry underwent little economic, social, and cultural modernization during the nineteenth century. The vast majority of Russian Jews
continued to live in small market towns (shtetlekh), and their everyday
lives conformed to traditional, preurban, preindustrial cultural patterns. Their needs for information, moral guidance, spiritual enrich-
ment, entertainment, and leisure activity were satisfied in the beys
medresh (house of study), the Hasidic shtibl (house of prayer) and
court, and, of course, home and neighborhood settings. Only on the
verge of the twentieth century did a significant proportion of Russian
Jewry become urbanized, industrialized, and secularized. The complexity and impersonality of urban life and the spread of a secular, ra-
tional worldview made the adoption of modern European cultural
forms, such as the newspaper, magazine, theater, and modern school,

possible and indeed necessary for Russian Jewry. The requisite social and economic conditions for the rise of a modern Yiddish culture did not exist until the turn of the century.[3]

The problem with this explanation is that its static and simplistic view of Russian Jewish life in the nineteenth century flies in the face of the facts. The urbanization and industrialization of Russian-Polish Jewry were well advanced by the 1860s, as was its cultural transformation. To cite just a few major developments, the secularizing influence of Haskalah ideology was pronounced in such centers as Vilna, Kovno, Berdichev, and Odessa. There emerged a sizeable Russified Jewish intelligentsia in St. Petersburg, Moscow, Odessa, and Kiev, and by the 1870s, Jews in Russian gymnasia and universities outnumbered yeshiva students. In Warsaw, a Polonized Jewish bourgeoisie assumed key positions in the Jewish community. A spectrum of modern Jewish schools — state-sponsored, private, and communal — arose, combining Jewish and general studies, and the Hebrew press (including, as of 1886, two dailies) flourished. However, these modern cultural trends expressed themselves overwhelmingly in Russian, Polish, and Hebrew, not in Yiddish.[4]

A second explanation is usually offered. It contends that the Maskilim and Jewish intelligentsia viewed Yiddish with disgust and contempt, as the living embodiment of the much-hated medieval past. The Maskilim therefore created their cultural outlets in Hebrew, which they worshipped as "the beautiful tongue, our last remaining remnant" *(ha-safah ha-yafah ha-seridah ha-yehidah)*, and, later, the Russian Jewish intelligentsia enthusiastically embraced Russian in its periodicals, schools, and organizations. Yiddish was supposed to wither and die, the sooner the better. At best, it was viewed as a necessary evil and relegated to the limited, transitory role of spreading enlightenment among the adult generations of unlettered Jews, for whom it was too late to acquire another language. With such a negative attitude toward the language, there was no ideological basis for the emergence of a modern Yiddish culture. Only at the turn of the century, primarily under the influence of the Jewish labor movement and its political arm, the Bund, did a segment of the Jewish intelligentsia change its attitudes toward Yiddish and begin to view it as a valued cultural medium or as a national cultural treasure. That is when the Yiddish press, school, and theater burst forth onto the historical arena.[5]

This ideological explanation, which was especially popular among Bundists who wished to lay claim to the emergence of modern Yiddish culture, is much too facile. From the 1860s on, a growing number of writers and intellectuals endorsed Yiddish as a tool for spreading enlightenment. Alexander Zederbaum, S. J. Abramovitsh, Moshe Leyb Lilienblum, Abraham Ber Gottlober, and Abraham Goldfaden are only the most famous early examples. They may have felt uneasy about writing in the despised *zhargon* and doubted its long-term viability and desirability, but nonetheless they plodded ahead, in the face of rather vociferous opposition by others. Even some Russified intellectuals such as Ilya Orshanskii and Menashe Margulis saw merit in advancing enlightenment by means of the folk idiom. After the pogroms of 1881–1882, a sizable segment of the Jewish intelligentsia shed its embarrassment or ambivalence toward the language. The view that Yiddish was a legitimate cultural medium with a valuable role to play in both the present and foreseeable future gained greater acceptance. Sholem Aleichem and I. L. Peretz were the preeminent converts to this view during the 1880s, but many others followed in their aftermath, including Y. H. Ravnitski, Simon Dubnov, and Shimon Frug. The favorable change in the attitude toward Yiddish occurred first among a segment of the bourgeois intelligentsia (in the 1880s) and only later among the Marxist and radical intelligentsia (in the 1890s).[6]

The requisite socioeconomic and ideological conditions for the flourishing of a modern Yiddish culture were in place perhaps by the 1860s, and certainly by the 1880s, yet no broad cultural renaissance arose until considerably later. I believe this delay was caused by an external factor: the problematic political status of Yiddish in tsarist Russia. The tsarist policy of banning and outlawing Yiddish in various contexts prevented the full-scale flourishing of modern Yiddish culture until the prohibitions were relaxed or removed.

STATE CENSORSHIP AND THE YIDDISH PRESS

During the nineteenth century, there was only óne Jew in all of tsarist Russia who was successful in obtaining a state permit to publish a newspaper in Yiddish: Alexander Zederbaum. Zederbaum had the necessary political connections in the government chancelleries and was an accomplished *shtadlan* (lobbyist) who knew how to persuade, reassure, and bribe imperial officials. Nonetheless even he encountered considerable official opposition to his publication of *Kol Mevaser*, the first modern Yiddish newspaper. His initial request to publish the weekly was rejected by the Ministry of Interior. He was only able to secure a legal status for the paper by issuing it as a "supplement in Jewish German" to *Ha-melitz*, the Hebrew weekly of which he was editor and publisher. For years, *Kol Mevaser* labored under the legal fiction that it was a supplement to *Ha-melitz* and that it was in German. In 1868 the imperial censors nearly discontinued publication of *Kol Mevaser* when they realized that, contrary to the original permit, the weekly was not in German with Hebrew letters, but in Yiddish. It took months of lobbying with the authorities, and an apparent editorial decision to recommit itself to Germanizing the language of *Kol Mevaser*, to save the paper from forced closure.[7]

When Zederbaum decided, and obtained permission, to move the Hebrew *Ha-melitz* from Odessa to the capital city of St. Petersburg, his petition to relocate the Yiddish *Kol Mevaser* along with it was refused. Zederbaum was forced to leave the Yiddish paper behind, in the hands of an inept editor who sealed its fate rather quickly. Once in St. Petersburg, Zederbaum faced an iron wall of bureaucratic opposition to his issuing a Yiddish newspaper in the capital. For years, his interventions were to no avail. Finally, during Count Nikolai Ignatev's brief term of office as minister of interior (March 1881–June 1882), Zederbaum obtained a permit for the publication of the weekly *Dos Yidishes Folksblat* (1882–1890). Zederbaum and Ignatev were long-standing personal acquaintances.[8]

The existence of a Yiddish-language press in Russia depended entirely on this one man's luck and perseverance. When *Dos Yidishes Folksblat* closed down (after it too was placed in the hands of an inept new editor), the 5.3 million Jews of tsarist Russia were again left without a single newspaper in Yiddish. All other applicants met with total failure. S. J. Abramovitz was frustrated time and time again during the 1860s, 1870s, and 1880s in his efforts to obtain permission to edit a Yiddish newspaper.[9] I. J. Linetski faced failure more ingeniously. He crossed over into neighboring Galicia (in the Hapsburg empire), joined forces with Abraham Goldfaden, and began publishing *Yisrolik* (Little Israel; Lemberg, 1875–1876), a newspaper expressly intended for readers in Russia. But before long, the tsarist authorities prohibited the mailing of the newspaper into Russia, and having lost its clientele, *Yisrolik* closed down. Mikhoel Levi Radkinzon followed Linetski's lead and published *Kol La'am* (The People's Voice; Koenigsburg, 1876–1879) from neighboring Prussia, with a Russian Yiddish readership in mind.[10] It seems likely that already in the 1870s, the Ministry of Interior had adopted a ban on the publication of Yiddish newspapers in Russia as a matter of policy (rather than mere bureaucratic obstructionism and foot dragging).

At least one contemporary observer, Aaron Lieberman (1842–1880), often referred to as the father of modern Jewish socialism, believed such a ban was in effect. In an 1877 letter to the Russian socialist V. Smirnov, he explained why he was publishing his newspaper *Ha-emet* (The Truth) in Hebrew rather than Yiddish. "Since we are talking about a legal newspaper, the Hebrew language had to be chosen. *Zhargon* is suppressed by the Russian government in order to Russify the Jews; and *zhargon* publications issued abroad encounter insurmountable hardships, regardless of their content."[11] Lieberman's assumption that the ban on Yiddish periodicals was designed to further the Jews' linguistic Russification was probably on the mark.

The picture is much clearer for the 1880s and 1890s. E. M. Feoktistov, the official in charge of press affairs at the Ministry of Interior, repeatedly turned down applications to issue Yiddish dailies or weeklies with the flat declaration that "there will never be a Yiddish newspaper in Russia." In his memoirs, Feoktistov claimed that Yiddish newspapers would have been impossible to control, since one couldn't find reliable censors for them. No one in the office of press affairs knew the language, and experience proved that Jews, even converted Jews, simply could not be trusted with the job of censorship. His successor, M. P. Soloviev, likewise opposed licensing any Yiddish newspapers and warned that "Yiddish is extremely dangerous from the state's point of view." Since Jews were well known to be revolutionaries, Yiddish newspapers would, if published, undoubtedly spread revolutionary ideas. He cited the underground Yiddish press of the Bund as proof.[12]

As a result, the requests to publish a Yiddish daily newspaper by Mordechai Spector in 1894, S. Rapoport (a partner in *Ha-melitz*) in 1896, Eliezer Kaplan (chief of the Warsaw publishing house Ahiasaf) in 1898, Leon Rabinovitz (editor of *Ha-melitz*) in 1900, and Zvi Prilutski in 1902 were all rejected. According to one account, the Ministry of Interior had thirty-five such requests on file in 1902.[13]

With no hope for a governmental permit, Kaplan resorted to the old ploy of Linetski and Radkinzon. His Warsaw-based publishing house issued a Yiddish weekly, *Der Yid* (1899–1903), which was edited by Y. H. Ravnitski in Odessa but was printed across the border in Cracow. From there it was mailed to readers in tsarist Russia.[14]

Salvation for the Yiddish press in Russia came from unexpected quarters. When Viacheslav von Plehve became minister of interior, in 1902, he decided to permit a single Yiddish daily in Russia as an experiment, in an attempt to counter the influence of the Bundist underground press. That is how *Der Fraynd*, the first Yiddish daily in Russia, came into being. A true explosion of Yiddish dailies and weeklies occurred during and after the revolution of 1905, when a greater measure of freedom of the press was instituted and mass-circulation dailies such as *Haynt* and *Moment* appeared on the scene.[15]

The internal social conditions for the emergence of a Yiddish-language daily press existed long beforehand. In Romania, with a fraction of Russia's Jewish population but without the interference of imperial authorities, a Yiddish daily first appeared in 1877, and numerous weeklies engaged in fierce competition during the late nineteenth century. And in Russia itself, two Hebrew dailies were published from 1886 on: *Ha-melitz* in St. Petersburg and *Ha-tsefirah* (The Herald) in Warsaw. (A third daily, *Ha-yom* [The Day], was short lived.) No doubt Yiddish, with its larger potential readership, could have sustained at least as many dailies, were it not for the tsarist ban on Yiddish newspapers during the late nineteenth century. The ministerial policy toward Hebrew was more lenient, precisely because Hebrew newspapers reached a much more limited reading audience.[16]

The same policy applied to literary and other journals in Yiddish.

According to tsarist administrative regulations, all periodicals—regardless of frequency, format, or subject matter—were subsumed under the category of newspapers. Hence there were no Yiddish magazines of any sort in nineteenth-century tsarist Russia. Sholem Aleichem's *Di Yidishe Folksbibliotek* (1888, 1889), and Mordechai Spector's *Hoyzfraynd* (Home Companion; 1888, 1889, 1894, 1895, 1896) were not journals (although they are occasionally referred to as such) but thick literary almanacs, which appeared no more than once a year. Each volume was considered by the tsarist authorities to be a separate book. The publication and censorship of books belonged to a separate section of the Ministry of Interior, and there was no administrative policy prohibiting the publication of books in Yiddish.[17]

The impossibility of publishing a Yiddish periodical of any sort led I. L. Peretz to a rather ingenious idea. He issued a series of pamphlets in 1894–1896, each one ostensibly in honor of a different Jewish holiday or fast day, and was thereby able to publish a de facto magazine, which historians of Yiddish literature refer to as the *Yontev Bletlekh* (The Holiday Pages). Legally, each pamphlet was a separate book, with its own title (*The shofar, Greens for Shavuos*, etc.). The only signs of continuity between one pamphlet and the next were the inscription "Peretz publication" on the title page and the typeface. Other Yiddish writers attempted similar projects.[18]

But such pseudojournals were difficult to negotiate through the censorship bureaucracy. The Ministry of Interior may have been wise to the schemes to circumvent the ban on Yiddish periodicals. In any case, the longer lead time for books between their composition and their review by the censors was an impediment to such devices. As a result, Yiddish magazines and journals only began to appear in the first decade of the twentieth century, when the press policy changed.[19]

THE FEAR OF THEATER

The most sensational tsarist decree against Yiddish was the comprehensive ban on Yiddish theater issued in August 1883. A secret memorandum from the Ministry of Interior to all provincial governors announced, "Taking into consideration that certain plays in the Yiddish language which were permitted to be performed are absolutely

inappropriate, it has been deemed necessary to prohibit the performance of plays in Yiddish in the theaters."[20] Enforcement of the ban was
put in the hands of the police authorities.

This curt and categorical directive is of little help in uncovering the
motives and reasons for the theater ban. A Soviet Yiddish scholar suggested that the ban was the result of denunciations by members of
the Russified Jewish bourgeoisie in St. Petersburg, who were offended
and embarrassed by the performance of Yiddish productions to packed
halls in the capital city. Others have suggested that Goldfaden's
operetta *Bar Kokhba*, which idealized the ancient Judean uprising
against Rome, was taken by the authorities to be a veiled allegory in
favor of revolution in Russia.[21] The latter explanation is more convinc-
ing, given Russian official paranoia over revolutionaries and, specifically, Jewish revolutionaries. It also seems to be supported by the text
of the ban, which alludes to certain plays that ought not to have been
performed.

The more important question is why the Ministry of Interior vigorously enforced the ban on Yiddish theater for seventeen years (until
1900), reiterated its validity in 1888, 1891, 1897, and 1900, and frequently invoked its authority in later years as well.[22] There is no evidence of a sustained denunciation campaign against the Yiddish theater on the part of the Russified Jewish bourgeoisie for nearly two
decades. Bureaucratic inertia can be given some share of the responsibility, but broader political considerations of state security must have
been involved as well. Since the official memorandums are silent on
the subject, we can only surmise. Jews were viewed in official circles
as treacherous and treasonous, plotting to destroy Russia, and the theater stage was recognized as one of the most influential and uncontrol-
lable of public forums. The poor and uneducated—the politically most
dangerous social classes—flocked to the theater, where they assembled in large numbers. Whereas the texts of books, newspapers, and
even plays could be censored, no one could control the content of what
actors actually said on the stage, in front of a large audience. The fear
of revolutionary propaganda being spread via the Yiddish stage must
have loomed large.

The ban of 1883 dealt a devastating blow to the brief flourishing of

Yiddish theater in Russia that began in 1878, when Abraham Goldfaden, the father of modern Yiddish theater, brought his troupe from
Romania to Odessa. His plays were smash hits, and before long Goldfaden's company was performing in cities and towns throughout the
Pale, and even in Moscow and St. Petersburg, where the general Russian press reviewed his work favorably. Rival theater groups sprang
up, some of them offshoots from Goldfaden's original cast, and plagia-
rized the master's repertoire. Odessan Jewry was in the throws of a
veritable theater mania when the ban was issued. Goldfaden traveled
to St. Petersburg and appealed to the authorities to reverse their decision, but had no success.[23]

The effects of the ban were felt rather quickly, and before long, the
best Yiddish actors (e.g., Jacob Adler, Boris Tomashevsky, Zigmund
Mogulesko) left Russia for England and the United States. Goldfaden
moved to Warsaw in 1886, where enforcement of the theater ban was
lax during the first few years. His company was able to perform there
on a quasi-legal basis, it being officially subsumed as part of a licensed
Russian theater company, with which it shared facilities. But by 1887
Goldfaden found this arrangement and the overall condition of Yiddish
theater in Russia intolerable, and he too left for America.[24]

One of the few Yiddish theater directors then remaining in Russia,
Abraham Fishzon, is credited with developing the stratagem of pre-
senting Yiddish plays under the mask of German theater, which saved
Yiddish theater in Russia from elimination. He submitted translated
German texts (of Goldfaden's operettas) to the censors and applied to
local police officials for permission to stage German plays in town.
This guise became the lifeline of wandering Yiddish theater troupes in
Russia during the 1880s and 1890s. But it was far from a panacea. In
most cities and towns, police officials were not willing to play the fool
and refused to grant permits to the bogus German performances. The
cities with larger Jewish populations (Warsaw, Vilna, Berdichev, Zhitomir, and others) were closed to Yiddish troupes. According to the
memoirs of writer Yankev Dinezon, there was no Yiddish theater in
Warsaw for eighteen years. Yiddish performances could not be staged
in entire provinces (Kiev, Chernigov, Vohlyn, Poltava, Grodno, and others) where police officials strictly enforced the ban. Wandering Yiddish

theater companies had better chances of obtaining (or, more accu-
rately, purchasing) a permit to perform in small God-forsaken towns,
where the local constable was less fearful of being caught by his superiors. Thus, Fishzon's troupe performed in the small town of Zvil (in
Russian, Novograd-Volynski) for half a year, because it could not find
anywhere else to go.[25]

There were problems even when permits were granted. The local
constable usually required that the performance be in German, and
would send a spy or come by himself to check what language was being used on the stage. If the actors were not speaking something ap-
proximating German, he would annul the permit after the first performance, or even worse, interrupt the play and confiscate the box
office. If, on the other hand, the actors did their utmost to speak German, the audience did not understand what they said, and after one or
two performances people stopped coming to see the show. Bribes were
essential to the existence of the Yiddish theater, in those years, and the
burden of paying a quarter or even a half of the ticket proceeds to the
constable led most troupes into bankruptcy.[26]

Yiddish theater existed in Russia under these severe constraints for
close to twenty years. All the while, waves of aspiring young actors and
actresses kept emigrating to America. Their career prospects in Russia
were bleak, with the doors of Warsaw, Odessa, and every other major
city closed to Yiddish theater, and actors leading a life resembling that
of fugitives on the run. The lure of emigration contributed further to
the instability of ensembles.

Officially, Yiddish theater was still contraband in Russia on the eve
of the revolution in 1917, and as late as 1904, the Russian senate considered (and rejected) an appeal by Fishzon to formally lift the ban.
But in fact, the police began to relax their enforcement of the ban in
many parts of the empire in 1900. That is when the first reviews of Yiddish plays began to be published in the Russian Jewish periodical
press. Shortly thereafter, impresarios started arranging special guest
tours for actors and troupes from America. In 1904, the censors at the
Ministry of Interior began to review scripts in Yiddish, without requiring that the texts be submitted in German.[27]

The renaissance of Yiddish theater in Russia began in 1905. The

Kaminski theater, starring Esther-Rokhl Kaminska, which had been for many years one of the struggling, wandering troupes in the empire, acquired its own building in Warsaw. Several ensembles revived the Goldfaden repertoire and staged the dramas of Jacob Gordin with considerable financial success. And in 1908, the Hirschbein Troupe, with its "literary" repertoire, was founded in Odessa and launched a successful tour throughout the major urban centers of the Russian Pale.[28]

The crucial factor behind the theater explosion of 1905 and later was political. The tsarist authorities loosened their reins, and this allowed pent-up cultural forces to flow.

SCHOOLS IN THE MOTHER TONGUE

Yiddish was the language of instruction in thousands of *heders* (religious elementary schools) across the Russian Empire whose curriculum consisted almost exclusively of *khumesh un gemore* (the Pentateuch and Talmud). But modern Yiddish schooling was a negligible phenomenon in tsarist Russia until shortly before World War I. The term modern Yiddish schools refers to schools where general subjects (such as mathematics, geography, and natural science) or modern Jewish subjects (such as Jewish history and Yiddish language and literature) were taught in Yiddish. The total absence of Jewish children's native language, Yiddish, is a striking feature of modern Jewish education in Russia in the nineteenth century. Classes were conducted in Russian, from the earliest grades on, although this created tremendous pedagogical difficulties. The idea of providing modern Jewish schooling in Yiddish first occurred to Ilya Orshanskii, the Odessan Jewish lawyer and historian, who wrote a memorandum on the subject to the Society for the Dissemination of Enlightenment among the Jews of Russia (Hevrat Mefitse Haskalah).[29] Others may have shared Orshanskii's opinion that teaching young children in a language they hardly knew was counterproductive, but there was little they could have done, given the educational policy of tsarist Russia.

After the Polish uprising of 1863, the tsarist Ministry of Education imposed Russian as the sole language of instruction in all elementary and secondary schools in the Kingdom of Poland and the western provinces. This step was primarily designed to uproot Polish and combat the spread of Polish nationalist sentiments among the younger generation. Secondarily, it was intended to preempt the independent cultural development of other languages, such as Ukrainian and Lithuanian. But it also had a direct impact on modern Jewish schools and their use of Yiddish.[30]

In the second half of the nineteenth century, three main types of modern Jewish schools existed (excluding the traditional religious school, the *heder*): (1) the network of state schools for Jewish children, originally established under Nicholas I; (2) private schools, led and underwritten by intellectuals and philanthropists; (3) Talmud Torahs, financed by local Jewish communities and intended for the poorest children in their city or town. According to state directives, Talmud Torahs were required to provide a program of general studies. All three types of schools were subject to the supervision of the tsarist Ministry of Education, which certified their teachers and regulated their curriculum. Like all other elementary schools in the empire, the mandatory language of instruction in all three types of schools was Russian. An exception was made for the Talmud Torah, which was a hybrid institution: half *heder*, half modern school. For half the day, general studies were taught in Russian, and for the other half, the traditional *khumesh un gemore* were taught in Yiddish.[31]

In the Jewish state and private schools, teaching in Yiddish was totally prohibited. Hirsz Abramowicz, who studied in a state school in the early 1890s, wrote, "All studies in the Jewish state schools were conducted in Russian, even religion ('*zakon bozhi*' [God's law]) and the prayers before the beginning of class. The children, especially in the first grade, didn't know a word of Russian. There was a regulation that in the first grade (and only in it) one could translate into Yiddish in an emergency, if a child couldn't understand. But the teachers, including Gozhansky [Abramowicz's teacher], almost never availed themselves of that regulation. They struggled long and hard in order to avoid using Yiddish."[32]

The traditional *heder*, on the other hand, was a bastion of Yiddish, thanks to the fact that it was exempt from ministerial regulation. In 1859, imperial law recognized the *heder* as a strictly religious institution, and from then on the authorities did not interfere in its curriculum and its language of instruction. The Russian Zionists took advantage of this loophole in the law to create the *heder metukan* (reformed *heder*) beginning in the 1890s. Since these schools were registered as *heders*, they were not subject to the regulations of the Ministry of Education. This enabled them to construct their own curriculum, and more importantly, use Hebrew as the language of instruction in classes of Hebrew language and literature, Jewish history, and Bible. Scores of such *hadarim metukanim* functioned in Russia at the turn of the century and formed the basis for the subsequent Hebrew-language schools of the Tarbut (Culture) network founded in 1917.[33]

Modern Yiddish schools had a much more difficult time emerging than their Hebrew equivalents. Because these schools were founded by secular socialists and nationalists, they did not teach religious subjects and could not pass as *heders*. (Usually, registration of a school as a *heder* required certification from the local crown rabbi.) The first Yiddish schools were therefore illegal, underground institutions. Avrom Reisin visited such a school in Warsaw in 1900, with twenty to thirty students, which functioned clandestinely in the building of a legally registered private Jewish school. In Nesviezh, a school in which all studies were conducted in Yiddish (with sixty students), existed for no more than two years before the police closed it down in 1903 and confiscated its possessions. Underground Yiddish schools also existed for short spans in Mir, Baranovich, and several other smaller towns. The first secret teachers' conference of Yiddish-language schools was held in Vilna in 1907, at which time the police arrested the participants, and their deliberations continued in prison.[34]

The first larger, stable Yiddish-language schools arose in the years before World War I—in Demievka, a suburb of Kiev, and in Warsaw. Both schools had several grades of classes and more than one hundred students. Their impact was limited, given the fact that they could not be written about in the then-flourishing Yiddish press. Because of their questionable legal status (the Demievka school was falsely registered as a *heder*, the Warsaw school as a Talmud Torah), it was considered wise not to attract too much publicity and attention. Thus a correspondent of a Bundist newspaper in Vilna lamented in 1913 that there was not a single Yiddish-language model school in Russia. "Despite all the

obstacles, it would not be impossible to establish such a school" he
wrote, apparently unaware that two such schools existed.[35]

The suppression of cultural, educational, and social activity in Yiddish was an integral feature of tsarist Russia's repressive policies toward the Jews. Official Judeophobia expressed itself not only in the
policies of restricting Jewish residence rights and occupations, insti-
tuting quotas on Jews in higher education, condoning outbursts of violence against Jews, and so forth, but also in the prohibitions against
Yiddish in print, on the stage, in schools, and in other public forums.[36]
Yiddish was, in a word, part of the "Jewish question" in tsarist Russia.

The struggle for the rights of Yiddish in Russia was taken up by virtually all the Jewish political movements, including the Russian Zionist
movement at its Helsingfors conference (1906). It also underlay the key
resolution of the 1908 Czernovitz conference for the Yiddish language,
whose text is rarely cited in full: "The first conference for the Yiddish
language recognizes Yiddish as a national language of the Jewish people, and demands for it political, social, and cultural equal rights."[37]

Yiddish was not the only language that was persecuted by the tsarist
regime. Polish was systematically hounded out of the schools and excluded from all official governmental functions in the Kingdom of
Poland. But the suppression of Polish was not as comprehensive; Polish theater flourished in Warsaw and other cities during the late nineteenth century, and the number of Polish-language periodicals grew
from twenty-two in 1864 to ninety-two in 1894. The treatment of
Ukrainian was harsher. In 1876, the tsarist regime proscribed the use
of Ukrainian in print—books, newspapers, and journals—and banned
Ukrainian theater (with certain very limited exceptions). The use of
Ukrainian in schools was, of course, prohibited. The status of Yiddish
was somewhere between that of Polish and that of Ukrainian.[38]

But Jews as a group were more modernized than Ukrainians—more
urbanized and secularized, in contact with modern culture and science. The prospects for a rich, modern cultural sphere in Yiddish were
greater than for Ukrainian in 1880. If such a culture did not come into
existence until the early twentieth century, the delay should be attributed first and foremost to the politics of Yiddish.

3

LANGUAGE AND REVOLUTION

HEVRAT MEFITSE HASKALAH IN 1905

On December 6, 1905, the Society for the Dissemination of Enlightenment among the Jews of Russia (in Hebrew, Hevrat Mefitse Haskalah; in Russian, Obschestvo Dlia Rasprostranenie Prosveschenie Mezhdu Evreami v Rossii, OPE) gathered in St. Petersburg for its annual general membership meeting. OPE was the oldest and most highly regarded Jewish organization in Russia. During the first three decades of its existence, OPE had supported the spread of enlightenment, education, and culture (all three of which were connoted by the terms Haskalah and *prosveschenie*) among the Jews by awarding stipends to Jewish students in Russian gymnasia and universities and supporting the publication of modern educational and belletristic literature in Hebrew and Russian. In the 1890s, the organization shifted its focus to the funding and supervision of various types of modern elementary schools under Jewish auspices. This was a tactical rather than ideological adjustment, motivated in part by the need to fill the financial and educational void created by the removal of state support from the network of Jewish crown schools. The schools receiving OPE support in the 1890s were still geared toward Jewish integration into Russian society and culture.[1]

At the turn of the century, with the rise of Zionism, OPE came under pressure from nationalist members, led by Ahad Ha'am and Simon Dubnov, to require more hours for Jewish studies (Hebrew, Bible, Judaism, Jewish history) from the schools that received its support. After sharp debates in OPE's Odessa branch between advocates of "national education" and proponents of "general and religious education," a compromise formula was reached, which increased attention to Jewish disciplines. Nonetheless, OPE's leadership remained staunchly loyal to integrationist and emancipationist ideals.[2]

At the time of its 1905 meeting, OPE sponsored or subsidized 117 elementary schools and allocated 39,098 rubles—or 40 percent of its total budget—toward their maintenance.[3]

The December 1905 meeting was held in the immediate aftermath of dramatic events that had consumed Russian Jewry during the course of the year. Revolutionary disturbances had swept across the empire beginning in January 1905, with the Bund leading a groundswell of demonstrations and strikes in the Pale of Settlement. The revolution shook the tsarist regime to its foundations and culminated with the October 17 Manifesto, in which Tsar Nicholas II made significant political concessions, including the introduction of freedom of speech and assembly and the creation of Russia's first freely elected parliament, or Duma. But in the days immediately following the October manifesto, counterrevolutionary groups vented their political rage by perpetrating pogroms in several hundred locales, killing more than twenty-five hundred Jews.[4]

As OPE met, Russian Jewry was in the throes of intense emotions: anger and indignation against the tsarist autocracy, sorrow and mourning over the hundreds of victims, and fervent hope that the old regime was nearing its end and that Jewish grievances would soon be aired and redressed in the Duma. These emotions, and the powerful revolutionary impulse to bring about radical change in public life, spilled over into the OPE annual meeting. In past years, these meetings had been relatively routine formalities, which approved the organization's budget and reelected members of its Executive Committee. But in 1905, the general membership meeting became a forum for intense conflict, as participants demanded the reform of OPE itself—its structure and governance and its educational and cultural goals. The issue that became the lightning rod of attention was language—specifically, the society's attitude toward Yiddish.

Public conflicts between OPE's Executive Committee, based in St. Petersburg, and its rank-and-file membership first surfaced in February 1905 and related to the unfolding revolution in the country. A group of seventy-seven members petitioned for an emergency general membership meeting in response to the general crisis. At the emergency meeting, they urged OPE to identify itself openly with Russia's oppositionist camp. M. Krol, a veteran Socialist Revolutionary, proposed that the society pass a resolution demanding equal rights for Jews and the establishment of parliamentary democracy in Russia. The politically conservative Executive Committee, led by its chairman Jacob Halpern, himself an official in the tsarist Ministry of Justice, opposed the resolution as dangerously ill advised, given the uncertain political situation in the country. After attempts to bury the resolution in committee failed, it was passed by an overwhelming majority of members, over the Executive Committee's objections.[5]

The divergent sensibilities of the Executive Committee and the rank and file regarding current events surfaced once again in late November. With the revolution and October pogroms just having occurred, the executive convened its regular membership meeting to review OPE's activities and budget, only to be fiercely rebuked by members in attendance that it was inconceivable to proceed with business as usual only a few weeks after the pogroms. They demanded that the meeting be devoted entirely to the pogroms. As one voice from the crowd declared, "The only report we are capable of listening to in these sorrowful moments is a report of the heavy losses we have suffered." Caught off guard, the executive hastily reversed its position and agreed to the proposal. The meeting was transformed into a protest rally with speeches by socialist, Zionist, and liberal members; it concluded with a unanimous resolution condemning the pogromists, the authorities, and the indifference of Russian public opinion.[6]

When the regular membership meeting was reconvened on December 6, the conflict between the Executive Committee and rank-and-file members did not subside, but shifted ground. It now concerned not political events affecting Russian Jewry but the goals and activities of OPE itself.

The critical tone of the meeting was set by Meir Kreinin, who re-

sponded to the executive's opening report with a speech on behalf of
the society's three-man Audit Committee, of which he was a member.
In the past, the Audit Committee had offered suggestions on the man-
agement of OPE's finances. But Kreinin, an active member who had
organized OPE's first teachers' conference in 1902 and was one of the
editors of the society's journal, *Evreiskaia Shkola* (The Jewish School),
used the occasion to launch into a frontal attack on the Executive
Committee.

Kreinin accused the Executive Committee, all of whose members
were from St. Petersburg, of being inert functionaries who were out of
touch with Jewish educational realities and needs in the provinces.
The executive's only interest in the organization's branches in the
provinces was as a source of donations and membership dues. It did
virtually nothing to encourage or stimulate local educational activity. If
80 percent of the dues from the provinces were spent locally, rather
than sent to St. Petersburg, as was required, the cause of furthering
Jewish education in Russia would be much better served. The society's
general membership meetings, which were the only forum for interac-
tion between OPE leaders from the capital and the provinces, were dry
rituals totally devoid of content. The organization was stagnant and
overcentralized; its membership figures had not grown in several
years.

OPE's remoteness from the problems of Jewish education was typi-
fied by its total disregard for the professional needs and opinions of
Jewish educators in the field. In fact, educators did not have the right
to participate in OPE meetings unless they paid the ten-ruble membership fee, a hefty sum for a schoolteacher in the provinces. OPE's publication policy, ostensibly geared toward the needs of Jewish education,
was whimsical and haphazard. There were no clear guidelines or pri-
orities regarding the kinds of literature OPE supported with grants.
Moreover, the Executive Committee stubbornly refused to support or
disseminate educational literature in *zhargon* (as Kreinin and all other
participants in the debate referred to Yiddish).

Kreinin chose to dwell on the latter point. The society's linguistic
ideology—that Jews should cast off Yiddish and use Russian for everyday matters and Hebrew for religious purposes—was an antiquated

relic of the Haskalah, he said. Moreover, it was totally unrealistic. According to the society's own statistics, only 12 percent of Jewish children attended modern schools where Russian was taught. Most children attended the traditional *heder* until age ten or eleven, and almost none mastered Hebrew sufficiently to read books in that language. How then could the society disseminate knowledge among the Jewish masses while prohibiting the use of Yiddish, which was the only language accessible to them? OPE's attitude toward Yiddish epitomized its distance and alienation from the realities of Jewish life in the provinces.

Kreinin's speech concluded with eight recommendations by the Audit Committee, which included the establishment of special commissions to reconsider the function of general membership meetings and the financial relationship between the OPE central bureau and the provinces. Teachers in OPE-sponsored schools should be automatically registered as members of the society after one full year of employment in an affiliated institution. Proposal number six was that "the Executive Committee should assign an equal role to Yiddish as it does to Hebrew and Russian in its future activity."[7]

In reply, the chairman of Executive Committee, Halpern, tried to minimize the importance of the differences between it and the Audit Committee. Of course the executive was interested in strengthening its ties with the provinces, and would support the creation of the commissions, although he reminded the assembly that according to the society's bylaws, the members of all commissions were selected by the Executive Committee. But on the point of giving Yiddish equal status with Russian and Hebrew, the Executive Committee felt compelled to voice its strongest objections.

The main speaker on behalf of the executive's position was Judah Leyb Katzenelson, a prominent Hebrew scholar and author and an Executive Committee member. Katzenelson defended OPE's long-standing language policy. The Jews did not live in a separate territory of their own, but in Russia, and knowledge of the state language was absolutely essential for their survival and opened up to them the riches of Russian culture. Knowledge of Hebrew was a link between contemporary Jewish life and the past and the best weapon in the struggle for spiritual and national survival. But what good was Yiddish, and why should anyone want to obstruct the natural process of its gradual displacement and disappearance from Jewish life?

Katzenelson conceded that OPE could use Yiddish in its non-school-based educational activity and could disseminate educational literature in Yiddish for adults. He offered an alternate resolution to that effect. But he insisted that there was no legitimate place for Yiddish in Jewish schools and stated that the resolution requiring that Yiddish assume an equal role with Russian and Hebrew was outrageous. Underscoring the gravity he attributed to the issue, Katzenelson concluded his speech with an ultimatum: if the Audit Committee's recommendation regarding Yiddish was passed, he would have no choice but to resign from OPE's executive.[8]

It is no coincidence that this rift within OPE erupted in 1905. The very divisions and radical impulses that underlay the Russian revolution of 1905 were now being reenacted in microcosm within the confines of the organization. The lines were drawn between two rival camps, the Executive Committee with its supporters, on the one hand, and the "opposition," as they were referred to in the Jewish press, on the other. The clash was between an entrenched establishment and those who demanded the organization's democratization, between the St. Petersburg elite and those who spoke on behalf of the masses in the Pale of Settlement, between a politically conservative leadership committed to Jewish integration into the existing social order in Russia and an activist intelligentsia, committed to new political and cultural ideals. And at the heart of the conflict was Yiddish, which epitomized the goals and values of the opposition: democratization, identification with the masses, social activism.

Jewish-nationalist themes, which were conspicuously absent from Kreinin's speech, were soon injected into the debate, as members from the floor spoke. Ber Brutskus, an economist and a leader of the Jewish Colonization Association, noted that whereas all nationalities in the empire were establishing institutions to develop their own languages and cultures, only the Jews were still following an assimilationist educational policy. Saul Ginsburg, a former secretary of OPE and editor of the Yiddish daily *Der Fraynd*, concurred.

The literary critic and scholar Israel Zinberg framed the issue as a clash between the aspirations of the Jewish intelligentsia and the people *(narod)*. For decades, the intelligentsia consisted of adherents of assimilation and Russification, who assumed that the people would follow their example and abandon Yiddish. But the people had a mind of their own. Instead, they had preserved the Yiddish language and developed its literature. The society had repeatedly rejected requests for subventions from Yiddish authors, beginning with Israel Aksenfeld in 1862 and down to Sholem Aleichem in 1895. In 1868, the leaders of its Odessa branch actually appealed to the Russian authorities to ban the publication of books in Yiddish. "But," said Zinberg, "the people have outlived the plans and designs of the *inteligenty*. OPE has no right to give orders to the people. On the contrary, it should listen to the demands of the people, and to the demands of life."[9]

Zinberg translated Russian populist and radical political rhetoric into Jewish cultural terms. It was time for the Jewish elite to listen to the Jewish people and accept their language—Yiddish.

As if to provide a concrete illustration of Zinberg's point about the need to "listen to the people," a visitor in the audience asked to be recognized. The chairman refused, stating that only members of OPE were allowed to participate in the membership meeting's deliberations. The ruling caused much commotion in the hall, since it seemed to confirm Kreinin's and Zinberg's point about the Executive Committee's arrogance. The question of the visitor's speaking was brought to a vote, and an overwhelming majority voted in favor of allowing nonmembers to speak. Two supporters of the Executive Committee then stood up and left the hall in protest. As they did, whistling and shouting erupted. The chairman, Halpern, then rose and declared that in light of the disturbances from the audience, the meeting could not continue and was adjourned.

The Executive Committee and its supporters left the hall, but many members and guests in attendance did not. Instead, a group of them mounted the dais and assumed the places of the executive. Kreinin was elected chairman of the rump meeting, and speakers began to lash out at the arrogant, lordly behavior of the Executive Committee, which first refused to allow nonmembers to speak and then unilaterally adjourned the meeting without a vote by the membership. There were calls to eliminate the "bureaucratic" and "philanthropic" spirit of the society and to dismiss its current leadership, which was concerned only about its own power and prestige, not with the problems of Jewish education. The rump assembly concluded with unanimous passage of a resolution declaring the executive's decision to cut off the meeting arbitrary and unfair and noting that it reflected a broader failure to take the membership's opinions into consideration.[10]

At first blush, the internal controversies on governance and procedure seemed to be a digression and distraction from the ideological debate on the position of Yiddish in Jewish education and culture. But in fact, there was an organic connection between them. To the opposition, recognition of Yiddish symbolized a commitment to the democratization of Jewish life and to "listening to the people." How could the people be treated with dignity, as equal citizens of the Jewish community, and be listened to if the language they spoke and read, Yiddish, was deemed illegitimate?

The disrupted meeting was rescheduled for January 29, 1906, and in anticipation of its resumption, both sides mobilized their supporters. A group of Zionists who were members of the OPE opposition sent out a circular letter asking like-minded people to "introduce fresh air into the OPE Executive Committee; new people, who will lead the Committee's activity in a new direction, in accordance with the demands of life." A member of the OPE executive sent out a circular letter of his own, warning that "outside agitators of a well-known orientation"— meaning Bundist radicals—were intent on exploiting OPE meetings for purposes alien to the society's goals, and were intimidating members into supporting their views. The letter warned that these persons wished to force Hebrew out of OPE-supported schools, replace it with Yiddish, and use OPE to publish socialist brochures. If members who were loyal to OPE's traditional ideals did not attend the next meeting, the organization would be hijacked by extremists.[11]

Meanwhile, as anticipation mounted for the public showdown between the OPE opposition and the establishment, the language debate shifted to the pages of the Jewish press. The main spokesman for the pro-Yiddish position was Yosef Luria, a well-known Russian Zionist and a former editor of the Zionist weekly *Der Yid*.[12] Luria published a seven-part series of articles entitled "Self-Determination" in *Der Fraynd*, in which he developed a full-blown nationalist argument on behalf of Yiddish. His basic thesis was that continued Jewish national existence in Russia depended on the Jews' preservation and development of their own language. Without a separate language, Jewish life would shrivel into a set of dried-up religious rituals and philanthropic societies, as had already occurred in western Europe.

Ideally, Luria admitted, the language of Jewish national culture should be Hebrew, so as to unite the Jews' past cultural treasures with the present. But no matter how much one might admire Hebrew, and speak of its national worth, one must recognize the fact that its use was declining. All efforts to introduce Hebrew as a spoken language in Russia had been dismal failures. The only setting in which such a revival was even conceivable was Palestine, where the conditions of Jewish life were totally different.

In Russia, the choice was between Yiddish and Russian, and the latter threatened to gradually push the former out of everyday use. Indeed, maintaining an attachment to the Yiddish language was essential to maintaining Jewish national bonds. It would be a national tragedy for the Jewish people to be fragmented into Russian speakers, Polish speakers, English speakers, and so forth. Surely Zionists should be the last to support that process, he argued.

Luria repudiated the "negation of the Diaspora" of some Zionists, according to which Jewish history and culture in the Diaspora were repulsive and shameful. "Our exile has been bitter, full of tragedies and suffering, but it was not disgraceful for us. . . . Our exilic history is a disgrace for the nations that tortured us, but not for us. There is much in that history with which we can take pride. We showed the world that we are morally a great nation, that we did not bow down before our enemies, that we remained loyal to the things which we considered holy, just and good."

Similarly, Luria concluded, there was nothing ugly or shameful about Yiddish, the language of Jewish exile. "The Jewish people poured into Yiddish a part of its soul, and feels Jewish when it speaks it. The folk calls it Yiddish, considers it its own, and loves it. The folk feels insulted when intellectuals are ashamed of it and reject it."

Indeed, Luria proposed that the Jewish intelligentsia should make Yiddish its own language of everyday discourse, not reserving it for communication with the uneducated masses. It was embarrassing that the conferences and meetings of Jewish communal organizations were held in Russian rather than in Yiddish.

Luria concluded his series of articles by returning to the issue that had stimulated the controversy in the first place: education. In the creation of modern, national Jewish schools, Yiddish should serve as the basic language of instruction for general and Jewish studies. And Hebrew should occupy a prominent place in the curriculum as a language discipline. In short, Luria, a Zionist without any socialist orientation, offered a nationalist argument for the maintenance and strengthening of Yiddish in Russia (and the advancement of Hebrew in Palestine).[13]

The rescheduled OPE meeting of January 29, 1906, took place in an atmosphere of drama and tension. Attendance was high, but in contrast to the previous meeting, only OPE members and professional educators were admitted into the hall. The proceedings began with a procedural debate: should the meeting be chaired by a member of the OPE Executive Committee (as was customary), or should the chairman be elected by the meeting itself, in light of the fact that the main item on the agenda was criticism of the executive's activity. The opposition's spokesmen on the procedural issue were, not surprisingly, also advocates of its pro-Yiddish position: Leon Bramson, a liberal-minded attorney who was elected a few months later to the Duma on the list of the Trudoviki party, and Mark B. Ratner, an active member of the Kiev branch of OPE and a founder of the newly formed Jewish Socialist Workers' Party (SERP). The procedural issue was decided in the opposition's favor.[14]

At the January meeting, more strident positions were voiced, as the establishment and the opposition grew further apart. L. Kliatchko of St. Petersburg took an explicitly integrationist position: *Zhargon* was helpful in moments of humor and laughter, but it was not really a language worthy of development. *Zhargon* was a deformed dialect, a language of slaves and cowards. "Jews must make the Russian language their own, and thereby fulfill their mission before humanity." Israel Zinberg responded by expressing his shock that such "antidemocratic views" could be voiced in 1906, when the slaves were rising up and struggling for their rights. Mark Ratner countered by connecting Yiddish with the Jews' revolutionary struggle in Russia. What Jews needed today was not enlightenment but national consciousness. The Jews would only achieve their liberation once they constituted a strong united force, and the only language that could unite them was Yiddish. Yiddish literature had played a valuable role in spreading the ideals of class conflict and revolutionary struggle among young Jews. Therefore, he concluded, the Audit Committee's proposal to provide an equal role for Yiddish alongside Hebrew and Russian was not only appropriate but quite modest.[15]

But the meeting was not to last very long. As Ratner began to read from the circular letter written by a member of OPE's Executive Committee, which accused the opposition of being led by Bundist agitators, Katzenelson interrupted him and declared that private letters should not be permitted to be read at a public meeting. Shouting then erupted throughout the hall, and after order was restored, a vote affirmed Ratner's right to read the letter. Katzenelson and the entire Executive Committee then left the hall in protest. Pushing, shoving, and pandemonium ensued. In the corridor, Dr. Yakov Eiger, a member of the executive, threatened a teacher: "Just you wait, we're going to expel all the *zhargonist* teachers from our schools." Inside the meeting hall itself, a supporter of the executive physically assaulted Saul Ginsburg, editor of *Der Fraynd.*

After a lengthy interruption, calm was restored, and the meeting was resumed in the absence of the members of the Executive Committee. Ratner concluded his remarks by attacking the establishment for using threats and violence; a resolution was passed condemning the physical assault of one OPE member on another.[16]

The third and final installment of the 1905 general membership meeting took place on March 30, 1906. The Executive Committee prepared itself for a showdown and recruited a large number of inactive St. Petersburg members to attend. The opposition, which drew its support from the provinces and professional educators in the field, was at an inherent disadvantage in bringing large numbers of supporters to St. Petersburg. This time all nonmembers, including non-dues-paying educators, were excluded from the meeting. Moreover, the executive convened the gathering in a school on the outskirts of the city, not accessible by public transportation, thereby limiting attendance by less-affluent members.

By now the identities of the rival camps had become firmly established. The Executive Committee and its supporters sat on the right-hand side of the auditorium, and were referred to by one newspaper report as "the defenders of the old regime." The opposition and its leaders sat on the left-hand side. The former outnumbered the latter two to one.

As twice before, the meeting was largely preoccupied by a lengthy and raucous procedural debate—this time on the minutes of the previous meeting and whether the concluding portion of the meeting, held after the executive's walkout, was valid and should be recorded in the minutes. Turning to the substantive issue at hand, Katzenelson spoke on the executive's behalf. He warned that the *zhargonists* spoke about the equality of the three languages but actually wished to establish the supremacy of *zhargon* and create all-Yiddish schools. This would be a disaster for Jews and Judaism. Katzenelson, himself an old-style Maskil and not a Zionist, appealed to the Zionist members of the society (many of whom were active in the OPE opposition) to recognize the danger *zhargon* posed to Hebrew. He concluded his forty-minute speech with a dramatic declaration: "If I forget Thee, Oh Hebrew, may my right hand whither—if I sign in favor of equality for *zhargon.*"

The chairman then declared that he would limit the time of all future speakers, because of the long list of individuals asking to be recognized. This sent the opposition into a fury, with Ratner protesting against the executive's suppression of speech. Katzenelson had spoken for forty minutes, and the opposition's time was being limited before it had even said a word. He proceeded to lead a walkout of thirty-three opposition members from the meeting.

With the opposition gone, the meeting went smoothly, and the Executive Committee's alternate resolution that it would "also include

Yiddish in its future work" was passed unanimously. The elections for vacant seats on the Executive Committee were also uneventful, as old members were reelected. But the meeting was not destined to end as a joyous victory for the executive. When Kreinin and other members of the opposition were reelected to the Audit Committee, they rose one by one and announced their refusal to serve, in protest against the executive's behavior. When the assembly then voted to induct a group of educators as OPE members, the educators followed suit, announcing one by one that they "declined the honor" of membership.[17]

The meeting was finally closed. The old regime had been victorious, and the revolution inside OPE had failed, much as the larger Russian revolution outside the hall would fail in the course of the next year. Yiddish—the issue that had galvanized the opposition—remained outside the curriculum of OPE-sponsored schools. But the surprising power of Yiddishism in OPE, the citadel of the Russian Jewish intelligentsia, had stunned its leaders and the Russian Jewish community at large. It signaled a major realignment of values and ideas.

This long-forgotten story, buried in the pages of the Russian Jewish press, illustrates some of the key tensions absorbing Jewry at the time. First, it exemplifies the central role the debate surrounding Yiddish occupied in Russian Jewish life beginning in 1905. The main cultural organization in Russian Jewish life was nearly torn apart over the demand that Yiddish be given equal standing with Russian and Hebrew. The issue would continue to divide the organization, and preoccupy its annual meetings, until and even during World War I.

Second, in 1905 the pro-Yiddish orientation was shared by a broad range within the Russian Jewish intelligentsia, by representatives of a variety of political and ideological movements, not only by the Bund or radical left. In fact, none of the participants in the debate described here were Bundists. At the time, the Bund dismissed OPE as an antiquated bourgeois organization and had nothing to do with it. The main Yiddishists in OPE were Meir Kreinin, a follower of Simon Dubnov, who joined his mentor a year later, in 1906, in establishing the Folkspartei; Israel Zinberg, a populist-oriented Diaspora Nationalist, who joined the liberal Jewish People's Group in 1907; and Yosef Luria, a leader of the Russian Zionist organization and editor (at first with

Shmaryahu Levin and then alone) of its official Yiddish organ, *Dos Yidishe Folk*. Several other figures in the pro-Yiddish opposition in OPE were Zionists (Ber Brutskus, Saul Ginsburg). The most radical member of this group was Mark Ratner, a leader of SERP, which, although socialist and revolutionary, criticized the Bund for the weakness of its national program. Whereas the Bund demanded Jewish cultural autonomy, SERP called for the creation of an officially recognized Jewish national parliament, or Sejm, in Russia.

Third, as one might expect from such a diverse group, the pro-Yiddish arguments differed from each other, and can be divided into three categories: (1) The pragmatic/utilitarian argument: Jewish children should be taught in their mother tongue, Yiddish, for the pure sake of pedagogical efficiency; (2) The populist argument: the Jewish intelligentsia must revise its attitude toward the Jewish masses, afford them respect and dignity, and—as a sine qua non of this process—afford legitimacy to their language, Yiddish; (3) The nationalist argument: the Jews' struggle for national survival and continuity, and the battle against assimilation, required the preservation and cultivation of Yiddish and its active adoption by the Jewish intelligentsia.

Fourth, the language feud was not a bipolar debate on the role of Hebrew and Yiddish but a tripolar one on the roles of Hebrew, Yiddish, and Russian. In OPE in 1905, the tension was sharpest between integrationists and nationalists, that is, between advocates of linguistic integration (who ascribed limited literary, scholarly, and religious roles to Hebrew) and supporters of linguistic nationalization, who pressed for the adoption of the Jewish tongue, Yiddish, as the basic medium of Jewish education, culture, and communal life.

Finally, the rise of the pro-Yiddish orientation was intimately connected with the political and social atmosphere in Russia and among Russian Jewry during and after the revolution of 1905, with the movements to democratize Russian society at large and Russian Jewish life in particular. Democratizing Jewish life meant opening up institutions such as the *kehile* (the community board) and OPE to public participation and scrutiny and reforming their internal governance to allow for popular decision making. It also meant assigning a greater role and greater significance to literary, cultural, and educational activity in Yiddish.

During the years 1905–1906, a social revolution took place inside the Russian Jewish intelligentsia, with groups demanding the toppling of old elitist approaches to Jewish politics and culture alike. The aspiring new elite signaled its goal to alter the social order and power structure in the Jewish community through its advocacy of Yiddish, the language of the people.

4

THE BUND'S
CONTRIBUTION

A 1907 article honoring the tenth anniversary of the General Jewish
Workers' Bund of Russia, Lithuania and Poland offered a glowing
evaluation of the movement's role in the rise of modern Yiddish culture. "The Bund created a modern Yiddish culture. . . . It turned the
market jargon into a language in which serious scientific matters could
be discussed. . . . The Bund taught the Jewish masses how to read. . . .
The Bund created a great circle of readers which needed good books
and newspapers, and it created a new literature for this circle."[1]

This self-congratulatory, partisan assessment was subsequently
adopted and elaborated on in Bundist historiography, and from there it
entered into mainstream scholarly literature and popular consciousness, where the close connection between Bundism and Yiddish culture has become a truism.[2]

Did the Bund lead or participate in the Yiddish renaissance at the
turn of the twentieth century? To answer this question, one needs to
compare the growth of Yiddish literature, journalism, and cultural activity inside Bundist circles with the growth in the nonradical segments of Jewish society and assess the influence of the former on the
latter. By and large, the evidence indicates that the growth of Yiddish
proceeded along analogous lines in the radical and nonradical segments of Jewish society. Indeed, most of the landmark events in the
history of modern Yiddish culture were not sponsored by the Bund nor
led by Bundists.

The first Yiddish literary thick journals (Sholem Aleichem's *Yidishe*

Folksbibliotek and Mordechai Spector's *Hoyz-fraynd*) were edited by bourgeois writers; the first daily Yiddish newspaper in Russia *(Der Fraynd)* was published by a group of Zionists; the first standing Yiddish theater company (traveling companies preceded it), the Kaminski theater, which established its base in Warsaw in 1905, had no radical or proletarian orientation; the Czernovitz conference for the Yiddish language was launched by the bourgeois Diaspora Nationalist Nathan Birnbaum, and its leading figures—Chaim Zhitlovsky and I. L. Peretz —had once been close to the Bund but had broken with it half a decade earlier and were sharply at odds with the Bund at the time of the conference.[3]

The Bund's Yiddish-language activity needs to be seen in context and in proportion. While Yiddish played a crucial role in the history of the Bund, the Bund did not play as central a role in the history of Yiddish culture as its partisan commentators believed.

THE USE OF YIDDISH BY THE BUND

The Bund would not have come into being were it not for the decision by Jewish social democrats in Vilna in the mid-1890s to shift the language of their activities from Russian to Yiddish. Instead of conducting Russian-language "circles," in which a select elite of Jewish workers were educated in Russian reading and writing, mathematics, and natural sciences, leading up to political economy and Marxism, Jewish socialists shifted their emphasis to political and economic agitation among workers in Yiddish.[4]

For the founders of the Bund, Yiddish was the sine qua non for creating a mass Jewish labor movement, the indispensable linguistic tool to disseminate their economic and political ideas. One of the Bund's founders, Shmuel Gozhansky, argued in his pioneering brochure "A Letter to the Agitators" (1893) that the leadership of the Jewish workers' movement should provide part of its training to agitators in Yiddish, to ensure their effectiveness in speaking to the workers, "who know Russian poorly and will need to learn everything in *zhargon.*" The Vilna-based Group of Jewish Social Democrats issued its first Yiddish brochures in 1894 and 1895, and their number increased substantially after the establishment of the Bund, in 1897.[5]

But until approximately 1905, the Bund's own use of the language was utilitarian and not a matter of ideology or principle. Indeed, the top echelon of the Bund's leadership consisted of Russified Jewish *inteligenty*, most of whom knew Yiddish quite poorly. One of the Bund's labor organizers and journalists, A. Litvak (pseudonym of Chaim Helfand), recalled that when he first met Alexander (Arkady) Kremer, the "father of the Bund," in 1895, the latter's Yiddish consisted entirely of a few juicy curses. As late as 1905, Bund Central Committee members Isaiah Eisenstadt, Vladimir Kosovsky, Pavel Rosental, and Vladimir Medem submitted their articles for the party's daily newspaper *Der Veker* (The Awakener) in Russian, from which they were translated by the editors, because the authors could not write them in Yiddish.[6]

The Bund's early Yiddish pamphlets and newspapers were composed by its second-tier leaders, such as Gozhansky, Litvak, and Israel-Mikhl Kaplinsky, who had not studied in Russian gymnasia and universities. Often former yeshiva students who had become "infected" with socialism, these autodidacts—or half intellectuals, as they were called—knew their readers' language, milieu, and mentality and were instrumental in translating the concepts of modern socialism into Yiddish.[7]

There can be no doubt that Bundist propaganda and agitation in Yiddish stimulated greater Yiddish literacy among the Jewish working class. Bundist agitators did indeed teach Jewish workers how to read, both literally and metaphorically. Consequently, the Bund's activity helped increase the demand for Yiddish literature by expanding its readership base. The Bund's underground pamphlet literature and press also played a major role in creating a modern Yiddish lexicon and "high register" (a style for serious topics) for the discussion of political, social, and economic problems. But the claim that the modernization of the Yiddish language first occurred in Bundist literature and then spread to non-Bundist Yiddish writing is highly questionable. A stylistic analysis of the Bundist *Arbeter-Shtime* (The Workers' Voice; Vilna, 1897–1905) and the Zionist weekly *Der Yid* (Odessa/Cracow, 1899–1903) would detect no noticeable difference in their language.[8]

While Yiddish was the language of the workers' circles and cells

and of the underground pamphlets and newspapers, Russian dominated as the language of party deliberations in the early years. Not a
single participant in the founding conference of the Bund in 1897
spoke in Yiddish. It was first afforded equal status with Russian at the
party's seventh conference, held in October 1906, at which all
speeches were translated from one language to the other. Only at the
eighth party conference, in 1910, did Yiddish become the official language of the proceedings.[9]

THE BUND AND YIDDISH LITERATURE

The Bund's early Yiddish publications were dedicated to political
and economic issues, with relatively little interest in literature and culture per se. Its underground newspapers, *Di Arbeter-Shtime* and *Der
Yidisher Arbeter* (The Jewish Worker; 1896–1904) published little poetry and virtually no imaginative prose. Indeed, the absence of belle
lettres from the early Bundist press was a feature that distinguished it
from legal Yiddish periodicals such as the weekly *Der Yid*, the daily
Der Fraynd, and subsequent newspapers, where short stories and seri-
alized novels were a mainstay. Of the ninety-one pamphlets published
by the Bund between 1897 and 1905, eighty-one were dedicated to politics, economics, and the history of socialism, four were anthologies of
revolutionary poetry, and six were works of literary prose.[10]

While the formal, organizational connection between the Bund and
Yiddish literature was quite weak, each drew strength and inspiration
from the other. Writers such as Peretz and Avrom Reisin were deeply
impressed by their encounters with organized Jewish workers in the
1890s and began to write with this new audience in mind. The Bund,
on the other hand, used several of Peretz's and Reisin's works (published legally, under Russian censorship) as tools to educate and agi-
tate among the workers. When, in 1895, Jewish socialists established
Yiddish workers' lending libraries in Vilna, Minsk, and Bialystok, their
holdings included the Maskilic satires of Mendele Moykher Seforim
and I. J. Linetsky, the radical stories and feuilletons of Peretz's miscel-
lanies (the *Yontev Bletlekh*), and the short stories on proletarian suffering and striving written by David Pinsky and Reisin. After the founding
of the Bund, its cells conducted literary readings *(forlezungen)* and

evenings *(ovntn)* to discuss works of Yiddish literature (as well as Yiddish translations of Russian and Western literature) and thereby cultivated an interest in modern Yiddish literature among the ranks of the labor movement.[11]

Yiddish poetry was central to the life of the Bund. The proletarian and revolutionary poems of Morris Vinchevsky, Dovid Edelshtadt, Morris Rosenfeld, and Avrom Reisin were extremely popular among organized workers and youth, and secret meetings of Bundist cells and trade unions usually concluded with the recitation or communal singing of their poems. The poems of workers' struggles were also posted on placards during strikes and sung at mass demonstrations. Recitation and communal singing at secret meetings and illegal public gatherings added to the emotional power of the poems and strengthened the workers' attachment to Yiddish poetry.[12]

There can be no doubt that a strong Yiddish literary culture grew within the ranks of the Jewish labor movement. But it was a very particular and selective literary culture. For, as Litvak noted in his memoirs on the *zhargonishe komitetn* (the *zhargon* committees that founded workers' libraries), their activists "viewed modern Yiddish literature merely as a tool for agitation; they attributed no intrinsic value to it."[13] For the Bund, poetry and prose were politics pursued by other means, and works of literature were measured according to their suitability for agitation. Pinsky and Reisin were read avidly and endorsed by the movement, while the works of Sholem Aleichem and Sholem Asch—both of whom were enormously popular among Russian Jewish readers at large—were neglected by the Bund's circles, because they were of no use to them in spreading their political ideas.

The Bund's attitude toward Peretz was tempestuous. He was their cultural hero during the mid-1890s, when he wrote radical stories and feuilletons, but his popularity among them dropped as his works shifted to national romanticism, neo-Hasidism, and symbolism. Peretz's 1906 essay "Hope and Fear," in which he warned that the revolutionary movement might prove to be as oppressive and intolerant as tsarism, caused grumbling among Bundists. And when he concluded his modernist drama *Bay nakht afn altn mark* (At night in the old market place; first version, 1908) with a wedding bard calling out *"in shul arayn!*" (back to the synagogue!), Bundists were appalled and attacked him for supporting a return to religion. They became similarly disillusioned and antagonistic toward S. An-sky, the author of the Bund's own anthem, "Di Shvue" (The Oath), when his writings developed in a neoromantic direction.[14]

Since the Bund valued Yiddish literature first and foremost as a vehicle for agitation among the masses, it had difficulty reconciling itself with the sophisticated and modernist Yiddish writing that arose after 1905. When the journal *Literarishe Monatshriftn* appeared in 1908, it was heralded by many as the beginning of a new era in the Yiddish cultural renaissance. The journal was self-consciously devoted to Yiddish art for its own sake and was explicitly aimed at an intellectual (rather than mass) readership. The composition of its editorial committee, which consisted of a Socialist Territorialist (Shmuel Niger), a Bundist (A. Weiter), and a Zionist (Shmaryahu Gorelik), signaled that Yiddish art and culture were independent values that transcended political divisions.[15]

For the Bund, the journal was a troubling development. Mark Liber, then a young member of the party's Central Committee, derided its apolitical posture. Politics and culture were inseparable, he wrote. Modern Yiddish culture was itself the product of class conflict within Jewry and of the rise of the proletariat, whether the journal's editors admitted to it or not. B. Vladek and Litvak launched frontal attacks on the *Literarishe Monatshriftn.* By championing art for art's sake, and excluding articles on social problems, the journal was a declaration of contempt for politics and political parties. By encouraging intellectuals to think only about themselves and their own edification, the journal cut the intelligentsia off from the masses. It thereby played into the hands of political reaction.[16]

THE NATIONAL PROGRAM

As Jewish national consciousness grew within the ranks of the Bund, Yiddish figured prominently in the movement's internal deliberations on adopting a Jewish national program. The first Bundist leaders to advocate "national equality" for the Jews of Russia, at the party's conferences in 1899 and 1901, explained the term as meaning freedom of speech, press, and assembly in Yiddish; protection against forced Russification; and securing the right of the Jewish masses to communicate with local and imperial organs of state in Yiddish. In these early formulations, Jewish national rights and Yiddish-language rights were nearly identical.[17]

Shortly thereafter, the nationally oriented wing of the Bund advanced a full-fledged program of Jewish national-cultural autonomy, based on the theories of the Austrian Social Democrats Karl Renner and Otto Bauer. But until 1903, a large part of the Bundist leadership objected to this program. Their opposition was based on many considerations, including doubts about the viability of Yiddish and the attachment of the Jewish proletariat to the language, as well as reservations about the desirability of perpetuating Yiddish among the Jewish working class. The debate reached a climax at the June 1903 fifth party conference, at which Sholem Levin, one of the opponents of national-cultural autonomy, declared, "The misfortune of the Jews in Russia today is that they are not allowed to assimilate. . . . Some here [at the conference] are connecting their national feelings with Yiddish, just as the Zionists aspire to the Hebrew language. But the masses aspire to the Russian language, and this is not because they are prevented from studying Yiddish. . . . If there were no discriminatory laws against the Jews, they would speak Russian."[18]

The authoritative Bundist statement on the subject came in Vladimir Medem's essay "Social Democracy and the National Question" (1904), which forged a compromise position. Medem professed neutrality on the long-term question of whether the Jews would maintain their nationality or assimilate. But he affirmed that the Jews were at present a national group and therefore argued for Jewish national-cultural autonomy in Russia.

In the essay, Medem associated nationality first and foremost with language and used a class-based analysis to argue that the granting of equal rights to all languages, including Yiddish was imperative. While the Jewish bourgeoisie had the time, financial resources, and inherent desire to become Russified, the Jewish working class knew no language fluently except for its mother tongue. By forcing Jewish workers to use Russian, a language they did not know, in their everyday lives, or to send their Yiddish-speaking children to Russian-language schools, the state imposed on the Jewish proletariat an inferior, disadvantaged existence. Thus, he concluded, securing equal status for Yiddish in the public arena and for Yiddish-language schools served both national and social objectives.

True equality of languages, Medem continued, could only be achieved and protected by removing those matters which were most contingent on language—education and culture—from the hands of the state authorities and handing them over to the jurisdiction of the nationalities themselves, who would establish public bodies to direct them. This was the meaning of national-cultural autonomy.[19]

The Bund formally adopted its program of Jewish national-cultural autonomy at its sixth party conference in October 1905. From that point on, it championed the cause of the recognition of Yiddish in the public arena. A resolution on the "struggle for equality of the Yiddish language," adopted unanimously at the eighth party conference in 1910, delineated the Bund's position:

(a) The distinction between official languages and tolerated languages is unacceptable.

(b) State institutions and organs of administration must communicate with the populous in the local languages. . . .

(d) In advance of the realization of national-cultural autonomy, . . . it is essential to attain the right for every national group to establish public schools in its own mother tongue.

(e) In the struggle for these demands, it is necessary to stress insistently the rights of the Yiddish language, which is more rightless than all others, and which is unrecognized even when other non-official languages are afforded partial recognition.[20]

From 1905 on, the Bund was more insistent in pressing this political agenda for the recognition of Yiddish than any other Jewish political party. In doing so, it raised public conscious about the dignity of Yiddish as a language.

BUNDISTS, YIDDISH NEWSPAPERS, SCHOOLS, AND
CULTURAL SOCIETIES

The revolution of 1905 was a turning point in the development of
Yiddish culture in Russia. As part of the state's concessions toward society, the authorities lifted the near-total ban on the Yiddish periodical
press and the long-standing prohibition of Yiddish theater. Yiddish
newspapers, books, and theaters flooded the cultural marketplace.
Meanwhile, the democratic and populist fervor that seized the Jewish
intelligentsia led to numerous calls for a positive reevaluation of the
role of Yiddish in Jewish life.[21]

The Bund itself was a direct beneficiary of the newly attained freedom of the press in Russia, which enabled it to publish a legal Yiddish daily of its own between late 1905 and 1907. (The Bundist organ
changed names from *Der Veker* to *Folkstsaytung* to *Di Hofenung* before
it was closed down and its editors arrested.) Even after the restoration
of political reaction in 1907, Bundist journals and newspapers were
permitted intermittently by state censors. But the party press never enjoyed mass appeal. The 1907 *Folkstsaytung* was printed in less than
ten thousand copies, compared to the fifty-thousand press run of the
liberal (and pro-Zionist) *Der Fraynd.* In an attempt to compete for
readers, Bundist newspapers and the party's newly established publishing house began to devote more space and resources to belle lettres. But this was an instance of the Bund following rather than leading the overall trend. Overall, the Bund's direct impact on the Yiddish
press and book publishing was surprisingly modest.[22]

By contrast, Bundists were the main pioneers in the establishment
of the first modern Yiddish schools in Russia. Although they conducted
this activity as private individuals rather than at the movement's be-
hest, or under its auspices, the schools they founded were an organic
extension of the Bundist tradition of workers' education, applied to
children and youth.

Bundists were at the helm of the Vilna Jewish evening school,
which was licensed to provide a Russian grammar school education to
workers above age sixteen, but which beginning in 1906 surrepti-
tiously taught all subjects in Yiddish, including the unmandated sub-

ject of Yiddish language and literature. The evening school, whose enrollment hovered between three hundred and six hundred in the years
prior to World War I, published the first—and most influential—
chrestomathy of Yiddish literature, the three-volume *Dos yiddishe vort*
(The Yiddish word; 1909), edited by the Bundist Moyshe Olgin. At
roughly the same time, Bundists in Warsaw established a Yiddish division of the Polish Society to Combat Adult Illiteracy, whose Yiddish-
language evening courses were attended by more than one thousand
students.[23]

Two of the first full-day Yiddish elementary schools were organized
by Bundists in 1912. In Vilna, the four-grade Dvoyre Kupershteyn
School, with 180 students, embraced a progressive pedagogical philosophy of holistic education. And in Warsaw, the four-grade Hinukh
Yeladim (Children's Education) school attracted teachers (Mordkhe
Birnbaum, Yankev Levin) who penned most of the first Yiddish textbooks for children. Both schools operated in violation of the law, which
stipulated that Russian was the only permitted language of school instruction. The Bundists' skills of concealment and subterfuge were
necessary to ensure their survival.[24]

In the years after the restoration of political reaction, Yiddish education became a focal point of Bundist activity and writing. Party-
sponsored publications devoted considerable attention to the ideological, psychological, political, and pedagogical issues surrounding this
newest type of Jewish school; Esther Frumkin was the most prolific author on the subject. Meanwhile, Bundist teachers in the field (mainly in
Warsaw and Vilna) experimented with curricula, developed Yiddish
terminology for teaching math and science, and applied their democratic ideas to student admissions, parent relations, and school governance.[25]

While qualitatively impressive, the quantitative scope of modern
Yiddish schooling prior to World War I was extremely modest because
of its illegal status.

The post-1905 years saw the legalization of various Jewish associations, including the St. Petersburg–based Jewish Literary Society
(Evreiskoe Literaturnoye Obschestvo), established in 1908. While the
society was officially dedicated to advancing Jewish literature in all

three languages (Hebrew, Russian, and Yiddish), its charter explicitly permitted it to conduct public lectures and programs in Yiddish—activities that were previously prohibited by law. By mid-1910, the society had fifty-five branches in the Russian Empire, which sponsored lectures, concerts, and dramatic performances overwhelmingly in Yiddish.[26]

The St. Petersburg leadership of the Jewish Literary Society consisted of liberals and Diaspora Nationalists, none of whom were Bundists. Indeed, for several years the Bund opposed, and refused to participate in, nonpartisan Jewish cultural associations such as the Jewish Literary Society. At the 1908 Czernovitz conference for the Yiddish language, Bundist Esther Frumkin vigorously opposed Peretz's and Zhitlovsky's attempts to establish a permanent umbrella organization for Yiddish culture, arguing that there could be no cultural cooperation between the bourgeoisie and proletariat, since each had distinctly different cultural conceptions and needs. Because of the Bundists' opposition, Peretz and Zhitlovsky were forced to settle for the establishment of a bureau that lacked the authority to conduct its own programs.[27]

But as the Jewish Literary Society's popularity grew, and local societies for Yiddish literature cropped up throughout Russia, and as the prospects of political organization and action diminished, the Bund was forced to alter its position. In late 1909, it began to encourage its members to become active in Jewish cultural associations, in order to exert an influence on their programs and orientation. In Warsaw, where the local branch of the Jewish Literary Society was chaired by I. L. Peretz, Bundists joined en masse and effectively took over the organization. Peretz was replaced by Bundist leader Bronislav Grosser. Shortly thereafter, the Jewish Literary Society (including its Warsaw branch) was forcibly closed by the Russian authorities. While the Bund did not initiate the creation of societies for Yiddish literature and culture, it eventually threw its organized weight behind this trend.[28]

YIDDISHISM

Until 1905, the language issue was not integral to Jewish party politics in Russia. The Bund was not Yiddishist (in the sense of being anti-

Hebrew), and the Russian Zionist movement was not Hebraist (in the sense of being anti-Yiddish). When the Bund first passed a resolution condemning Zionism as a bourgeois, reactionary political movement, at its third conference, in 1901, the resolution specifically excluded the (mainly Hebrew) cultural work of Zionist groups from its condemnation, noting laconically that "the conference relates to it as it does to any legal activity." Meanwhile, the Zionist Ahiasaf publishing house issued the Yiddish weekly *Der Yid*, which served not only as an organ for Zionist news and views but also as a forum for the best of modern Yiddish literature—including the works by Sholem Aleichem, Peretz, and Asch.[29]

While Yiddishist views were propagated at the turn of the twentieth century by Chaim Zhitlovsky, his idea of a Jewish national renaissance based on the Yiddish language was too overtly nationalist for the Bund at the time.[30]

In the years after 1905, Yiddishism enjoyed support across a large part of the Jewish political spectrum. Its leading spokesmen included liberal Jewish nationalists such as Nathan Birnbaum; socialist Diaspora Nationalists associated with the Jewish Socialist Workers' Party (SERP), such as Zhitlovsky himself; Socialist Territorialists, such as Shmuel Niger; and socialist Zionists, led by the father of Poale Zion, Ber Borokhov. Even in the leadership of the general Russian Zionist movement, there were Yiddishist voices, notably Yosef Luria, an editor of *Der Yid* and of the official Zionist weekly, *Dos Yidishe Folk* (Vilna, 1906–1907), and the young Yitzhak Grünbaum—who caused a storm when he insisted on addressing the fifth conference of Russian Zionists in 1909 in Yiddish.[31]

The divide between Yiddishists and Hebraists was not between Bundists and Zionists per se, or between socialists and nonsocialists, but between those movements (or factions of movements) that affirmed the perpetuation of Jewish national existence in the Diaspora and those who rejected this goal. Thus, there was a non-Yiddishist minority wing of the Bund (those who were not Jewish nationalists) and a Yiddishist wing of the Zionist movement, mainly among socialist Zionists (who affirmed perpetuation of Jewish nationality in the Diaspora). It was no coincidence that Luria and Grünbaum were both champions of the Helsingfors platform, passed at the 1906 conference of Russian Zionists, which endorsed Jewish national rights (i.e., autonomy) in the Diaspora.[32]

The Bund's contribution was to champion after 1905 a version of Yiddishism that was staunchly Marxist, secularist, and anti-Hebrew. Its major spokesmen were Bundist "young Turks" who rose up the movement's ranks after 1905, such as Moyshe Rafes and Esther Frumkin.

The Bund's radical Yiddishism came to the fore at the 1908 Czernovitz conference for the Yiddish language. On the main issue that engulfed the proceedings, the question of the status of Yiddish, Frumkin proposed the most extreme of the five alternate resolutions: "The conference recognizes Yiddish as the only national language of the Jewish people. Hebrew has the significance of a historical monument, whose revival is a utopia." The Bundist resolution was rejected in favor of a resolution that Yiddish was *a* (not *the*) national language and that the conference took no position on Hebrew.[33]

Also at Czernovitz, Frumkin scoffed at Sholem Asch's proposal that the conference endorse creation of a new literary translation of the Bible into Yiddish, to ensure that the riches of ancient Jewish culture would reverberate in the Yiddish renaissance. In the eyes of the Jewish proletariat, said Frumkin, the Bible was material for historical scholarship; its Yiddish translation was no more important than the translation of other classics of world literature. Writing after the conference, she alluded to the proposal as having been a bit of Zionist propaganda. But as with the resolution on the status of Yiddish, Frumkin was in the minority at Czernovitz; the conference enthusiastically supported Asch's project.[34]

A major forum for Yiddishist-Hebraist debates in those years was the annual conference of OPE. A Yiddishist opposition first arose in the organization in 1905, which argued for setting aside a place for Yiddish both as a language of instruction and as a discipline in modern Jewish schools. Its most prominent spokesman was the literary critic and historian Israel Zinberg.[35]

When Bundists joined OPE in 1910 (after the movement's decision to join Jewish cultural associations), they voiced a much more radical position than the Yiddishists who had preceded them. At the 1911 conference, Moyshe Rafes argued that Jewish schools should use Yiddish as their only language of instruction and should exclude religious subjects from their curriculum, such as Bible and Hebrew. Moreover, echoing Medem's "neutralism," Rafes argued that Jewish schools should not have any specifically national objectives, such as strengthening Jewish identity, but should be natural products of the Jewish environment, by virtue of their use of Yiddish as the language of instruction. Rafes's resolution was resoundingly defeated. But the resolution that passed in its stead was the first Yiddishist victory in OPE. It stated,

> (a) All Jewish schools must teach Bible and Hebrew.
> (b) In those places where the Jewish masses speak the Yiddish language, the latter must occupy a place as a language of instruction and as a discipline.[36]

Thus, the Bund's radical Yiddishism after 1905 was not the dominant position among Yiddishists.

The Bund did not pioneer in the rise of Yiddish literature or journalism; it participated in a linguistic-cultural trend that engulfed most of Russian Jewry. The Bund's ideological commitment to Yiddish language and culture arose from 1905 on, when it became a thoroughly Yiddish-speaking and Yiddish-writing movement, which stressed Yiddish language rights as a part of its political program.

After 1905, the Bund gave voice to a radical version of Yiddishism, which was opposed to the revival of Hebrew and advocated the separation of Yiddish culture from the Jewish religious tradition. By adopting this posture, the Bund contributed to the polarization and politicization of the language question within Russian Jewry.

Even within the Yiddish cultural movement, the Bund occupied a politically sectarian position. It was reluctant to participate in Yiddish cultural organizations it could not dominate or control, and it was troubled by the rise of modernist Yiddish literature that did not serve the ends of political struggle. While the Bund tugged Yiddish culture to the political left, its positions did not dominate the Yiddish literary and cultural scene during the period between 1890 and 1914.

5

REINVENTING
COMMUNITY

At the turn of the twentieth century, a broad range of Jewish intellectuals in Russia embraced the ideal of Jewish national revival in
the Diaspora, an ideal they considered to be compelling, heroic, and
ultimately more realistic than the Zionist dream. They shared a common consciousness of representing a third path in Jewish life between
Zionism and assimilation, between those who affirmed Jewish nationhood but denied its viability in the Diaspora and those who affirmed
their attachment to Russian society and culture but denied the principle of Jewish nationhood. These intellectuals often referred to themselves as Diaspora Nationalists (in Yiddish, Golus-natsionalistn).

Within the Diaspora Nationalist stream, there were political and
cultural wings—much as there were within Zionism. The cultural
wing, founded by Chaim Zhitlovsky, emphasized the role of Yiddish
language and literature as the vehicles of Jewish national revival. It
was the task of Yiddish to serve as the main unifying, binding force of
the Jewish people, in an era when religion could no longer serve that
function and when territory/sovereignty could not yet (and might
never) do so. For Zhitlovsky and his disciples, building the Yiddish cultural infrastructure—literature, the press and periodicals, schools (including, eventually, universities), theater and the arts—and expanding
the use of Yiddish in Jewish social and communal life were the primary tasks of modern Jewish nation building.[1]

The political wing of Diaspora Nationalism strove for a transformation of the Russian state into a federation of nationalities

(nationalitäten-stadt), with equal recognition of all national groups, including the Jews. For Simon Dubnov and others, the attainment of autonomy in eastern Europe rather than sovereignty in a territorial homeland was the Jews' most pressing political goal. Their demands included: (1) guarantees for the use of Yiddish and Hebrew by government agencies in their communications with the Jewish population and the right of Jews to use Yiddish and Hebrew in official institutions, such as the courts; (2) proportional representation of national minorities, including the Jews, in all elected political bodies; (3) establishment of Jewish national self-government on the local and statewide levels, through the agency of modern *kehiles* and a Jewish National Assembly; (4) recognition of national-minority schools, including Jewish ones, as institutions of public education.

This neat intellectual typology of Diaspora Nationalists is by necessity a schematic simplification. Reality was much more complex. Most Diaspora Nationalists embraced both the political and cultural agendas, with varying degrees of emphasis. Many of them supported the process of cultural renaissance in both Yiddish and Hebrew, with varying degrees of emphasis on the former or the latter. Some of them even bridged the gap between "autonomism" and Zionism by considering autonomy in the Diaspora a step or stage on the road to territorial concentration and statehood. The boundaries were not always clear or absolute. The passion that Diaspora Nationalists dedicated to their cause is captured by the words of their founding father, Simon Dubnov, upon concluding his first sustained essay on the subject:

> I call out to the Jewish intelligentsia and say: Here is a concrete ideal which will restore to your life its lost meaning. Regarding this ideal one can cite the words of our great teacher, "For this commandment which I command you this day, it is not too hard for you, neither is it too far off. . . . Neither is it beyond the sea. . . . But the word is very close to you, in your mouth and in your heart, that you may do it" [Deuteronomy 30:11–14].
>
> Our historical survival does not depend upon the external forces which oppress us today—no matter how mighty they may appear to us— nor upon distant, dubious plans whose realization are beyond our control.
>
> Our national revival does not depend upon the repressive policy of

one regime or another, or upon the fantasy that the Sultan and the world powers will agree to cede Palestine to us. It depends on "our mouth and our heart," upon those concrete actions that we will take everywhere in the diaspora to preserve and develop our nation.

We must reject the weary politics of waiting—waiting for equal rights, waiting for anti-Semites to come to their senses, waiting for the beneficence of the Turkish Sultan. Our program is a program of action, of stubborn, day-to-day effort, often hidden from view, and of endless struggle for our human and national rights.

Every exertion of effort in the present is also a step toward the future. Every consolidation of our national energy, every institution which strengthens our legitimate autonomy, every school permeated with the Jewish national spirit, every new circle for the study of Hebrew, Jewish history and literature brings us a step nearer to our sacred goal. . . . Our goal is the internal revival of Jewry in all lands where it is dispersed.[2]

Although Diaspora Nationalist ideas were extremely popular and widespread, their adherents were organizationally divided, because of the differing positions they took in general Russian politics. Dubnov and his Jewish Folkspartei (founded in 1906) were close to the Russian Constitutional Democratic Party and advocated the gradual and peaceful transformation of Russia into a liberal democracy, while eschewing class politics and social violence. Vladimir Medem and other leaders of the Bund followed the Russian Social Democratic Labor Party in general political matters. As Marxists, they supported the struggle of the proletariat (including the Jewish proletariat) against their economic exploiters and believed that they would lead the battle to overthrow tsarism and replace it with socialism. The leaders of the smaller Jewish Socialist Workers' Party (SERP), Moyshe Zilberfarb and Mark Ratner, were allied with the Socialist-Revolutionary Party, which was radical but non-Marxist. As a result of these political divisions, there was no overarching Diaspora Nationalist organization.

Diaspora Nationalists devoted much of their thinking, especially between the revolutions of 1905 and 1917, to conceptualizing a modern *kehile* and Jewish national autonomy. These topics were addressed at the conferences of all Jewish political parties and debated in the Jewish press. Reform of the *kehile* was the subject of a conference of Jewish communal leaders held in Kovno in November 1909, attended by

120 delegates. Organized by the Jewish liberal politicians Henryk Sliozberg and Maxim Vinaver, the conference helped stimulate public debate on the kind of *kehile* Jews wanted and needed. A second forum devoted mainly to this question was the monthly Russian-language journal *Vestnik Evreiskoi Obshchini* (Herald of the Jewish Community), which appeared between August 1913 and the outbreak of the First World War, a year later.[3]

Most of this discourse was predicated on the expectation that tsarist rule would come to an end in the not-too-distant future and that new forms of social organization would soon become possible.

THE DUBNOVIAN FOUNDATION

The father of the movement to revive and renew the *kehile* was the historian Simon Dubnov, who developed this idea in a series of essays, "Letters on Old and New Jewry," published between 1897 and 1907. Dubnov considered the *kehile* (in Russian, *obshchina*) to be the central feature of the Jewish historical experience in the Diaspora, where it had served as the surrogate for statehood, unifying Jews and giving them internal discipline. In Dubnov's view, the central tragedy of the modern era of emancipation was the Jews' voluntary abandonment of the *kehile* as the framework for their social and cultural life and its abolition by the modern centralized state as a legally autonomous entity. Revival of the *kehile*, in a modern, democratic, and secularized form, was the task of the new era of national renaissance now dawning upon Jewry.[4]

Dubnov's ideal of autonomy was romantic and utopian. Not unlike Zionism, it called for a return to a model of Jewish existence from the distant, unremembered past. It idealized the unity and cohesiveness of premodern Jewish life and sought to recapture those virtues by reviving, in adapted form, an institution that had flourished in the "golden era" of Polish Jewry (1501–1648). According to Dubnov's historical conception, the *kahal* (communal) system had degenerated in the eighteenth and early nineteenth centuries. Since the *kahal* had been formally abolished by the Russian authorities in 1844, the harmonious self-governing community was well beyond the personal memory of Dubnov and his contemporaries.[5]

Dubnov forged his mythos of the *kehile* as a protective and preserving force in Jewish history in part under the influence of Russian populism, which had expounded a mythos of the Russian peasant commune as a powerful and harmonious community in the face of external adversity. But unlike the Russian populists, for whom the commune was a model of primordial socialism, Dubnov's utopian ideal was national rather than social. The revived *kehile* would endow the Jews with unity and inner strength, which were preconditions for their success in the struggle for external security.[6]

Seen against the backdrop of Jewish social thought in the nineteenth century, Dubnov's proposal to revive the *kehile* was a bold departure. For decades, the Russian Jewish intelligentsia had vilified the *kahal* (and its post-1844 heirs and continuations) and had identified itself in opposition to the latter. The institutions built by Maskilim and the Russian Jewish intelligentsia—schools and modernized synagogues, the Hevrat Mefitse Haskalah, the Russian Jewish press, the Odessa Committee of the Hibat Zion movement—were established to circumvent the *kahal* leadership of the Pale of Settlement and as alternatives to *kahal*-sponsored institutions. In the nineteenth century, Jewish intellectuals had migrated from the towns of the Pale to the new cities of St. Petersburg and Odessa in part to escape the oppressive rule of communal elders.[7] Dubnov called on Jewish intellectuals to return to the institution they had hated and avoided for so long, to reform it and reinvigorate it, for the sake of the higher cause of national unity. Reconstitution of the *kehile* system required a radical shift in the Jewish intelligentsia's pattern of social organization and demanded that it place communal unity above its particular ideological causes.

Dubnov's thinking on the *kehile* evolved over the course of the decade in which he published his "Letters on Old and New Jewry." In the earlier "Letters," published before the revolution of 1905, Dubnov envisioned the modern *kehile* as a voluntary association, which would thrive or languish depending on the level of the Jews' collective will to survive. The major obstacle to the establishment of such a *kehile* was the absence of freedom of assembly and association in Russia. Writing in cautious, oblique terms (tsarist censorship of the press remained in force until 1905), Dubnov looked forward to the removal of the restrictions that prevented Russian Jews from creating modern membership-based *kehiles*. Meanwhile, he chastised German, Dutch, and British Jews for not creating what was already permitted to them.[8]

Dubnov's conception of the *kehile* was transformed under the influence of Austrian Socialist Karl Renner, who developed the theory of extraterritorial autonomy for national groups in the Hapsburg empire. Renner argued in his 1899 pamphlet *Nation and State*, and more fully in his 1902 book *The Struggle of the Austrian Nations Against the State*, that given the mixed ethnic composition of many regions in the empire, the nationalities problem could not be solved on a territorial basis, but should be addressed in functional terms. The state should cede authority over educational, cultural, and certain other affairs to associations representing the various national groups. Each citizen of the empire would, in turn, be required to declare his personal affiliation with the national association of his choice. (Hence Renner coined the term national-personal autonomy.)[9]

Renner's theory led Dubnov to conceive of the modern *kehile* as a public and compulsory institution. The scheme of Jewish communal autonomy that he published in December 1905, in the midst of the political euphoria over the revolution, represented a translation of Renner's ideas into Jewish historical terms. The Russian state would recognize the *kehile* as the local unit of Jewish self-government, which would be responsible for directing all institutions dealing with Jewish education, philanthropy, and religion. The *kehile* would be a democratic community, consisting of all adult Jews, and would be authorized to extract compulsory membership dues. A Jewish National Assembly, or *va'ad* (echoing the *va'ad arba aratsot* [Council of Four Lands] in sixteenth- to eighteenth-century Poland), would be established to address Jewish needs and concerns on the national level and to engage in nonparliamentary representation of the Jewish people to the imperial government. Dubnov proposed that a Jewish constituent assembly be convened immediately, to establish bylaws for the operation of the local *kehiles* and Jewish National Assembly.[10]

This Dubnovian concept of communal autonomy was embraced by a number of leading Russian Zionists in 1905, including Shmaryahu

Levin and Menahem Ussishkin, who saw the political unification of
Russian Jewry in *kehiles* and a National Assembly as a desirable (albeit
limited) step in the process of Jewish national revival. The young
Vladimir Jhabotinsky actively propagated this idea in the Zionist press
and proposed that *kehile* autonomy be formally incorporated into the
political platform of the Russian Zionist Organization. This was indeed
done at the third conference of Russian Zionists, held in Helsingfors in
November 1906.[11]

Dubnov's 1905 plan, although rich in imaginative detail, also had
numerous ambiguities and gaps. On the one hand, it proposed that the
Jewish National Assembly consist of three hundred delegates, each
representing a district of ten thousand adult Jews. On the other hand,
it skirted over fundamental questions of constituency, authority, and
operation. An entire discourse developed among Diaspora Nationalists
to refine and resolve the questions his initial scheme left open.

THE COMMUNITY'S CONSTITUENCY, OR WHO IS A JEW?

Perhaps the most perplexing issue was the question of membership, or constituency: Who would be considered a member of the modern *kehile?* As progressive intellectuals, Diaspora Nationalists agreed
on the need for a democratic community, in which all Jews would be
equal citizens, with no means tests for membership or for office hold-
ing, as had been typical of the traditional *kahal.* As secular Jews, they
rejected schemes, such as that of Henryk Sliozberg at the Kovno conference, that would have tied *kehile* membership to membership in a
synagogue and would have entrusted the election of the citywide *kehile* leadership to synagogue elders. And as post-Rennerian nationalists, they insisted that *kehile* membership be required by law of all
Jews rather than being a voluntary affiliation. Their common slogan
was "an autonomous, democratic, and secular *kehile.*"[12]

But this slogan raised more questions than it answered. Just what
did it mean to say that all Jews would belong to the *kehile?* Who was a
Jew and how would that be determined?

In part, this dilemma was aggravated by the reality that the Russian
Empire did not register its inhabitants by nationality or ethnicity. Inter-

nal passports and birth certificates recorded their religion *(verois-pove'danie)*, and the census also recorded their mother tongue *(rodnoi yazik)*. According to Russian law, Jews were a religious category, and thus no mechanism existed by which to record a person's Jewish nationality.

Dubnov's own Folkspartei (which was in fact not a party but a circle of public intellectuals), could not agree on the matter of membership in the *kehile* and published two alternate membership planks in its platform. The majority proposed that anyone "factually and officially" recorded as a Jew be considered a member of the *kehile*. This meant accepting the government's religious definition of Jewishness, as inscribed in people's passports. It also tied departure from the *kehile* to conversion to another faith. If a Jew did not convert, he would belong to the *kehile* and be subject to its fees or taxes. (Tsarist passports did not allow a category of atheist or religionless under religion.) If he converted, he was outside the *kehile*. Underlying the majority plank of the Folkspartei was what might be called a neomedieval definition of Jewishness.

A more liberal-minded minority in the Folkspartei accepted religion (as recorded in one's passport) as the basic criterion of Jewishness, but also allowed for admission into the *kehile* on an administrative basis. It stipulated that individuals "of non-Jewish origin or non-Judaic faith" could join the *kehile* through submission of a written declaration of affiliation. Conversely, a Jew could resign from the Jewish community (and join another national group, such as the Poles or Russians) without converting, through submission of a statement.[13]

Practically speaking, the main bone of contention between the two factions of the Folkspartei was the status of Jewish converts to Christianity, many whom had embraced Christianity to advance their education and careers but still identified with Jewry. In the first decade of the twentieth century, when harsh quotas on Jewish students in the universities were enforced, such conversions became a significant phenomenon among the younger generation, and their number increased during the period of reaction between 1907 and 1915, when the alleviation of quotas and other discriminatory measures seemed remote. The question of whether to shun converts as traitors or accept them as wayward children was hotly debated in the Jewish press and spilled over into the discussions of the future *kehile*. The majority of the Folkspartei refused to grant membership in the *kehile* to this group (called *meshumodim* in the Yiddish press) unless they reconverted to Judaism, something that was legally possible from 1905 on. The minority would have allowed apostates into the *kehile* based on a written statement of Jewish affiliation.[14]

The issue of membership was also considered from a more ideological perspective by figures in the Bund, which began to take an active interest in the question of *kehile* autonomy in 1909. In a programmatic article in the Bundist journal *Tsaytfragen*, Vladimir Medem confessed that the question was a thorny one, at least until the creation of a reliable Jewish national register. For the foreseeable future, the basic criterion for membership in the *kehile* would have to be one's officially recorded religion. But this was merely a matter of administrative convenience. As a matter of principle, Medem allowed for departure from and admission into the *kehile* by written declaration, that is, on a secular basis. In other words, Medem's position was identical to that of the liberal-minded minority of Dubnov's Folkspartei.[15]

For Medem, the issue of admitting individuals recorded as Christians into the *kehile* had a poignantly personal dimension. He had himself been baptized by his parents at birth and was registered as a Christian on his identity papers. Only during his early adulthood did he consciously choose to identify with Jewry. Medem did not refer to his own personal saga of return in his article on the *kehile*, but it was just beneath the surface of his statement that "there is no reason to close the door of the *kehile* to those 'national converts' [*natsionale geyrim*] who belong officially to a different faith." Medem may also have been thinking of non-Jews active in the Jewish socialist movement, such as Rudolph Rocker in New York.[16]

Medem noted that the acceptance of written declarations regarding national affiliation would solve an opposite problem as well: it would allow "Poles and Russians of the religion of Moses" who did not consider themselves part of the Jewish national group to freely leave the *kehile* and join the Russian or Polish associations. There was no point in forcing assimilationists to belong to a national group they disavowed.[17]

Nonetheless, Medem's acceptance of religion as the basic criterion for Jewishness is noteworthy and probably psychologically revealing, reflecting a lingering personal feeling of guilt about his baptism. His position was attacked from the left by the Bundist journalist and labor organizer A. Litvak, who, unlike Medem, had been educated in a traditional *heder* and several yeshivas. In a counterarticle, "On Questions of the Jewish *kehile*," Litvak polemicized,

> We consider Jews to be not a national-religious group but a nation. . . .
> The Jewish religion has ceased to be the Jews' culture; their culture is
> now a secular one. . . . There are already many Jews who have nothing
> to do with faith, who are in fact religion-less, but who are Jews by culture. . . . We cannot accept religion as a criterion for membership in the
> Jewish community, because we support secularization. We cannot demand that the *kehile* should be a secular institution and at the same time
> make religion a criterion for membership. That is a contradiction which
> will confuse people's consciousness.[18]

Litvak proposed instead that the declaration of Yiddish as one's mother tongue (in the census) be used as the basic criterion for membership in the *kehile*. Language was a secular trait closely tied to nationality, and its use would avoid introducing "religious confusions" into the *kehile*. Admission and departure by written declaration would also be allowed.

Medem had considered the language option in his article but had rejected it on the grounds that language was a divisive issue among the Jewish intelligentsia, and many "real, non-assimilated" Jews would either fail to declare Yiddish as their mother tongue or refuse to on ideological grounds. Litvak retorted that, first of all, many of those who would refuse to declare Yiddish as their language were Poles and Russians of the Mosaic persuasion, who staunchly denied belonging to the Jewish nationality and who would therefore not want to belong to a national *kehile* in the first place. And as for the Hebraists, they were by virtue of their rejection of Yiddish "objective assimilationists," who were harming the survival of the Jewish people in the Diaspora. In any

event, Litvak argued, the practical difference between the two membership criteria, religion and language, was very small. More than 96
percent of the Jews (by religion) in the Russian Empire had declared
Yiddish as their mother tongue, and those Jews who would not be admitted to the *kehile* based on the language criterion could submit a
written declaration of affiliation to join the *kehile*. The inconvenience
caused to the 2–3 percent of Jews who were staunch anti-Yiddishists,
and who would need to submit a declaration, was a small price to pay
for the principle of secular Jewish nationality.[19]

RANGE OF AUTHORITY

A second issue of contention among Diaspora Nationalists was
defining the range of the *kehile*'s jurisdiction and authority: which
powers and responsibilities would be ceded by the state to the nationalities, particularly to the Jewish *kehiles*. Dubnov's original 1905 formulation was brief, ambitious, and highly problematic: "The local *kehile* council directs all local institutions for education, philanthropy
and religion, and appoints from among its members the leaders or
trustees of every institution."[20]

The first problem with Dubnov's formulation was that of *kehile* cen-
tralism, or statism. It subordinated all local communal institutions to
the *kehile* council. The *kehiles* were to appoint their leadership and de-
termine the course of their activity. The subsequent program of the
Folkspartei eliminated this centralized, hierarchical vision of the Jewish polity and replaced it with a more open and flexible system: "The
organs of Jewish autonomy, both local and central, have the right to
establish, guide, and/or support a variety of institutions and corpora-
tions." This formula allowed for much greater individual institutional
freedom. Not every institution had to be created or directed by the *kehile;* grassroots voluntary initiatives were not ruled out.[21]

The second problem with Dubnov's original formulation was its reference to religious institutions being directed by the *kehile*. Here as
well, the Folkspartei program of 1906 retreated from Dubnov's preliminary position of 1905 and deleted religious affairs from the list of areas of *kehile* jurisdiction. Dubnov noted in his introductory essay to the

program that "in accordance with the dominant secularization of the national idea, it [the *kehile*] will be separated from religion."[22] But just what this vague formulation meant was open to interpretation. How total would the separation of *kehile* from religion be? Would the *kehile* fund religious schools (under education), synagogues and their clergy (under culture), or religious charities (under philanthropy)?

The question of religious affairs was part of the larger debate among Diaspora Nationalists on the scope of activity that would be included under the rubric of autonomy. Jewish political parties diverged on this question. The narrowest definition was provided by the Bund during the first few years after it embraced this idea in principle in 1901. The Folkspartei occupied a middle ground, and SERP offered the most ambitious vision.

Vladimir Medem articulated the Bund's early position in his 1904 series of articles, "Social Democracy and the National Question" (subsequently issued in pamphlet form). Medem associated nationality first and foremost with language. Since the Jewish, Polish, Lithuanian, and other working masses knew no language well other than their own respective mother tongues, it was crucial to secure equal status for all languages in Russia. This could only be done by removing those matters that were most contingent on language—education and culture—from the authority of the state and handing them over to the jurisdiction of the nationalities themselves, which would create separate organs for directing them. But Medem and other Bundists adamantly opposed authorizing those organs to deal with social or economic issues, which should be left to the general political organs of the state. National groups, including the Jews, had no common economic or social interests as such. In these areas, the cardinal division in society was along class lines, between the bourgeoisie and the proletariat, and not between nationalities. The Bund therefore advocated national-cultural autonomy, using the phrase in a restrictive sense: culture and only culture. It cautioned against constructing *klal yisroel* (general Jewish) institutions that ignored, and thus weakened, class divisions within Jewry.[23]

In this early stage of the development of Bundist thought on Jewish national autonomy, Medem and his colleagues did not use the term *kehile* or *obshchina*, and it seems that they had in mind something much narrower—a kind of Jewish educational-cultural association.

In contrast, the most expansive vision of autonomy was offered by the leaders of SERP, who were popularly referred to as the Sejmists, because of their support for the idea of national parliaments, or Sejms, in a reconstituted Russia. Moyshe Zilberfarb, the party's foremost spokesman on the subject, criticized the Bund for the meekness and halfheartedness of its national program. National groups were entitled to full political autonomy, meaning jurisdiction over all internal affairs, however the members of the given national group defined them, as long as their autonomous organs did not violate or contradict the law of the land.[24]

The range of areas of Jewish national autonomous jurisdiction enumerated in SERP's 1906 party program included not only education and culture but also public health and welfare (hospitals, soup kitchens, child-care centers), economic and labor policy (credit, insurance, job training), the propagation of agriculture among Jews, and, finally, the regulation and financing of Jewish emigration abroad—with the goal of effecting compact territorial concentration. In this vision, Jewish national autonomy in the Diaspora would allocate funds toward the building of the Jewish national home.

Zilberfarb argued that implementing such an ambitious agenda required the creation of not only a national parliament but also a ministry for Jewish affairs in the Russian government. But this point was not included in the SERP party program. (Little did Zilberfarb know that in 1918 he would himself become minister for Jewish affairs in the government of independent Ukraine.)[25]

The growing national orientation in the Bund after the revolution of 1905 led its leaders to further develop their position on national-cultural autonomy and to embrace the revival and reform of the *kehile*. In his 1910 essay, Medem argued that it would be a mistake to restrict the *kehile* to the supervision of education and culture alone. Until just and democratic institutions of state administration were firmly established throughout Russia, the *kehile*'s authority would have to be broad and include responsibility for health, philanthropy, and emigration.

Otherwise, Jews would be discriminated against in the area of social services by Polish and Russian municipalities. His respondent, A. Litvak, had no principled qualms about the *kehile* dealing with such matters even indefinitely, as long as it did not address economic issues, where Jews' interests divided along class lines.[26]

On one matter, SERP members and Bundists fully agreed: religious affairs had no legitimate place in the activity of the modern *kehile*. Zilberfarb anticipated a difficult struggle against the bourgeois elements in Jewish society to establish the principle of "separation of religion from nationality." Bundists championed the cause of a fully secularized *kehile* at the Kovno conference, much to Sliozberg's chagrin. Litvak argued that the *kehile* would "not support rabbis, cantors, and ritual slaughterers. For religious affairs, there will have to be separate religious societies. . . . We maintain that Jews are a nation, and that the main tasks of the *kehile* will be national and cultural. Religion is a private matter."[27]

Litvak was confident that there would be adequate private contributions to support religious institutions and functionaries. There were rich Hasidic merchants and an Orthodox middle class. He noted, only half in jest, that since the introduction of full separation of church and state in France, "not a single priest has died of starvation."[28]

Dubnov, the father of the *kehile* idea, injected himself into the discussion of this point in the pages of the Russian-language Diaspora Nationalist weekly *Evreiskii Mir*. He warned that the exclusion of religious affairs from the *kehile*'s functions was both unjust and harmful. It would constitute a form of discrimination against the cultural needs of the Orthodox sector of the community. Moreover, it would lead to a new schism in Jewry, as the Orthodox would construct parallel religious communities to satisfy those needs and would withdraw from the *kehiles*, thereby undermining the goal of Jewish unity that was the very purpose of the modern *kehile* movement.

Dubnov argued that secularization of the *kehile* meant demoting religious affairs from their previous position of primacy or domination to a position of parity with other spheres of communal life. Secularization meant that rabbis would have no veto or privileged voice in *kehile* deliberations. But the modern *kehile* should have a commission for reli-

gious affairs, just as it would have commissions for education, philanthropy, and mutual aid. He reminded his readers that religious affairs
meant not only synagogue-congregational affairs but also marriages,
burials, and circumcisions—ritual services that, he noted, were employed by virtually every Jew, including the most secular. It was best to
have a single authoritative agency, recognized by all, to supervise such
matters.[29]

FINANCING THE KEHILE AND REFORMING IT

The third basic question that concerned Diaspora Nationalists was
the mechanism through which the modern *kehile* would obtain revenue for its activities. The Folkspartei program proposed a dual revenue system. On the one hand, the local *kehile* and Jewish National
Council would have the power of compulsory taxation over their
members. On the other hand, they would be entitled to receive proportional funds from the general state budget for education and for other
state functions that were ceded to them.[30]

On the issue of internal Jewish taxation, Socialists such as Zilberfarb hastened to add that it should be in the form of a progressive income tax and not a flat membership fee. Progressive taxation was a
passionate cause for Jewish socialists, because the existing form of
Jewish taxation in the Russian Empire at the turn of the twentieth century was still the *korobka* (the so-called basket tax), a consumption tax
on kosher meat, which financed existing communal synagogues, rabbis, cemeteries, *shehita* (slaughter of kosher meat), and so on. Because
of certain peculiarities of the Jewish community, the *korobka* was
even more regressive than other consumption taxes. Nonobservant
Jews who did not purchase kosher meat avoided paying. In addition,
certain categories of Jews, such as university graduates and members
of the merchant guilds, were officially exempted from paying the *korobka* and were entitled to an annual end-of-year cash refund. Since
the nonobservant and exempted groups overlapped, many of the latter
received a windfall *korobka* income: a refund for taxes they had never
paid. Abolishing the *korobka* was a point on which all reformers of the
kehile agreed.[31]

There were voices within the Bund, and elsewhere, that opposed internal taxation altogether and argued that all *kehile* funds should be obtained through proportional allocations from the state budget. The Jewish working masses were simply too poor to shoulder a double tax burden, from the state and from the *kehile*. But Medem warned that denying the Jewish community the means to raise its own revenue was a formula for national dependence, not national autonomy. If all *kehile* funds would have to be extracted from the general state budget, the state would have effective control over the Jews' national budget. Medem called this "autonomy with one's hands tied." He went to great lengths to demonstrate that there was enough of a Jewish middle class in Russia to shoulder a progressive *kehile* income tax.[32]

Litvak agreed that both internal taxation and proportional state allocations were needed to finance Jewish national autonomy. But he proposed an additional revenue mechanism for the *kehile* and other nationality associations: a corporate tax on private businesses, in which the revenues would be allocated to the various nationalities according to the ethnic composition of the labor force of the given business.[33]

For the participants in this discussion, revival of the *kehile* was not only a matter for the messianic future, in a free and democratic Russia, but a matter for immediate action as well. Some of them called for the drafting of a new law on the Jewish community and its submission to the Duma to replace old, outdated legislation. But even without new legislation, much could be done to reform existing *kehile* structures — to make them more equitable and responsive to public needs.

Zilberfarb was the trailblazer for this line of thought. He pointed out that a neglected existing law allowed Jewish communities to collect an "auxiliary *korobka*" from the rental of property, industrial production, and legacies. Nothing prevented communities from lowering the meat *korobka* to a nominal level and activating the auxiliary *korobka*, thereby replacing a regressive tax on the poor with a progressive tax on the wealthy. There was also no legal obstacle to altering the outlay budget set by Jewish communal leaders so that it would include support for modern Jewish schools, cultural institutions (such as libraries and theaters), job training, cooperatives, and even emigration.[34]

The main irreparable defect of the existing system, according to

Zilberfarb, was its unrepresentative nature. In most locales, the *korobka* and the Jewish communal budget were controlled by self-perpetuating boards, made up of members of wealthy families who worked closely with the local municipal authorities and were totally unaccountable to the Jewish community. The first task, Zilberfarb argued, was to raise public consciousness and to exert public pressure on the existing oligarchies to open up the *kehile* process to the community at large. For too long had the Jewish intelligentsia been indifferent toward local communal affairs, thereby giving free rein to the oligarchies. "In our time, we should already have learned to look upon our *obshchina* as not merely a remnant of the historical past, but as the basic cell of our future national-autonomous organization. It would be naive to imagine that the transition from our current situation to autonomous national existence will be a single jump from the kingdom of national slavery to the kingdom of national freedom."[35]

Medem and Litvak likewise considered public enlightenment on *kehile* affairs and the mobilization of public opinion on behalf of *kehile* reform to be the first necessary steps in the revival of Jewish communal autonomy.[36]

By 1913, the *kehile* movement had accumulated enough momentum to establish a monthly journal of its own, *Vestnik Evreiskoi Obshchini*, with the active participation of Dubnov, Zilberfarb, Jacob Lestschinsky, the Bundist A. Kirzhnits, the Zionist Yitzhak Grünbaum, and others. The opening editorial announced the journal's credo: "From representatives of various social groups and ideological tendencies one hears voices proclaiming, more and more frequently and loudly: Back to the *kehile*! Back to the organization that, since ancient times, served us as a common shield against enemies and a common roof for cultural creativity. . . . At the current difficult moment in our history, it would be a crime to retreat from this loyal and historically tested position. It is necessary now, before it is too late, to begin the work of strengthening the *kehile* and gradually restoring its past might."[37]

In retrospect, the discourse on the revival of the *kehile* was more theoretical than practical. It succeeded, however, in transforming Jewish public opinion and consciousness. By the time of the Russian Revolution and Paris peace conference, the concept of Jewish communal autonomy was firmly embedded in the minds of east European Jews as their unquestionable natural right. It was, in fact, the one national idea that enjoyed the support of Jews across party lines, from Zionists to Bundists and in between. Through it, Jewish-nationalist intellectuals gave expression to the psychic community of *klal yisroel* and sought to give it concrete political form. And in the course of their discussions, they grappled with many of the issues of identity and communal existence that have bedeviled Jews in Israel and the Diaspora down to this day.

PART II

POLAND
BETWEEN THE
WORLD WARS

6

NEW TRENDS IN INTERWAR
YIDDISH CULTURE

While the destruction and dislocation endured by east European
Jews during World War I and its aftermath hampered Jewish
cultural activity, the end of tsarist rule created great opportunities for
Yiddish expression. In the Polish territories that were under German
occupation from 1915 to 1918, the authorities sanctioned and even encouraged the development of Yiddish culture. In the territories that
remained under Russian control, the revolution of February 1917
brought with it the immediate lifting of a wartime ban on Yiddish publications. Moscow, which had been outside the now-abolished Pale of
Settlement, became a center of Yiddish culture for the first time. But
probably the most impressive flourishing of Yiddish culture during the
war years was in the short-lived independent Ukraine (1917–1920),
where a Ministry for Jewish Affairs existed briefly and was succeeded
by a nonpartisan (or multiparty) umbrella organization for Yiddish culture, called Kultur-Lige (Culture League). In 1919, the Kultur-Lige
system included sixty-three Yiddish schools, fifty-four libraries, and
numerous choruses, drama clubs, and people's universities. In Kiev,
the organization sponsored professional studios for Yiddish theater,
music, and art and a publishing house that issued books, newspapers,
and magazines on education, culture, and the arts.[1]

From 1920 through 1939, the Jews of the former Russian empire
were divided between Poland and the Soviet Union, each with between 3 and 3.5 million Jews, with much smaller communities in independent Lithuania and Latvia. Yiddish culture flourished in both

Poland and the Soviet Union, as Warsaw and Moscow competed over which city was its prime center.

Before turning to interwar Poland, a few remarks are in order on Yiddish culture in the Soviet Union, where dramatic shifts took place in the trilingualism of Jewish culture. Hebrew literature, press, and education were banned by the Soviet authorities from 1921 on, since Hebrew was considered the language of Jewish clericalism and Zionism. Distinctively Jewish literature and cultural activity in Russian were also branded as bourgeois and were increasingly suppressed. Yiddish culture, on the other hand, was recognized as the official culture of the Jewish national minority in the Soviet Union and enjoyed state support. The numbers for Yiddish cultural institutions in the USSR were impressive: In 1931, 120,000 Jewish children attended Soviet Yiddish schools, and there were twenty Yiddish theater companies. In 1935, 437 Yiddish-language books were published in the Soviet Union, as were forty-one Yiddish newspapers and periodicals.[2]

But the new social and political conditions of Soviet life encouraged Jewish linguistic and cultural Russification. Foremost among them were the removal of all restrictions on Jewish participation in Soviet higher education and government service and the rapid influx of Jews into these spheres; the sizable migration of Jews to Moscow and Leningrad, where they constituted a small minority of the population; and the regnant Communist ideology of internationalism, accompanied by the suppression of expressions of Jewish nationalism and religion.

As a consequence, Yiddish culture flourished under state sponsorship during the 1920s and 1930s, while Yiddish itself declined. In 1926, 70.4 percent of the Jews in the Soviet Union declared Yiddish as their mother tongue; by 1939 this figure dropped to 39.7 percent. Among young Jews serving in the Red Army, the proportion of Yiddish mother-tongue claimants in 1939 was only 21 percent.[3]

In addition, Soviet Yiddish culture thrived only in the manner and form sanctioned by the authorities and as long as the state considered it desirable. For instance, since the authorities considered Yiddish mainly a medium to spread Communism among the Jews, 213 of the 437 Yiddish books published in 1935, or 45 percent, were translations from Russian, mostly of Soviet political literature and textbooks. More-over, given the intensely Communist, Soviet, antinationalist, and an-tireligious content of the Soviet Yiddish press, books, and schools, it is an open question whether they perpetuated their audience's interest in Yiddish language and culture or eased the transition to Soviet cul-ture and education in Russian. The latter seems more likely.

In 1937–1938, Yiddish culture was struck severely by government purges: the central Yiddish daily in Moscow, *Der Emes* (The Truth), was "liquidated" and its editor, Moyshe Litvakov, arrested; the Yiddish schools in Belorussia were ordered closed, and those in Ukraine were cut back; the Yiddish scholarly institutes in Minsk and Kiev were elim-inated; and many members of the Yiddish cultural elite (including the well-known author Moyshe Kulbak) were arrested and killed as "ene-mies of the people." By 1939, Soviet Yiddish culture was the target of creeping official liquidation.

In Poland, the social and political conditions were quite different and more favorable for the preservation of Yiddish. The dense concen-tration of the Jewish population remained intact, with Jews constitut-ing 30–40 percent of the residents in major cities; anti-Semitism was widespread; the Jews' access to Polish higher education was limited by quotas, and employment in the government sector was nonexistent; and Jewish national self-consciousness was high. Consequently, lin-guistic acculturation was slower than in the Soviet Union, especially in the eastern borderlands, the *kressy*, where Jews had previously gravi-tated toward Russian (rather than Polish) culture. In the 1931 census, 80 percent of the Jewish population in Poland claimed Yiddish as its mother tongue. Even among young people, 53 percent of Jewish high school students claimed Yiddish as their mother tongue in 1937.[4]

In Poland, Yiddish culture never received state support or recogni-tion and was the product of Jewish commercial and independent so-cial activity. The total amount of printed output was impressive. In 1934, 281 Yiddish books were printed, along with fourteen Yiddish dailies and fifty-eight other periodicals. The social constituency of the Yiddish printed word showed signs of both expansion and decline. On the one hand, Orthodox Jewry, the most conservative sector of Jewry, now issued dailies, weeklies, and magazines in Yiddish—a new phenomenon. Zionists of all stripes also published most of their periodical literature in Yiddish during the interwar years. Indeed, the era of the Hebrew daily and weekly press in eastern Europe virtually came to an end. Only one Hebrew newspaper appeared in interwar Poland—during some years a daily, during others a weekly, and during others defunct.[5]

If Yiddish clearly outstripped Hebrew, it faced increasingly serious competition from Polish. Most Jews became fluent in Polish during the interwar years and gravitated toward reading as much, or perhaps even more, in Polish as in Yiddish. A study of major Jewish lending libraries in 1926 indicated this trend: 43.4 percent of the books taken out by readers were in Yiddish, whereas 41 percent were in Polish. Not only did Jews read general Polish literature, but a strong Polish-language Jewish press grew in readership and prestige. While Yiddish culture was strong to the end, there were ample signs that raised doubts about its long-term durability and elicited concern among Yiddishists.[6]

TRENDS IN YIDDISH ARTS AND LETTERS

In interwar Poland, Yiddish arts and letters underwent a process of professionalization. A Union of Yiddish Writers and Journalists in Poland was founded in Warsaw in 1916 and established criteria for membership, a system of dues, and rights and privileges for its members. The union protected the professional interests of the members of the writing trade and settled professional disputes. Its headquarters at Tlomackie 13 in Warsaw became a bustling social hub for Yiddish writers and the bohemian circles that revolved around them. Thanks to the union's activities, the distinction between professional writers and amateurs became firmly entrenched. A similar process took place in the Yiddish theater, under the auspices of the Yiddish Actors' Union, founded in 1919.[7]

The growth and professionalization of the Yiddish writing craft was most evident in the Warsaw Yiddish press. The editorial staff of the largest daily, *Haynt* (from 1920, a Zionist newspaper), consisted of twenty-eight journalists and writers in 1928. In addition, the paper maintained correspondents all across Poland, in Palestine (at one point there were five Palestine correspondents), Paris, London, Berlin, New York, Prague, The Hague, and Salonika. The production and business departments of *Haynt* were each as large as the writing staff. In all, the newspaper had more than 140 people on its payroll in the 1930s, some of whom worked on special weekly sections; on affiliated publications, such as the weekly *Velt-shpigl* (World Mirror); and in the newspaper's publishing house, Yehudiah. *Haynt*'s Yiddish publishing empire was a far cry from the days of Alexander Zederbaum's *Kol Mevaser.*[8]

The rise of bona fide Yiddish publishing houses, which had their own production facilities and staffs, editors, and business departments, was itself further indication of professionalization. Gone were the days when Yiddish authors both edited and sold their own books. The two most prestigious Yiddish presses in Poland were Kultur-Lige (in Warsaw), and Vilner Farlag fun Boris Kletskin (until 1925 in Vilna, afterward in Warsaw). Kultur-Lige launched the Yiddish literary weekly magazine *Literarishe Bleter* (Literary Pages; 1924–1939, modeled after the Polish *Wiedomosci Literacki*), which was the central forum for the Yiddish intelligentsia on problems of literature, theater, and art. The Kletskin Farlag undertook ambitious projects, such as the first European editions of the collected works of Sholem Aleichem (in twenty-eight volumes) and I. L. Peretz (eighteen volumes). The professionalism (and relatively low cost) of Yiddish publishing in Poland led major American Yiddish writers, such as Joseph Opatoshu and H. Leivik, to publish their latest books and collected works in Poland, rather than in the United States. The Yiddish publishing houses in Poland thus serviced a worldwide book market, including America.[9]

Both popular, mass culture and refined, high culture expanded, as the gap between them grew and mutual resentments intensified. On one end of the spectrum were the afternoon tabloid newspapers in Warsaw, such as *Hayntike Nayes* (Today's News); *Radio*; and *Undzer Ekspres* (Our Express), which published shorter news reports and sensational human-interest stories in a simpler language; and the musical/comic revues performed at Warsaw's Central Theater, which were branded as trash *(shund)* by literati. On the other end of the spectrum were the *Literarishe Bleter*, the journals published by literary groups such as Khalyastre (The Gang) and Yung Vilne (Young Vilna) and the highbrow dramatic theater companies: the Vilna Troupe and the Warsaw Yiddish Art Theatre, led by Ida Kaminska and Zigmund Turkow.[10]

The artistic achievements of Yiddish literature and theater were numerous. Two of the best-known works were S. An-sky's expressionist drama *The Dybbuk*, written during the war years but first performed in Yiddish in 1920 by the Vilna Troupe and after enormous critical and box-office success made into a Yiddish feature film in 1938, and Isaac Bashevis Singer's dark novel, *Satan in Goray*, published in 1933, which launched Singer's literary career and was awarded the literary prize of the Union of Yiddish Writers and Journalists in Poland.

Cutting across the spectrum between popular culture and high culture, and supporting all of it, was a network of local institutions dedicated to collective cultural consumption and activity—first and foremost, libraries and reading rooms. Virtually every local branch of every Jewish political party or trade union, and every local cultural association, sponsored a library. In larger communities, there were also commercial or not-for-profit lending libraries. The Yiddish reading culture in interwar Poland was quite intense, especially considering the economic poverty and low formal educational level of the reading public. Then there were amateur choruses and drama circles, which were likewise usually linked to cultural associations or political parties and which created intense social bonds between their participants. Choral singing and amateur choral concerts were so popular that they surpassed performances by professional vocalists as the primary medium of Yiddish musical culture in Poland.[11]

One novel feature of Yiddish culture during this period was the strong interest of the Yiddish intelligentsia and general public in European literature and theater. According to one calculation, more than 20 percent of the Yiddish books published in Poland in 1923 were translations from European literature. More than half of the repertoire of the Warsaw Yiddish Art Theatre consisted of translated dramas (by Moliere, Andreyev, Hugo, Chekhov, Roman Rolain, Dostoevsky, and others). The pages of *Literarishe Bleter* were replete with translations of, and criticism on, European writers—an indication that this interest was widespread not only among the monolingual masses but also among the Yiddish intelligentsia. As a result, the consciousness spread that Yiddish culture was an integral part of European culture, facing the same problems of life and art, rather than a totally separate Jewish realm.[12]

The maturation of Yiddish literature in Poland led to an important expression of international recognition—the establishment of a Yiddish section of the International PEN (poets, essayists, novelists) organization, based in Poland. The formation of the Yiddish section, in response to a petition and memorandums by Yiddish writers, was the first case in which PEN recognized a literature without a state, rather than the literature of a country. The decision was in part a consequence of the exclusion of Yiddish writers from the Polish PEN club. PEN chartered the Yiddish club to be based in Vilna, rather than in the capital city of Warsaw, where the Polish club existed. The arrangement aptly reflected the estranged relations between the two literatures between the wars.[13]

But despite the signs of maturation, a closer look at Yiddish culture in Poland reveals its youth and underdevelopment. One striking feature was the lack of specialization among members of the Yiddish cultural elite. Writers and intellectuals engaged in astonishing combinations of high and low forms of writing and of literary and nonliterary activity. It was rare to find a playwright, even the most famous, who was not also a prose writer or critic; it was rare to find a scholar, even the most accomplished, who was not also a journalist. Thus Zalmen Rejzen, a philologist who was one of the codirectors of the Yiddish Scientific Institute (Yiddisher Visnshaftlekher Institut; YIVO), in Vilna, was also the editor of a local daily newspaper, *Der Tog* (The Day). Alter Kacyzna, one of the best Yiddish playwrights in Poland, was also a novelist and poet, but he made his living as a photojournalist for the New York Yiddish daily *Forverts* (Forward). Kh. Sh. Kazhdan, one of the heads of the Central Yiddish School Organization (Tsentrale Yidishe Shul Organizatsye; TsISHO) and editor of its pedagogical journal, was also a critic and contributor to *Literarishe Bleter*, and he was the translator (from Russian) of several volumes of Simon Dubnov's *World History of the Jewish People*, for YIVO.[14]

The absence of clear-cut professional boundaries was in part a consequence of the weak economic base of Yiddish culture in Poland. Intellectuals needed to "dance at many weddings" in order to make a living. The daily press and popular theater were the only financially secure cultural institutions. But the lack of specialization among intellectuals also reflected the lack of long-standing institutional traditions in the various spheres of Yiddish cultural endeavor and the absence of psychological space separating them. A professor could be a journalist, and a pedagogue could be a literary critic, because in the intellectuals' own minds, they were all engaged in aspects of one activity—advancing Yiddish culture.

EDUCATION

The virtual nonexistence of modern Yiddish-language schools was the single greatest gap in the Yiddish cultural system before World War I. Yiddish had been passed on from generation to generation orally, with little, if any, formal, institutionalized instruction. This put Yiddish culture in an anomalous situation in many respects. It meant that most Yiddish speakers had never studied how to spell correctly or write grammatically and that there was little awareness of linguistic norms. Even the name of the language itself was spelled differently in different publications—as *yudish*, *idish*, or *yidish*. The absence of schools also meant that Yiddish speakers had never formally studied Yiddish literature, and familiarity with the literary cannon was not widespread. Perhaps most ominously, the nonexistence of Yiddish schools meant that acculturation was a precondition for obtaining a modern education. This situation encouraged Russification and Polonization and relegated Yiddish to a lower status compared to "proper" modern languages.

This situation changed during the interwar years. A modern Yiddish educational system arose on all levels: elementary and secondary schools, technical and professional training, and some forms of higher education. This educational endeavor was driven by Yiddishists, who considered the language and its literature to be central Jewish values. For them, the creation of a Yiddish school system was essential in order to transmit Yiddish language and literature to the next generation and combat "linguistic assimilation." As Yiddishists, they viewed the creation of a comprehensive Yiddish cultural system, with education at its foundation, as an inherent goal.

Yiddish schools were the newest form of Jewish schooling to arise in eastern Europe. (Bilingual Hebrew-Russian schools had existed since the 1890s in tsarist Russia.) After an initial period of spontaneous and disorganized growth under the German occupation, they coalesced into TsISHO, founded in Warsaw in 1921. In the fierce, cutthroat partisan rivalry that characterized interwar Polish Jewry, TsISHO soon came under the control of two parties: the Bund and the Poale-Zion-Left, both of which were Marxist. The other, non-Marxist, Yiddishist parties—the liberal Folkspartei, led by Noyekh Prilutski, and the moderately socialist Fareynikte (a conglomeration of the prewar Sejmists and Socialist Territorialists)—were not significant political forces in the 1920s and 1930s. Consequently, the TsISHO schools identified themselves as proletarian schools and had a strong socialist and secularist orientation. Religious subjects and Hebrew were, as a rule, not taught.[15]

In Vilna, the third-largest Jewish community in Poland, the situation was different. Yiddishism had a broader social base in Vilna and a local tradition of Yiddish educational activity dating back to 1905. Consequently, the Yiddish schools there arose independently of the political parties and united into the Central Education Committee (Tsentraler Bildungs-komitet; TsBK) in 1919. The TsBK schools defined themselves alternately as modern Jewish schools and as secular Yiddish schools. As a rule, they taught Bible "from a cultural-historical perspective," as well as Hebrew language, and celebrated Jewish holidays. From 1921 on, TsBK was an autonomous, local division of TsISHO.[16]

The TsISHO schools struggled with the practical, real-life implementation of Yiddishist ideology. They needed to strike a balance between the teaching of three curricular blocks: Polish language, literature, and history—taught in Polish; Jewish subjects (Yiddish language and literature, Jewish history)—taught in Yiddish; and general subjects (world history and geography, math and science)—also taught in Yiddish. Textbooks needed to be composed for the Jewish and general subjects. Rules of Yiddish spelling and grammar needed to be established and disseminated. And the schools needed Yiddish terms to teach chemistry, algebra, and other advanced general subjects in Yiddish. The question of the schools' attitude toward Judaism and the Jewish religious tradition also loomed large.[17]

The TsISHO schools were pioneers in introducing progressive educational ideas and practices, such as coeducation, physical education, nonfrontal learning through activity (arts and crafts, music, science experiments, and excursions), student governance, parent committees, and attention to educational theory and developmental psychology.

While impressive in their achievements, the numeric scope of the Yiddish school system was modest and grew little during the interwar years. Of the 180,181 children who attended Jewish day schools in Poland in 1936 (who were themselves approximately a third of all Jewish children in Poland), 16,486, or 9 percent, attended the TsISHO schools. There were many reasons for the relative weakness of the school system. Yiddish schools, like other modern Jewish schools in Poland, received no government funding and had to charge a poverty-stricken parent body tuition. Moreover, the Yiddish schools in particular were harassed and persecuted by the Polish authorities, who considered them to be nests of Communism. Many schools were forcibly closed, and the graduates of the TsISHO schools were not awarded state-recognized diplomas that would enable their advancement to high school or university.

Since Yiddish-language education was a new phenomenon, it was also viewed with apprehension by many parents, who were concerned that it would hinder their children's career prospects: their children would either not know Polish well enough or would receive a second-rate education. Finally, the overtly partisan nature of the TsISHO schools narrowed their constituency to the children of Socialist parents. (In Vilna, where the Yiddish schools were nonpartisan, 41 percent of all children attending Jewish day schools were enrolled in the TsBK schools.) For all of these reasons, schools remained the weakest link in the Yiddish cultural system.[18]

The scope of modern Yiddish-language education during the interwar years was broader, and more developed, than the TsISHO and TsBK schools alone. From 1928 on, a small bilingual (Yiddish-Hebrew) school system, called Shul-kult, functioned in Poland, with three thousand students. Moreover, ORT (Obschestvo Remesslenogo Truda), the Jewish society for crafts and technical professions, founded in 1880, developed a network of technical schools that used Yiddish as their language of instruction. At its pinnacle was a polytechnicum in Vilna, which published Yiddish literature on mechanics, engineering, electronics, and other fields. Taken together with Yiddish-language crafts schools, agricultural schools, a nursing school, a conservatory, a theater school, and the Yiddish teachers' seminary, the annual enrollment in Yiddish-language professional schools in Poland was about five thousand on the eve of the war.[19]

A FLOWERING OF SCHOLARSHIP

Another entrenched gap in the Yiddish cultural system before World War I was the absence of scholarly literature. Rabbinic scholarship, in both its traditional and modern (critical) forms, had always been composed in Hebrew. And modern Jewish scholarship, as embodied in the Jewish Historical-Ethnographic Society and its journal *Evreiskaia Starina* (Jewish Antiquities), had been published in Russian. While a few scholarly works on Yiddish language and literature were published in Yiddish after 1905, they were isolated publications, and their authors lacked any institutional base or organizational center.

The idea of establishing a Yiddish university or academy had been the utopian dream of Yiddishists ever since it was first proposed by Chaim Zhitlovsky in 1899. Consequently, the formation in 1925 of YIVO attracted broad public attention and was seen as the capstone event in the rise of modern Yiddish culture. The institute itself was located in Vilna, but some of its research divisions were based in Berlin (until 1933, when they moved to Paris), and an active American branch functioned in New York. YIVO was, in the words of its scientific secretary, Max Weinreich, "the highest scientific agency of the Yiddish speaking community worldwide."

In its structure and operation, YIVO was modeled after an institute of the academy of sciences of a European country. It had four research divisions: Philology, History, Economics and Statistics, and Psychology and Pedagogy. The expansion of Yiddish-language scholarship beyond the first field, Yiddish philology, was itself a major departure. The research agenda of each division was set by its members, an elite group of scholars, most of whom (with the exception of the division secretary) were not on YIVO's salaried staff. Each research division edited and published its own series of collected studies—*Historishe shriftn fun YIVO, Filologishe shriftn fun YIVO*, and so on—as well as monographs, sources, and other materials. In 1931, YIVO began to publish a journal called *Yivo Bleter*, with each research division responsible for the submission, refereeing, and editing of its own materials.

YIVO's research agenda reflected the secular, Yiddishist, and Diaspora Nationalist orientations of its founders and heads. The Division of Philology studied Yiddish language and literature, not Hebrew literature, let alone Bible or rabbinics; the Division of History focused overwhelmingly on the history of east European Jewry and conducted virtually no research on Jewish history in antiquity and the middle ages and the like. But within the parameters of its research agenda, YIVO struggled mightily to be nonpartisan, objective, and pluralistic in its methods and conclusions.[20]

The Division of Philology was particularly active, in part because YIVO's Executive Committee in Vilna consisted of three philologists: Max Weinreich, Zalmen Rejzen, and Zelig Kalmanovitch. The division had under its auspices two special subunits, called commissions. The first was the Folklore Commission, which conducted fieldwork, distributed questionnaires, and collected one hundred thousand items of Jewish folk creativity—songs, stories, proverbs, idiomatic expressions, jokes, customs, and folk art. The second was the Terminological Commission, which maintained seven hundred terminological lists: of words used in traditional Jewish crafts and trades and of new terms for use in the Yiddish schools in the fields of mathematics, technology, and the natural sciences.

The Division of Philology was also the prime mover in establishing the rules of standard Yiddish spelling. A basic set of rules was passed by TsISHO in 1921 and expanded and modified at a YIVO conference in 1928; the final rules were codified in a joint conference of YIVO and TsISHO in 1936. Since YIVO was not a state agency, it did not have any means of enforcement at its disposal, and adherence to the YIVO spelling system was uneven at best. Most periodicals and books eliminated the silent letters *hey* (the equivalent of *h*) and *ayin* (the equivalent of *e*), as required by YIVO, and wrote *yidn* rather than *yiden, ershter* rather than *ehrshter*, and so on. But the large daily newspapers did not follow suit in implementing these reforms. Very few publications, other than YIVO's own, used diacritic signs over the letters *feh* (the equivalent of *f*) and *vet* (the equivalent of *v*) as required by the rules. The Division of Philology had somewhat greater success in propagating adherence to stylistic and grammatical norms among the Yiddish intelligentsia, through articles in YIVO's newsletter, in *Yivo Bleter*, and in a special magazine called *Yidish far Ale* (Yiddish for All; 1938–1939). A primary objective of YIVO's language-normative work was to distinguish Yiddish from modern German and combat the Germanizing style known as *Daytshmerish*.[21]

The Division of History was headed by Elias Tcherikower, a close disciple of the founding father of Russian Jewish historiography, Simon Dubnov. YIVO considered itself to be following in the Dubnovian tradition and translated the master's major works from Russian into Yiddish. Consequently, Tcherikower's research interests had a Russian Jewish slant (history of pogroms in the Ukraine, the early history of the Jewish labor and socialist movements). Major Polish Jewish historians, such as Majer Balaban, who dealt with Jews in the old Polish kingdom and the history of Jews in Lublin and Cracow, remained distant from YIVO and published their scholarship mainly in Polish. This estrangement was partially overcome during the 1930s, when a younger generation of historians arose, who became active in the division's Historical Commission for Poland.[22]

In general, YIVO's mode of operation—a small salaried academic staff who combined research with administrative duties, reinforced by circles of affiliated, nonsalaried scholars (the members of the divisions)—encouraged the conduct of collaborative research projects and the writing of articles, rather than the production of major monographs by individual scholars.

Besides the research and publications conducted by the divisions, much of YIVO's institutional energy was invested in developing its library and archive. Both were built up largely thanks to the volunteer efforts of *zamlers*, YIVO collectors, who received instructions from the institute's staff on what kinds of materials to collect and send to Vilna. Thanks to energetic public campaigns, the library also received free copies of most Yiddish books published in Poland, eastern Europe, and the United States from their publishers. As YIVO's prestige grew, many Jewish organizations in Poland designated YIVO as the depository for their past records. On the eve of World War II, the YIVO library had forty thousand books and ten thousand volumes of Jewish periodicals, and the archive had accumulated 175,000 catalogued files.

The last component of the YIVO structure to be introduced (in 1936) was its graduate training program, or *aspirantur.* Students studied and worked under the direction of members of YIVO's research staff and in some cases also studied simultaneously at Vilna's Stephan Bathory University. Fifty-three students participated in the program during the three years of its existence.

YIVO's intense attention to detail, precision, modern academic methods, and high standards were shocking novelties in Yiddish culture. Perhaps this institution-wide feature is best exemplified through the workings of its library and Bibliographic Center, which aspired to register every Yiddish book published in the world. The Bibliographic Center conducted meetings and issued guidelines on the proper form of full bibliographic description in Yiddish. The guidelines provided instructions on such matters as the use of commas, semicolons, parentheses, brackets, and ellipses and the transcription and translation of authors and titles. The YIVO library was the first Jewish book repository in the world to use the Dewey decimal system and issued working papers on the system's modification to meet YIVO's specific needs. In this and other respects, YIVO compensated for the lack of a modern Yiddish scholarly tradition and the absence of a state imprimatur by maintaining standards that were as high as, or higher than, those of a state university or national library. In doing so, it sought to raise the status of Jewish research and the Yiddish language in the eyes of skeptical Jews and Poles alike.

Yiddish culture in interwar Poland developed in an environment marked by intense nationalism, both Polish and Jewish. Since the Jews had no state and their political influence in Poland was weak, their cultural institutions were important sources of pride and self-validation. The Yiddish cultural institutions—the press, literature, theater, schools, YIVO—were considered proof that Jews were a nation, a people deserving of collective dignity and national rights. The maintenance of Yiddish culture was considered as advancing a Jewish political goal, whether it was the recognition of the Jews' right to equality and autonomy in Poland or their right to sovereignty in Palestine.

Consequently, the intelligentsia often used the language of political struggle in discussing Yiddish culture. A Yiddish newspaper or theater company was an important "cultural position," which needed to be protected and fortified. Choruses and drama circles were engaged in "cultural work" and needed to mobilize as many "forces" as possible. Yiddish intellectuals discussed the state of affairs "on the cultural front" (the name of a book by the editor of *Literarishe Bleter*). At its worst, this rhetoric engendered a mechanistic attitude toward culture, whose main concern was with numbers, not with content or quality. At its best, the language of struggle created a broad public awareness among Polish Jewry that culture was an independent value that uplifted Jewish and human life. More often than not, the rhetoric of struggle used concerning Yiddish culture in Poland aptly reflected the anxieties of a community whose language, and whose physical survival, were felt to be in a state of perennial danger.

7

THE JUDAISM
OF SECULAR
YIDDISHISTS

The explosion of Yiddish-language creativity in the early twentieth century was accompanied by the rise of ideological Yiddishism. Yiddishism synthesized nationalist and populist ideas drawn from the Russian, Polish, and broader east European milieu, applying them to the Jews. Like other east European ethnonationalist movements, it placed great emphasis on the Jews' spoken language as one of their defining markers as a national group, which bound them together across time and space. It celebrated and championed the fact that Yiddish, like other east European vernaculars, was undergoing a process of modernization and becoming the vehicle for a modern national culture encompassing literature, the performing arts, education, social and political discourse, and scientific scholarship. Yiddishists considered the suppression or nonrecognition of Yiddish by the Russian and Hapsburg empires to be a national injustice against the Jews, and they viewed the abandonment of Yiddish by certain groups of Jews themselves as a national tragedy or, worse, a form of national treason.

Perhaps the most succinct proclamation of Yiddishism as a Jewish version of east European ethnonationalism was made by I. L. Peretz in his opening speech at the Czernovitz conference for the Yiddish language in August 1908:

> The state which used to devour smaller and weaker peoples—as *molekh* devoured its children—that state is now losing its luster. . . . Small op-

pressed peoples are awakening and fighting for their language, their uniqueness. And we, the weakest of all, have joined their ranks. We do not wish to be anyone's servant. . . . We do not want to fracture ourselves any more, and sacrifice parts of ourselves to each *molekh*-state.

We call out to the world and say: we are a Jewish people and Yiddish is our language, and in that language we will create our cultural treasures, arouse our spirit, and unite ourselves culturally across lands and generations.[1]

Diaspora-oriented ethnonationalism was a key component of Yiddishism, but the former did not necessarily lead to the latter. The Hebraist movement, most famously represented by Ahad Ha'am, aspired to establish Hebrew as the dominant language of Jewish education, culture, and communal life in Russia and was equally rooted in east European ethnonationalism. Indeed, for many Hebraists, the cause of Hebrew was separate from and more immediate than the cause of establishing a Jewish national home in Palestine. They contended that regardless of the prospects for Jewish settlement and sovereignty in the land of Israel, Jewish life in the Diaspora needed to be Hebraized so that it would retain its national authenticity and unity.[2] And there were Diaspora Nationalists who stressed other components of national identity (such as historical consciousness and communal autonomy) above and beyond language, such as the historian Simon Dubnov.

The second essential ingredient of Yiddishism was Jewish populism. Like its Russian and Polish counterparts, Jewish populism celebrated the Jewish masses, as opposed to the modernized elites. The masses were imbued with the virtues of wisdom, beauty, strength, humor, and nobility, whereas the modern Jewish bourgeoisie and intelligentsia were considered morally decadent and culturally shallow. This contrast applied to their respective levels of national identity as well. The masses were unwavering in their Jewishness, whereas the modern elites had cut themselves off from the Jewish people and assimilated, in a quixotic quest to be accepted by Poles and/or Russians. If the Jewish people continued to survive, it was thanks to the masses, not the elites. Of course the masses were in certain respects backward and benighted, but this was in no small measure due to their "abandonment" by the intelligentsia. It was incumbent upon the new, nationally conscious intelligentsia to return to the masses and unite with them, in a relationship in which they would be inspired by the masses and learn from them, while also guiding and teaching them.[3]

This reevaluation of the Jewish masses brought with it a reevaluation of their folk tongue, Yiddish, which was now viewed as the quintessential product and reflection of the folk genius. As such, it was to be cherished and cultivated. Uniting with the Jewish masses meant, in concrete cultural terms, that the intelligentsia should make the language of the masses its own. Not only should it learn it (as was often necessary) and use it to convey ideas to the less educated, but the Jewish intelligentsia should adopt Yiddish as the language in which it conducted its everyday lives and public endeavors. This meant speaking Yiddish at home and at the meetings of Jewish associations, rather than Russian or Polish, and composing the most sophisticated artistic, philosophic, and scholarly literature in Yiddish, rather than in Russian or Hebrew.

The populism inherent in Yiddishism brought with it a revision of the Jewish literary and cultural cannon, in which folklore was elevated to the status of the Jews' most precious national treasure, since it was the truest expression of the folk spirit. Yiddish folktales, folk songs, and proverbs were now collected, published, performed, analyzed, adapted, and imitated by members of the intelligentsia who were eager to link up with the spirit of the masses.[4]

Yiddishists entertained a range of attitudes toward Hebrew language and literature, from negative to neutral and even positive. But all agreed that Hebrew would never become a living, spoken language among the Jews of eastern Europe and that it would at most be a language known and used by an elite of writers and scholars there.

What were the Yiddishists' attitudes toward the Jewish religious heritage—the Bible and rabbinic literature, the Sabbath and religious holidays, religious rituals and faith? Conventional wisdom has it that the Yiddishists were archsecularists, that they rejected traditional Judaism in its entirety and sought to replace it with a new, modern European culture in Yiddish. This image is a simplification and distortion, more a caricature than a portrait. The complexity is illustrated in the thought of two founding fathers of Yiddishism, Chaim Zhitlovsky and I. L. Peretz.

TWO COMPETING FORCES IN YIDDISHISM

Zhitlovsky and Peretz were the central personalities at the 1908 conference for the Yiddish language held in Czernovitz, at which Yiddish was declared a Jewish national language. While the two men cooperated closely at the conference and shared the core Yiddishist perspective, their outlooks differed significantly.

Zhitlovsky (born in Vitebsk in 1865, died in Canada in 1943), was the father of the culturally radical version of Yiddishism. In a series of influential articles and lectures written between 1897 and 1914 in Russia, Switzerland, and the United States, Zhitlovsky affirmed Jewish nationality while supporting its total separation from the Jewish religion. Religion could no longer serve, in the modern era, as the binding force that united the Jewish people in the Diaspora, because it flew in the face of modern science, philosophy, and morality. On the other hand, the Jewish people could not rely on territorial concentration and political sovereignty as binding national forces, at least for the foreseeable future. It was therefore imperative that language, specifically Yiddish, serve as the basis for Jewish national unity.

The task of Jewish nation building, according to Zhitlovsky, was to create a comprehensive modern culture in Yiddish, so that the Jewish people could satisfy all of its intellectual and cultural needs in its own tongue. Zhitlovsky looked forward to the creation of Yiddish-language universities and himself composed a two-volume history of world philosophy in Yiddish as well as translations of works by Friedrich Nietzsche. For Zhitlovsky, the rise of Yiddish, and its displacement of Hebrew, symbolized a cultural revolution taking place in Jewry—the end of the era of religious Judaism and the dawn of the era of free, secular Jewish culture. The new Yiddish culture would be Jewish by virtue of its language, not by virtue of its particularist content. It would be Jewish just as French culture was French because of the language in which it was created, without being Catholic or focusing on exclusively French problems. Indeed, Zhitlovsky went so far as to argue that a Yiddish-speaking and Yiddish-reading Jew could choose whatever metaphysical or religious system he preferred, including Christianity, and remain a Jew by nationality.[5]

Peretz, on the other hand, articulated a national-romantic version of Yiddishism during the decade between 1905 and World War I, in numerous articles in the Warsaw Yiddish press and in public addresses. As a religious agnostic, Peretz stripped the Bible and rabbinic literature of their status as products of divine revelation and as codes of binding religious law. But he reenshrined these works as national repositories of wisdom, beauty, and moral-ethical values. It was incumbent on modern Yiddish literature and culture to inherit the positive elements of the old religious heritage, as sources of inspiration and as idioms of expression. In Peretz's conception, Yiddish literature was the newest link in a cultural chain going back to the Bible and should reflect the unique way the Jewish people have seen and felt reality throughout the ages.[6]

At Czernovitz, Peretz argued that one of the most urgent tasks awaiting modern Yiddish culture was preparation of a complete literary translation of the Bible and of other classical Jewish texts into Yiddish. This would ensure that the newer generation of Jews, and, most importantly, of Yiddish writers, who did not know Hebrew, would not lose access to the ancient tradition. In addition, he felt that Yiddish could not legitimately claim the status of a Jewish national language so long as the greater part of the Jewish national literary canon was not available in it. Peretz himself composed Yiddish translations of the five Biblical scrolls (the Song of Songs, Ruth, Lamentations, Ecclesiastes, and Esther) and of several medieval liturgical poems.[7]

The tension between the radical and national-romantic versions of Yiddishism runs through the history of this movement and even through the thinking of individual Yiddishists.[8] While this tension was expressed in ideological pronouncements and reflected in literary works, it expressed itself most concretely, and on a socially influential plane, in the schools the Yiddishists created. There they faced head-on the questions, What Jewish subjects and material were to be included in the curriculum, and how were they to be taught? What was the Judaism or Jewish culture that should be instilled in children?

YIDDISH SCHOOLS AND THEIR JEWISH CURRICULUM

Differing perspectives on the Jewish education to be offered in Yiddish schools were articulated as early as 1910 on the pages of the
Bundist journal *Tsaytfragen*. Esther Frumkin, the first theoretician of
the Yiddish school movement, articulated the culturally radical position. There was no need for particularly Jewish national subjects to be
taught in Yiddish schools; the schools were naturally and inherently
Jewish by virtue of their language of instruction. Frumkin scoffed at
celebrating the Sabbath and Jewish holidays as part of the children's
education, noting that it would be utter hypocrisy for a modern person
to bless Sabbath candles, take his children to the synagogue, or tell
them stories about heaven and hell. There were new proletarian holidays to celebrate, new anniversaries of revolutions to commemorate,
and new stories to tell about the heroes in the struggle for progress.

While Frumkin did support teaching Jewish history, because it
would help Jewish children understand their contemporary condition,
she contended that teaching arithmetic in Yiddish was just as important an act of national education, and perhaps even more important.[9]

In her rhetorical crescendo, Frumkin stated, "I believe that in place
of the old dying Judaism [*yidishkayt*], a new Judaism is sprouting up.
Jewish life is creating new forms. And when I see the old dying—the
Judaism of messiah, Yom Kippur, and the *tashlikh* and *kapores* rituals
[on the High Holidays]—I rejoice. Because I know that the old is ob-
structing the new, and that the old must be overcome, so that the new
may flourish."[10]

The opposing position was taken by Boris Levinson, also a Bundist
but a member of the Bund's national wing. While conceding that there
was no place for supernaturalism or synagogue prayers in the modern
Yiddish school, he asserted that there was a need to include national
customs in the homes and schools of Jewish workers and radical *inteligenty*, so that these groups would not cut themselves off from the
Jewish historical experience and from the Jewish community at large.
The Sabbath could be observed by spreading a white tablecloth and by
lighting candles without a blessing. Passover should be celebrated as
the festival of freedom, and on the agricultural festival of Shavuot,

homes and schools could be decorated with green leaves, in accordance with tradition. The Jewish holidays could be filled with human cultural significance.

Levinson argued that the developmental and psychological needs of Jewish children demanded that they have moments of elevation and joy, such as the Jewish holidays, to break with the grayness of everyday life. And as for literature and reading material, young children were attracted to stories of the mysterious, the fantastic, and the heroic. The Bible was therefore the most beautiful children's book of all, and ancient Jewish history was filled with dramatic and heroic moments.[11]

Already in Levinson's brief article, one can detect the main techniques used by national-romantic Yiddishists to incorporate ancient religious texts and practices into secular Yiddish education: the transformation of the Bible (and other hallowed texts) into a corpus of ancient Jewish history, literature, and folklore and the transmutation of religious festivals into national holidays with humanistic messages and of religious commandments into national customs.

At first glance, the TsISHO schools were the embodiment of Esther Frumkin's approach. The official elementary school curriculum issued by TsISHO's Pedagogical Council in 1921 had only one required Jewish-studies subject: Yiddish. The remaining subjects were Polish, natural science, mathematics, history and geography, art, crafts, music, and gymnastics. Subjects one might expect to find in a Jewish day school were not enumerated in the curriculum. There was no study of Bible. Jewish history was not listed as a separate discipline and was subsumed under the general rubric of history (along with Polish and world history). Hebrew was an optional subject that schools could choose to offer beginning in the fourth grade.[12]

The official TsBK curriculum differed from that of TsISHO in Jewish studies. Hebrew was taught in all schools beginning in the second or third grade, for more weekly hours than was allotted for it as an elective by the TsISHO program. Bible was listed as a constituent part of teaching Hebrew ("Hebrew [with Bible]"), and Jewish history was a separate subject, apart from Polish and world history.[13]

To a certain extent, the apparent radical secularism of the TsISHO curriculum, and the absence of traditional Jewish subjects, were an optical illusion created by the labels given to disciplines. The level and nature of the schools' Jewish content is revealed by the textbooks they used to teach Yiddish literature and Jewish history.[14]

TWO TEXTBOOKS AND WHAT THEY TEACH US

The first major school anthology of Yiddish literature was a three-volume series called *Dos yidishe vort* (The Yiddish word), which was published in Vilna in 1912 and went through eight printings by 1921. *Dos yidishe vort* was compiled by Moyshe Olgin, a Bundist educator who later gained fame as editor-in-chief of the New York Communist Yiddish daily *Morgn Frayhayt* (Morning Freedom).[15]

Volume 1 consisted of selections from numerous Yiddish authors. Most prominently represented were Mendele Moykher Seforim, I. L. Peretz, Sholem Aleichem, and Sholem Asch, whose portraits adorned the book's cover to highlight their status as the four classics of modern Yiddish literature. The portraits of Shimon Frug, Chaim Nachman Bialik, and Avrom Reisin were printed inside the book, affording them a privileged second-tier position after the classics.

The first volume's subtitle, and its organizing principle, was *The Jewish Shtetl, the Seasons of the Year, and the Holidays* [*yomim toyvim*]. It opened with a story by Sholem Aleichem about a boy's first day in *heder* and the popular song "Oyfn pripetchik" about the rebbe (teacher) teaching children the Hebrew alphabet, thus inviting the book's readers to see themselves in a symbolic continuum with students in Jewish religious schools from the past. *Dos yidishe vort* went on to include stories and poems set around the Sabbath and the holidays of Sukkot, Simhat Torah, Hanukah, Purim, Passover, and Lag Baomer. While ostensibly, and in fact, an anthology of Yiddish literature for the school, modern Yiddish literature was used by *Dos yidishe vort* as a vehicle to teach about the Jewish holidays and to instill an appreciation of their symbols and rituals. The rituals were transformed into folkways and customs characteristic of the *shtetl*, the Jewish heartland of the recent past. Besides the holidays, it included positive stories on old-world characters and artifacts: a preacher, a Hasidic rebbe, a penitent, a rabbinic library, a Jewish cemetery.

Dos yidishes vort did not include stories that satirized or criticized the *shtetl* as backward and superstitious, but rather materials that highlighted its positive values. On the other hand, the book did not teach children to perform the Sabbath or holiday rituals per se or intend for them to return to the lifestyle of the nineteenth century *shtetl*. It attempted to implant in them favorable images of the rituals, figures, and objects of the old way of life as part of their Jewish national consciousness.

Perhaps even more surprising, *Dos yidishes vort* extended the boundaries of Yiddish literature to include material that was not originally Yiddish and not, strictly speaking, belletristic literature. The opening section of volume 1 included, immediately after the *heder* material, a number of Talmudic legends on the life of Rabbi Akiva, and tales about the Talmudic sage Hillel were also interspersed in the volume.

This tendency culminated in volume 3 of *Dos yidishes vort*, intended for higher grades and deceptively subtitled *Model-Works from Major Literary Genres*. Included in the prose section were a fragment from the biblical book of Kings (as a chronicle), part of Ahad Ha'am's essay on Moses (translated from Hebrew), two historical selections by Simon Dubnov—one on the siege and destruction of Jerusalem by the Romans and the other on the founder of Hasidism, Israel Ba'al Shem Tov (translated from Russian), and a meditation on Jewish spirituality by Hillel Zeitlin called "The Longing for Beauty in the Old Jewish Way of Life." All of this in an anthology of Yiddish literature edited by a Bundist. The parameters of the Jewish literary legacy that could be taught under the formal curricular rubric Yiddish were broader and more flexible than the name implied.[16]

Another example of a textbook that stretched the secular Jewish curriculum to surprising limits was *Yidishe geshikhte*, two volumes of Jewish history by Mordkhe Birnbaum and David Kassel, two of the most prolific authors of Yiddish textbooks and children's literature, who were active in Warsaw during the second and third decades of the twentieth century. *Yidishe geshikhte* was first published in 1916 and went through seven printings by 1929.[17]

Under the rubric of history, the book provided a Yiddish adaptation of the five books of Moses for children. The cover page projected this message visually, through traditional iconography. It featured the tablets of the Ten Commandments in the upper center, with lions facing them on both sides—a symbol commonly found above the ark in the synagogue. Behind the tablets and lions lay an opened scroll, evidently of the Torah.

The first volume of *Yidishe geshikhte* was entitled, without any intent at irony, *Jewish History from the Creation of the World until the Judges*. In their brief introduction, written in smaller typeface and intended probably for teachers, Kassel and Birnbaum offered a modern critical sketch of the ancient Semitic peoples from which the Jews descended. The introduction noted that each of these peoples had its own legends on the creation of the world and of man, and on the rise of nations, but Kassel and Birnbaum stopped short of stating that the material that followed in *Yidishe geshikhte* was legendary. Instead, the introduction concluded by shifting back to the affirmation of basic national myths: the Jews were the descendents of Abraham and had embraced monotheism, while all other Semitic peoples remained idolaters. In sum, the introduction took an ambiguous position on the historicity of the biblical narrative.

What followed in the next one hundred pages was quite traditional: the biblical stories of creation, Adam and Eve, Cain and Abel, Noah and the flood, the parting of the Red Sea, the giving of the Torah at Sinai, down to what it called "the conquest of Palestine by the Jewish People" and the death of Joshua. Select rabbinic Aggadot were included in the textbook, in chapters specifically marked as *legendes* (legends). But the overall impression left by *Yidishe geshikhte* was that the biblical narratives themselves recounted the course of Jewish history. Perhaps sensing that the textbook had gone too far in embracing religious language and myths, the authors or publishers revised its title in later editions to *Yiddishe geshikhte in dertseylungen un legendes* (Jewish history in stories and legends).

Tensions and clashes between the radical and national-romantic orientations within TsISHO were an ongoing theme in the organization's twenty-one-year history. On the whole, the radical trend dominated in the Warsaw organization and the romantic-national trend in the Vilna-based TsBK.

THE CELEBRATION OF JEWISH HOLIDAYS

TsISHO's official first-grade curriculum included the celebration of three Jewish holidays—Sukkot, Hanukah, and Pesach. The omission of Rosh Hashanah, Yom Kippur, Purim, and Shavuot was conspicuous. As a rule, Jewish holidays were marked in the schools through assemblies featuring communal singing, literary readings, and a dramatic performance. This format allowed for flexibility in interpreting a holiday's significance.

Hanukah provides a good example of the transformation of a holiday's meaning in the TsISHO schools. In her 1910 essay, Esther Frumkin made special allowances for celebrating Hanukah with Jewish proletarian children, despite the fact that she was opposed to Jewish holiday celebrations in general. In the proletarian Yiddish school, Hanukah would not focus on the miracle of the oil, as was the practice among Orthodox Jews, and would not instill the ideal of Jewish political independence in the land of Israel, as the Zionists did. Instead, Hanukah would be celebrated to mark a people's armed struggle against oppression, on behalf of freedom. This reinterpretation of Hanukah, as a symbol of progressive social and political struggle, was widely appropriated by the TsISHO schools. A teacher in a Warsaw TsISHO school recalled with joy and pride that her pupils told her after their Hanukah play, "When we Judeans fought with our swords and bayonets against the Romans, we imagined that we were standing on the barricades in Warsaw and fighting against the exploiters of the working class."[18] A nationalist holiday was thus given a universal, and specifically socialist, meaning.

The traditional ritual associated with the Hanukah holiday was eliminated: no Hanukah candles or menorahs were lit in the TsISHO schools. This was considered to be a religious act—since it was accompanied by the recitation of a blessing—that commemorated an alleged supernatural event—the miracle of the oil. As such, it had no place in a secular Yiddish school.[19]

This approach to Hanukah reflects the centrist approach within TsISHO—to celebrate select Jewish holidays by fusing them with the socialist values of struggle, freedom, and labor. The radical wing of the school organization celebrated no traditional Jewish holidays at all. The TsISHO children's home in Warsaw reported matter-of-factly in 1927, "The [Jewish] religious and national holidays are obviously not celebrated or cultivated by us. However, we also don't do anything to weaken their influence on our children. . . . Our children's home celebrates a Peretz holiday, a Sholem Aleichem holiday, a May Day holiday. . . . The second priority is occupied by nature holidays: a spring holiday, a winter holiday, a planting holiday."[20]

On the other end of the organization's spectrum were the Vilna schools, which marked nearly all Jewish holidays in one way or other. An interesting example is provided by the celebration of Purim. Purim had been rejected by Zhitlovsky and other cultural radicals as a chauvinistic celebration of Jewish vengeance, whose festivities were characterized by a frivolity devoid of social value. But in the early 1920s, students in the Vilna Yiddish Teachers' Seminary introduced the custom of performing a traditional Purim *shpil* (play) for the student body and faculty, using folklorized versions of the biblical stories of Joseph and Esther. This revival of the Purim *shpil* spread from the Teachers' Seminary to the TsBK schools and became quite popular. However, when a leader of the Warsaw TsISHO attended the first Purim *shpil* in the Teacher's Seminary, he was appalled. He publicly rebuked the seminary for observing a religious holiday and staging a biblical play in a secular institution. This in turn provoked a counterprotest by the seminary's director, Avrom Golomb, and its instructor of Yiddish, Dr. Max Weinreich, who had inspired and guided the performances.[21]

BIBLE WITHOUT RELIGION, HEBREW WITHOUT SPEAKING

Most of the TsISHO schools that taught biblical narratives did so under the rubric of Jewish history. Avrom Golomb recalls joining the staff of a Bundist-oriented elementary school in Warsaw in 1921, midyear, as a substitute teacher. While Hebrew and Bible were "strictly forbidden" in the school, Jewish history was not. On the first day of class, he asked his pupils what point they had reached in Jewish history, and they replied, "the part when Joseph is sold by his brothers."[22]

In the intermediate grades, biblical history was presented in terms of the development of social institutions: the priesthood and its sacrificial cult, the tribes and their judges, the history of the monarchies of Judea and Israel, the evolution of rituals and holidays. This social history approach entailed naturalizing biblical history and deleting accounts of divine revelation and miraculous events. An alternative approach among Yiddish educators was to consider the Bible not as a source of history but as the repository of ancient Jewish folklore, whose beauty lay precisely in its imaginative fables. As one leading TsISHO educator noted, "If we teach our children Grimm's fairy-tales, and introduce them to folk-creativity, then all objections to the Bible fall aside." This approach shifted the curricular framework in which biblical narratives were taught to Yiddish language and literature, which included both Jewish and world folklore.[23]

Recasting hallowed narrative texts as folklore was a popular device. Following in Peretz's footsteps, national-romantic educators saw a continuous tradition of Jewish folk creativity running from the Bible, Agadah, medieval legends, and Hasidic tales and culminating in the riches of Yiddish folktales, folk songs, and idioms. Shloyme Bastomski, a prolific anthologizer of Yiddish folklore for the schools, also composed Yiddish translations of rabbinic Agadot and Hasidic tales.[24]

Whether Bible was taught as history or as folklore, TsISHO educators stressed that "the study of Bible carries a non-confessional character in our schools. . . . The boys do not cover their heads." In practice, the commandments contained in the Pentateuch were given the least attention.[25]

A related, but nonetheless distinct, dividing line within the school organization was over the instruction of Hebrew. Most advocates of teaching Hebrew, such as Dr. Israel Rubin and Avrom Golomb, maintained that the primary educational objective of Hebrew-language instruction should be the attainment of reading fluency in the Bible. Golomb constructed a Hebrew curriculum for grades 3 through 7 in which the readings consisted almost entirely of biblical texts. As Yiddishists, Rubin, Golomb, and most others dismissed the cultivation of active Hebrew speech among the students as a pointless enterprise and considered modern Hebrew literature to be of secondary importance in the Jewish literary canon. "Hebrew for the sake of Bible" was their slogan.[26]

Other educators did not link the inclusion of Bible with Hebrew language instruction. From their perspective, it was sufficient to teach biblical texts in Yiddish translation in the framework of Jewish history or Yiddish literature, just as Russian and French literature were taught in TsISHO schools in Yiddish translation. Full comprehension of biblical Hebrew was unattainable, given the limitations of time, and it was better to spend the classroom hours teaching Exodus or Isaiah in Yiddish.[27]

Ultimately, for the national-romantic educators in TsISHO, teaching Hebrew was of ideological and symbolic importance, above and beyond the concrete skills and knowledge that were imparted in class. Kh. Sh. Kazhdan, one of TsISHO's leading educators, put the matter quite starkly: "Eliminating Hebrew from our schools can only be the desire of those whose slogan is: 'liberate our schools at any price from all traces of our ancient culture.' But in our view, this means flattening our culture, degrading Yiddish to the level of a mundane utility-language, and blocking all paths for the development of a modern, independent [Yiddish] culture. Such education is full-fledged betrayal of the nation and its future. Breaking with Hebrew means breaking with the path of our cultural creativity."[28]

LITERATURE AND THE ABSENCE OF GOD

Yiddish was the central Jewish subject in the TsISHO curriculum and was afforded the largest weekly number of teaching hours. But the cannon of Yiddish literature to be taught in the schools was by no means set or stable and was a subject vigorously disputed by radical and national-romantic educators.

The national-romantics gave preference to literary works that drew upon traditional Jewish culture and reflected the antiquity of Jewish wisdom and ethical values. Peretz's *Hasidic Tales* and *Tales in the Folk Spirit* and Sholem Asch's *A Shtetl* and *Kidush Hashem* (Martyrdom) were the key works of their cannon. They conceived of modern Yiddish literature as, at its essence, a continuation and culmination of earlier phases of Jewish culture. In Kazhdan's words, "The beauty which Peretz and Asch brought forth to the world, lay beforehand (and lies still today) in the people. These treasures of word, image, experience and thought were accumulated over generations; they were refined and enriched over time. . . . The great artist expresses and reveals merely that which the people prepared for him."[29]

Cultural radicals, on the other hand, gave preference to works that reflected a break with the Jewish religious tradition and an embrace of modernity and works that dealt with modern social issues. They called for ideological consistency between the TsISHO schools' secular orientation and the Yiddish literature taught in its curriculum. One educator warned, "Works that smell of religious romanticism, such as Peretz's *Hasidic Tales* and *Tales in the Folk Spirit*, and Sholem Asch's *A Shtetl*, must not occupy any place in our schools. Why on earth should our schools be teaching Hasidism? Gorky belongs to our literature, not Sholem Asch of the *Shtetl* and *Der tehilim yid* (Salvation). The Peretz of 'Bontche the Silent' belongs to our literature, but not the Peretz of the *Hasidic Tales* and 'Three Gifts.'"[30]

The national-romantic wing of Yiddishism, in theory and in educational practice, exhibited a deep and complex relationship toward Judaism. Nonetheless, there were clearly drawn lines that were not crossed even by its most traditionalist members. Foremost of these was the issue of God. Yiddish schools defined themselves as secular. Discussion of God as creator, master of the universe, or providential force was beyond the pale of acceptable discourse. Consequently, prayer and religious ritual were likewise anathema. The Hebrew liturgy was not taught (even as a literary document), and no blessings were recited. Children were not familiarized with the synagogue and its service, although the latter was sometimes addressed indirectly, in Yiddish literary texts.

While much of the religious tradition could be recast in national terms, the aversion to religion per se remained nearly total. At a TsISHO teachers' conference on the teaching of natural sciences, Avrom Golomb proposed that one of the objectives should be to instill in the students "a healthy religious feeling toward nature." When colleagues fiercely objected to use of the word religious, Golomb explained that he used it to signify "an exalted and inspired attitude by the individual toward the world." He went on to argue that the students' accumulation of knowledge about nature, without such feelings—upon seeing a blade of grass, a butterfly emerge from its cocoon, or the transformation of elements—was educationally deficient. The majority of those present, however, voted to delete the words "religious feeling" from the resolution, on the grounds that the word religious was compromised.[31]

Seen from a historical distance, it can be argued that the varieties of modern Jewish cultural nationalism—those ideological trends that placed greater importance on national culture than on national politics—were, unwittingly, influenced by the Jewish religious tradition. For it was the religious tradition that had established this priority of the spirit over the material, and it was the rabbis who had symbolized and championed the primacy of spiritual values throughout the centuries. The underlying, and often concealed, force of the religious tradition thus resonated in the cultural nationalism of Ahad Ha'am and Bialik, Peretz, and Zhitlovsky alike.

However, on the overt, explicit level, the Judaism of secular Yiddishists, even of the national-romantic variety, was a Judaism without religion and a Judaism without God.

8

COMMEMORATION AND CULTURAL CONFLICT

THE VILNA GAON'S BICENTENNARY

The Jewish community of Vilna first organized a series of public events to pay tribute to its most famous son, Rabbi Elijah, the gaon (1720–1797), on the occasion of his two hundredth birthday, in April 1920.

Although Rabbi Elijah was frequently invoked throughout the nineteenth century as the spiritual father and cultural hero of *Yerushalayim de-lita* (the Jerusalem of Lithuania), earlier centennial anniversaries of his birth and death passed quietly, with little fanfare. In traditional Jewish religious culture, great individuals were recalled at the time of their *yortsayt* (the anniversary of their death), and not on their birthday, and no particular significance was attributed to round-numbered anniversaries, such as a person's fiftieth or one hundredth *yortsayt*.

Nonetheless, by the time the one hundredth anniversary of the gaon's death rolled along, in 1897, modern forms of commemoration had taken hold among Vilna Jews. A local book dealer used the occasion to issue facsimiles of a well-known portrait of the gaon, seated against the backdrop of his library with a pen in hand, and sold thousands of copies to bookstores and individuals. The Hebrew writer and educator Zalman Epstein proposed in the Hebrew weekly *Ha-melitz* that the one hundredth *yortsayt* anniversary be marked by "collecting all the tales and legends on the Gaon, and compiling all the information in the possession of the elderly generation, so as to compose a comprehensive and systematic biography of this great man." He suggested that the wardens of the Vilna community announce a competition, with a prize for the best biography of the gaon. But the proposal apparently fell on deaf ears.[1]

The bicentennial commemorations of 1920 display vividly how the various segments of the Jewish community related to rabbinic Judaism. The Orthodox, Zionists-Hebraists, and Yiddishists marked the occasion with varying degrees of emphasis and interpreted the gaon's enduring significance along sharply divergent lines. Vilna's secular Yiddishists confronted, perhaps for the first time, the problem of how to relate to the gaon and, by extension, to their community's history of piety and rabbinic learning.

The commemorations took place in a highly charged political environment. Jewish-nationalist sentiments were strong, and celebrating the deeds of Jewish heroes from the past was considered de rigueur. But several factors cast clouds over the anniversary.

In 1920, Vilna Jewry was just beginning to emerge from the economic devastation and communal trauma caused by World War I, during which the city's Jews had endured successive German, Lithuanian, and Bolshevik occupations, followed by Polish conquest. The Polish takeover of the city, in April 1919, had been accompanied by a bloody pogrom, and mutual tension and accusations abounded in the ensuing months. As a result, the Jewish community had little time or peace of mind and few financial resources to organize large-scale public commemorations.

In addition, Vilna Jewry of 1920 was riven with internal divisions, between religious and secular, Zionists and Bundists, Yiddishists and Hebraists. These divisions permeated all spheres of communal life, from the *kehile* board elected in December 1918, to the Yiddish daily press, to elementary and higher education. No public commemoration of a national hero could avoid becoming involved in the tangle of Jewish partisan and cultural politics, and the Vilna Gaon was hardly a unifying historical figure, whose name could easily bring together all sectors of the community. He had, after all, led the campaign to ban and suppress the Hasidic movement in the late eighteenth century and was hence a combatant in one of the great internal Jewish schisms in history.[2]

The gaon's forthcoming anniversary was first brought to the public's attention in January 1920—ironically, not in a Jewish communal forum but in a municipal one, at a meeting of the Vilna City Council's commission on street names. In the aftermath of the Polish conquest, the new authorities were intent on changing all of the city's street names from their prewar Russian to Polish ones. At the commission's first meeting, on January 6, 1920, Shaul Trotsky, a city councilman elected on the list of the Jewish Craftsmen's Association, proposed that three streets be named after local Jewish personalities. First in the order of priority was renaming the Second Glaziers' Street (Vtoraia Stieklanaia Ulitsa) as Gaon Street. Trotsky explained that the street was the site of the house in which the gaon had lived and bordered on the synagogue courtyard (shulhoyf) where he had prayed. He stressed the symbolic importance of naming a street for the Vilna Gaon in the bicentennial year of his birth.

Two other Jewish street names were proposed. Edimanska Alley (also known as Shavelska Street) was to be changed to Strashun Street, after the Talmudic scholar, bibliophile, and communal leader Matityahu Strashun, and Tsaritsinska Street (in the Shnipishok section) was to be renamed Fuenn Street, after the Hebrew author, Maskil, and educator Shmuel Yosef Fuenn. Councilman Trotsky noted that all three name changes had been approved by the previous Lithuanian-led city council in 1918.

Several Polish members of the commission objected on principle to having Jewish street names in Vilna and argued that the proposed names were not familiar to the general population. In response, Trotsky presented the biographies of the Vilna Gaon, Strashun, and Fuenn to the commission and stressed that their names were well known to the entire Jewish population of Vilna, which constituted 40 percent of the city's population.

After some deliberation, two of the three changes were adopted—Gaon Street and Strashun Street. But the proposed naming of Fuenn Street was deferred, pending further investigation of his biography in the municipal archives. Several members of the commission had objected that Fuenn—who had been closely associated with the tsarist authorities in Vilna, as an instructor in the State Rabbinical Seminary and in other capacities, and who had supported Jewish Russification (rather than Polonization)—had been an enemy of Poland.[3]

The decision to create Gaon Street was lauded in the local Zionist weekly *Ha-hayim* as an important milestone. At a time when the memory of the gaon was in decline, along with traditional rabbinic learning in general, such symbolic acts were of great value, wrote the Hebrew educator Y. A. Trivush.[4]

But it is clear that much more was at stake here than the memory of the Vilna Gaon himself. He was a symbol, and his anniversary was an instrument for local Jewish politicians. At issue was whether the new Polish authorities would attempt to recast Vilna's urban landscape in exclusively Polish terms. (Besides eliminating Russian street names, the commission also endorsed the removal of Russian monuments, including one to Alexander Pushkin.[5]) The debate over Jewish street names was a debate about public recognition of the Jewish position in the city. The sharp objections voiced by some city council members, and the ultimately mixed decision taken by the commission, reflected the uneasy attitude of many Poles on the subject.

Moreover, municipal officials were slow to implement the change and attach a new street sign to Gaon Street. Whereas other street signs in the city were changed in the first half of April 1920, in anticipation of the celebration of Vilna Liberation Day on April 18, Gaon Street did not bear a sign with its new name until many months later.[6]

Within the Jewish community, the initiative to commemorate the gaon's two hundredth birthday was taken by the rabbinate. In anticipation of the anniversary, which fell on the first day of Passover (April 3, 1920), the Va'ad Ha-rabonim (Committee of Rabbis) issued a lengthy proclamation *(kol kore)* in Hebrew and Yiddish, which was hung in local synagogues and on the streets of the old Jewish quarter. The Va'ad Ha-rabonim also organized special communal prayers in the gaon's *kloyz* (house of prayer) on the first day of Passover. As an act of homage, all the members of the Vilna rabbinate, close to forty rabbis in all, assembled for the morning prayers in the *kloyz.* (Normally, each rabbi prayed in a different synagogue.) With an unusually large congregation in attendance, the official preacher of the Vilna community, Rabbi Menachem Krakowsky, spoke before the reading of the Torah on the life and works of the gaon.[7] The secular leadership of the Vilna *kehile* played no role in the organization and conduct of the gaon's bicentennial commemorations. Neither its chairman, the Zionist Dr. Jacob Vigodski, nor its vice-chairman, the Diaspora Nationalist Dr. Tsemach Shabad, spoke, wrote, or issued proclamations in honor of the anniversary.

The secular communal leadership was preoccupied at the time with a different anniversary, which fell on the very same week of Passover, 1920—the first anniversary of the Vilna pogrom of 1919. In an event that sparked international protests, Polish legionnaires had raided Jewish homes and killed fifty-three Jews, including the Yiddish writer and former Bundist leader A. Weiter (Isaac Devenishvki). In the spring of 1920, tensions between Poles and Jews mounted in the city, as Poles planned to celebrate the anniversary of Vilna's liberation and Jews planned to mourn and protest the killing of Jews by Polish forces. Planning the venue, format, and content of the commemoration was extremely sensitive, as the Jewish community sought to manifest its pain and anger and at the same time avoid provoking yet another pogrom.[8]

In the end, the format selected was a memorial evening for the martyred writer A. Weiter, sponsored by the Association of Yiddish Journalists and Writers, on Saturday, April 10, the eighth night of Passover. More than one thousand people packed the municipal theater, in an event that was part political protest rally, part literary-cultural evening. The program, which was chaired by Dr. Vigodski, the head of the Vilna *kehile*, opened with a large photograph of Weiter, framed in black, being displayed on the stage. After Vigodski's opening remarks, the sounds of Beethoven's funeral march were heard, and a stream of delegations of cultural, educational, and political organizations laid wreaths at the base of Weiter's photograph. Several speeches on Weiter's life, writings, and tragic death followed. After an intermission, the Vilna Yiddish Theatre Society performed Weiter's last drama, *In umglik* (During the catastrophe).[9]

In April 1920, the commemoration of Weiter's death, and all that it symbolized, overshadowed commemoration of the Vilna Gaon's birth and all that it symbolized, for the secular segments of the community.

The special prayer services and fund-raising campaign launched in memory of the gaon were the first public demonstrations by Vilna's Orthodoxy after the end of the Great War. Most of the city's rabbis, such as Rabbi Krakowsky and the revered Rabbi Chaim Ozer Grodzensky, had fled Vilna with the retreating Russian army in 1915, to avoid the anticipated hostilities, and had returned to the city in 1918–1919. The Orthodox sector had been without leadership for three crucial years, and the rabbis' moral authority in the community at large had suffered because of their wartime abandonment of Vilna.[10] By evoking the memory of the gaon, and of past rabbinic greatness in Vilna, on the occasion of his bicentennial, the rabbis sought to rally and mobilize religious Jews on a broad basis and to demonstrate to the community at large that orthodoxy was "back" and would strive to be a major force in communal life.

The proclamation issued by the Vilna Committee of Rabbis began in a celebratory tone, referring to the gaon's birthday as "the day on which the light of dawn broke for Israel and its Torah." But it quickly reverted to plaintive and combative language. "At this time, when darkness covers the land, and most of the people of Israel have turned their back on their great rabbis and on all that is sacred, we cannot pass by this great moment." The rabbis explained that one of the purposes of celebrating the gaon's bicentennial was to set before the younger generation an example of a true Jewish leader and hero, unlike the false leaders and heroes who were now widely admired and followed by the youth.[11]

Rather than depicting the figure of the gaon himself, the proclamation used him as a symbol of the rabbinate and of Orthodox Judaism, to polemicize against secular Jewish ideologies: "We must always recall that the Torah, and only the Torah, gave us the strength and the power to endure all that befell us. Only it gave us the desire and the courage to be the people of the book, throughout all our horrible wanderings. And only the giants of the Torah, with their remarkable powers, dedication, and love of their people were the exclusive captains of the ship of Israel in the stormy seas."

While the occasion of the proclamation was celebratory, several passages were quite somber and dejected: "Now, new winds have arisen which threaten to extinguish the light of Torah, the eternal light of Israel. We the disciples of Rabbi Elijah's disciples must protect the last spark of light, lest it be extinguished, God forbid. . . . And we call upon all those in whose hearts the last spark of Torah has not been extinguished, to join us."[12]

Specifically, the Committee of Rabbis announced a fund-raising campaign to establish two new institutions in the gaon's memory: an institute of advanced Talmudic studies (a *kolel*), to be named Aliyos Eliyohu, and a religious orphanage for local children, to be called Beys Eliyohu.

In an interesting aside, the rabbinic proclamation noted that the first *yortsayt* of the April pogrom would also be marked during Passover and reminded the community that nothing had been done to commemorate its martyrs. The rabbis proposed that the orphanage Beys Eliyohu would be a worthy monument for the martyrs of 1919, since it would house children who had been orphaned by the pogrom. The orphanage would thus serve to commemorate both Vilna's "day of light" two hundred years ago, and its "day of darkness" just one year ago. This combination of anniversaries reflected an awareness on the rabbis' part that the anniversary of the pogrom was more on the community's mind than was the gaon.

In fact, the Committee of Rabbis failed to raise funds to establish the Talmudic academy and religious orphanage. Despite appeals for contributions at yizkor (memorial) services on the last day of Passover, and subsequent reminders in the local Yiddish press, the campaign was a failure. The reasons were discussed by the Vilna correspondent of the Warsaw Yiddish daily *Moment*, M. Nokhumzohn. It reflected, he wrote, the decline of Orthodoxy, the diminished moral authority of the rabbinate, and the acute economic crisis plaguing Vilna Jewry. But the correspondent also suggested that there was a deeper moral malaise plaguing the community. During the past few years, Vilna Jewry had become accustomed to financial dependence on donations from America. Even projects that enjoyed public support were met with passivity and replies that "America will provide." Vilna's inability to build an enduring monument to the gaon, wrote Nokhumzohn, revealed that it had adopted the role and the mentality of a *shnorer* (beggar).[13]

Vilna's modern Jewish intellectuals reacted with varying degrees of interest to the gaon's bicentennial. The Yiddish daily *Tog*, which was Diaspora Nationalist, Yiddishist, and politically left of center, published the Committee of Rabbis' news releases on the synagogue commemorations but did not print a single article on the life and works of the gaon. On the other hand, it dedicated several articles in early April 1920 to the fifth *yortsayt* of I. L. Peretz, the Yiddishists' central cultural hero. The local Yiddish literary monthly *Lebn* apparently recalled the gaon's anniversary at the last minute and inserted a two-page biographical note on Rabbi Elijah into its April issue just before going to press. The featured items in the issue were stories by Moyshe Kulbak and Alter Kacyzna and an article on the staging of *The Dybbuk* by the Vilna Troupe theater company.[14]

Thus, Vilna's Yiddishists in 1920 were enthralled by Peretz's Hasidic tales and by S. An-sky's depiction of a suffering Hasidic master and his followers in *The Dybbuk*, but they were left uninspired by the figure of the Vilna Gaon. The unfamiliar world of Hasidism was to them mythic, poetic, and exotic, while the gaon represented the real-life rabbinic Orthodoxy they knew all too well and had sharply rejected. As the man renowned for persecuting Hasidism, he was singularly unsuited for them as a cultural hero, despite the fact that he hailed from their own community, from Vilna.

While *Der Tog* hardly noticed the gaon's bicentennial, the rival daily *Yidishe Tsaytung*, which was published by the Vilna Zionist Organization, attributed much more significance to the occasion. It published a special six-page illustrated section on the Vilna Gaon in its April 23 edition, which featured eight articles, four original illustrations, and reproductions of the Hebrew inscriptions found on the gaon's seat in his *kloyz* and on his tombstone in the old cemetery. Two of the articles were by figures from the Orthodox sector of the community (including one by Rabbi Krakowsky on a unknown kabbalistic manuscript by the gaon) and three were by the editor and staff writers for *Yidishe Tsaytung*.

The lead article was by Dr. Joseph Regensburg, a German Jewish physician and Judaic scholar who had settled in Vilna in 1914 and become a central figure in its communal life. Besides being the editor of *Yidishe Tsaytung*, Regensburg was director of Vilna's Hebrew Gymnasium (Gimnasia Ha-ivrit), and a member of the three-man Executive Committee of the Vilna Zionist Organization.

Regensburg opened his article with a mixture of homage and distancing, by stressing the "deep chasm" that separated modern Jews from the world of the Vilna Gaon. "No matter how highly we may regard our religion, rabbbinic study and prayer, we must admit, that these matters no longer occupy the center of our personal and national interests. Seclusion and asceticism are also not the ideals of modern man. . . . And yet. Despite our negative view of many specifics in the Vilna Gaon's life and activities, and even despite our negative view of his entire world-view and philosophy of life, nonetheless, the remarkable spiritual figure of the Gaon will always elicit from us feelings of great admiration and awe. . . . Most of all, are we in awe of the mystical deepness of his complete, moral personality."[15]

Regensburg did not gloss over the features of the gaon that were unappealing from his perspective: opposition to rationalist philosophy and attachment to *kabbalah*, stringent *halakhic* (legal) rulings, and insistence on ritual minutiae. He reserved his admiration first and foremost for the gaon's personality—his modesty, righteousness, and self-denial. Regensburg compared the gaon to another great son of the Jewish people—Benedict de Spinoza. Both took pleasure in the world, but theirs was an intellectual pleasure not a physical one. Both lived in secluded simplicity and poverty; both strove for total intellectual freedom and independence; both avoided public lecturing and communal responsibilities, although they were endowed with a deep love of mankind; and both were absolutely consistent in living according to their ideas. "No matter how great the chasm is between the views of God and life held by our most brilliant philosopher and our near-greatest Talmudist . . . we can detect in these two opposites the common blood of our race. . . . Our nation should take pride in such spiritual and moral figures as these, and even more should we take pride in the historical force which created them—Judaism!"[16]

In evaluating the Vilna Gaon's enduring influence, Regensburg highlighted the connecting strands between Rabbi Elijah and modern Jewish culture. As the inspiration for the Volozhin yeshiva (founded by his student Hayyim of Volozhin, in 1802), Rabbi Elijah built a bastion of rabbinic rationality against Hasidic mysticism. And the Jewish intelligentsia that was raised in Volozhin and other yeshivas gave birth to virtually all of modern Hebrew and Yiddish literature and to modern Jewish scholarship in Russia. As opposed to the yeshiva-trained intelligentsia, the Jews who had attended Russian universities were inert and alienated from a Jewish national perspective. The gaon also exerted a direct impact on the development of secular Jewish culture in Lithuania. His study of science contributed greatly to the development of the Lithuanian Haskalah, and his scientific text criticism of the Talmud had laid the groundwork for modern *hokhmat yisrael* (Judaic scholarship).

Regensburg concluded his article with a jab at contemporary Orthodoxy, which had strayed from these aspects of the Vilna Gaon's legacy. "His influence today has sunk greatly. Not because he has been surpassed, but because in many respects, contemporaries lag behind him. . . . Rabbi Elijah went up to heaven, and many of his past and present disciples and admirers inherited nothing from him, except for his cane and a few of his rags. Unfortunately, they inherited neither his critical approach to Talmudic studies, nor his sympathy for the general sciences."[17]

Regensburg offered an appreciation of the gaon according to the standards of modern, secular, Jewish cultural nationalism. The gaon was praised as a second Spinoza, as a father of the Haskalah, and as the progenitor of the modern Jewish national intelligentsia. Much like the Committee of Rabbis, Regensburg could not avoid using the gaon to score polemical points against his ideological opponents, in his case against the Orthodox.

Yidishe Tsaytung also published an article by Chaikl Lunski, a respected, beloved, and unifying figure in Vilna's Jewish cultural life. Lunski was director of the Jewish communal library, the Strashun Library, and secretary of the S. An-sky Historical-Ethnographic Society, a *kehile*-sponsored agency that collected Hebrew manuscripts and documents and maintained the Jewish communal museum. He straddled the fence between various Jewish movements, maintaining close ties with old-world Orthodoxy (in which he had been raised), Zionism (to which he belonged), and modern Yiddish culture (in which he was active). He represented the synthesis of Vilna's varying streams.

Lunski took a very different approach toward the Vilna Gaon, by placing him in the ahistorical realm of legend and myth. His article, which recounted several tales told about the Vilna Gaon, intentionally obscured the issue of whether they were factual or fictitious. "All we know about the Gaon's life are legends, his whole life-story is wondrous and legendary. Even the few true facts about his life appear to us ordinary people to be legends, such as the fact that at age seven, he presented a *khiluk* [Talmudic insight] in Vilna's Great Synagogue which astonished the city's great scholars."[18]

By employing a quasi-ethnographic approach, Lunski left it unclear whether he was writing in praise of the gaon himself or in praise of the Jewish folk imagination and the values expressed by the folk through their tales about the gaon. This ambiguity was a perfect strategy for Lunski, given his role and position in the community.

In subsequent years, Lunski made further efforts to spread Vilna Gaon lore among secular Yiddishists, and particularly in the Yiddish schools, where his children studied and his sister was a popular educator. In 1922, Lunski published an expanded collection of tales on the gaon in the TsBK youth magazine, and his collection was issued in book form, as instructional material, under the organization's auspices in 1924. By presenting the gaon as a folk hero, he made him palatable to secular Yiddishists, who had very little sympathy for the rabbinic elite but had great love for Jewish folk creativity. Several of the tales he collected and related were reminiscent of tales about Israel Ba'al Shem Tov and Hasidic masters. These included stories about miraculous events that occurred to Rabbi Elijah's mother while she carried him in the womb and a story of how the gaon's prayers during the Kosziuszko uprising of 1794 prevented a bomb, which fell in the packed Great Synagogue, from exploding. The battles between the gaon and Hasidism virtually disappeared from the Jewish folk imagination, at least as it was presented by Lunski.[19]

Lunski's approach, of making the Vilna Gaon into a second Ba'al

Shem Tov—a mythic folk hero who was the subject of enchanting miracle tales—scored some successes among the Yiddishist intelligentsia. The Vilna-based Yiddish children's magazine *Grininke Beymelekh* (Little Green Trees) published stories about the gaon, and its editor, Shloyme Bastomski, included such tales in some of the readers he composed for the TsBK schools. But in 1920, this Yiddishist appropriation of the gaon had not yet taken hold, and even later, it would not take root as strongly as the movement's appropriation of the Ba'al Shem Tov.[20]

The commemoration of the two hundredth birthday of the Vilna Gaon reflected in microcosm many of the problems and conflicts of the Vilna Jewish community in 1920. The effort to name a street for the gaon, while successful, served to highlight the tense relations between Poles and Jews, as each group harbored a sharply different historical vision of the city. The virtual neglect of the gaon's anniversary by the Yiddishist and socialist sectors of the Jewish community reflected their distant and uneasy attitude toward the rabbinic tradition as a whole. The commemorations conducted by the rabbinate, while dignified and impressive, revealed to all the limitations of Orthodox influence on the Vilna community. Meanwhile, secular nationalist intellectuals struggled to find a way to fit the gaon into their pantheon of heroes, either by stretching historical facts or by removing the gaon from history to the realm of national mythology. Given the external pressures facing the community, and the cacophony of voices emanating from within it, the celebration of the two hundredth birthday of the Vilna Gaon was an event riddled with ambiguity.

9

MAX WEINREICH
AND THE DEVELOPMENT
OF YIVO

The Yiddish Scientific Institute, YIVO, was conceived of and developed in 1925 by four scholars, who constituted its original organizing committee: Nochum Shtiff, Elias Tcherikower, Zalmen Rejzen, and Max Weinreich. A fifth scholar, Jacob Lestschinsky, joined this cohort and was appointed secretary of YIVO's research division for economics and statistics at a planning meeting in Berlin in August 1925, before the institute itself was officially founded.[1]

The founders of YIVO were divided by geography: the Berliners were Shtiff, Tcherikower, and Lestschinsky, and the Vilners were Weinreich and Rejzen. The establishment of a Yiddish academic institute was the brainchild of Shtiff, who composed a lengthy memorandum on the subject in February 1925, shared it with other émigré Yiddish intellectuals in Berlin, and sent copies to colleagues in Poland and the United States. The most energetic and detailed response came from the Vilna-based Rejzen and Weinreich, who formulated a document of "theses" that modified Shtiff's plan. The Berlin and Vilna groups disagreed on the crucial issue of where the institute should be based, with each side arguing for its own place of residence.

But looking beyond personal and local ambitions, the commonality of the Berlin and Vilna founders of YIVO is striking. There were no major differences of opinion between them on the institute's research agenda or on its cultural and communal orientation. Their varying places of residence were the result of personal decisions they made during the years of war and revolution and did not reflect deeper differences in ideology or scholarly approach. The Vilna-based Max Weinreich had lived in Berlin between 1919 and 1923, and the Berlin-based Shtiff had spent the years of the war and revolution in St. Petersburg and Kiev, before arriving in Berlin in 1922.

Indeed, the founders of YIVO were a relatively homogeneous group. If there was a geographic factor in the group's composition, it was the fact that they all were products of the Russian Jewish intelligentsia. No scholars from Poland or Galicia were to be found among them. It is noteworthy that such well-established Polish Jewish scholars as Majer Balaban, Isaac (Ignacy) Schipper, and Noyekh Prilutski were not included in the inner circle of YIVO founders. The institute's research agenda and social orientation might well have been different had these scholars been involved in YIVO's conception. The Division of History would have been strengthened were Balaban at its helm. (The history division's activities were complicated by Tcherikower's residing in Berlin, away from Poland and the Vilna headquarters.) The division would also have published more studies on Polish Jewish (as opposed to Russian Jewish) history. And had Prilutski been a cofounder and leader of YIVO's Division of Philology, it would have given greater stress to Yiddish grammar and dialectology, as opposed to the history of Yiddish language and literature.

YIVO's relationship with Jewish communal bodies and political movements in interwar Poland would have been closer, and carried a different complexion, if Balaban (a leading general Zionist), Schipper (a leader of Poale Zion-Left), and Prilutski (the head of the Folkist party) had been among YIVO's founders. However, YIVO was the brainchild of Russian Jewish intellectuals, who were somewhat alienated and marginal vis-à-vis the Polish Jewish political arena, centered in Warsaw, which arose after World War I.

A more instructive division of YIVO's founding five would be according to their fields of research. They consisted of one historian (Tcherikower), one statistician-demographer (Lestschinsky), and three philologists (Shtiff, Weinreich, and Rejzen). With such a makeup, it was predictable that the Division of Philology would emerge as YIVO's strongest branch. Of the 2,529 items published under YIVO auspices between 1925 and 1941, 709 were in the fields of Yiddish language and literature, while only 509 were in the field of Jewish history.[2] The emphasis on philology as opposed to history was a reflection of YIVO's core Yiddishist ideology, which saw the language, its lore and literature, as more central features of the Jewish people than its shared historical experience. This scholarly Yiddishism represented a break with earlier Russian Jewish scholarship, as represented by the work of Simon Dubnov and the Jewish Historical-Ethnographic Society he founded in St. Petersburg in 1908, in which history occupied a clear position of primacy.

But the division of YIVO's founders according to discipline obscures the fact that Weinreich was in many respects a category unto himself. He belonged to a different generation, with a different life experience and education. Weinreich was the youngest of the five founders of YIVO, being thirty-one years old at the time. Shtiff was fifteen and Lestschinsky eighteen years older. Weinreich was also the only founder of this academic research institute who held a doctoral degree.

The biographical differences between Weinreich and the others shed light on the peculiar development of modern Jewish scholarship in early-twentieth-century Russia. Shtiff, Tcherikower, and Lestschinsky all belonged to the generation of Russian Jewish youth who entered the stormy arena of Jewish politics and public affairs in the years just before the Russian revolution of 1905. The three distinguished themselves in various Jewish socialist parties and circles and as writers in the nascent Yiddish press. Shtiff was one of the heads of the Jewish Socialist Workers' Party (SERP). Lestschinsky was a member of the central committee of the Zionist-Socialist Party (Sotsialisty Sionisty, founded in 1906), which, its name notwithstanding, was territorialist and Marxist. Tcherikower traveled in Socialist-Zionist circles, then joined up with Russian radicals in St. Petersburg and was arrested at a conference of Mensheviks in 1907, leading to a year in prison. All three were political activists before their interest turned to scholarly research. They did not receive a systematic higher education, or formal training, in the research areas that interested them. The rigid state quotas limiting the admission of Jews to Russian universities and the tumultuous times of pogroms, revolution, and social upheaval presented objective and subjective obstacles to their pursuing systematic training in their fields.[3]

These founders of YIVO did not lack modern higher education altogether. Shtiff studied chemistry and engineering in the Kiev Polytechnicum and received a law degree from the Kiev Lyceum of Jurisprudence. Tcherikower graduated from the Odessa Artists' School and was admitted to St. Petersburg University shortly before his arrest. Lestschinsky spent half a year at the University of Bern, Switzerland, studying philosophy and social sciences. But Shtiff had no professional training as a philologist, nor did Tcherikower as a historian, nor Lestschinsky as a social scientist.[4]

The three men shifted from political activity and journalism to scholarship and research after the failure of the 1905 revolution. For Tcherikower, the break was total and abrupt. After his release from prison, he abandoned politics and began a new life as an author and editor in the field of Jewish history. For Shtiff, the move from politics to scholarship was bridged by literary criticism, which became his main source of livelihood after the 1905 revolution. His reviews gradually became less overtly political and led him to the study of the history of Yiddish literature. Lestschinsky's transition was smoother and more organic. As a leader of the Zionist-Socialist Party, he had written extensive statistical analyses of the Jewish working class in Russia, using a Marxist approach to prove that its economic crisis could only be resolved by territorial concentration. After the collapse of the 1905 revolution, Lestschinsky became a journalist specializing in Jewish economic affairs and began to compose broader studies of Jewish demography and statistics. In their scholarly methods, all three men were essentially autodidacts.

Weinreich's biography stands out in contrast. Born in 1894, in Kurland (today's Latvia), he grew up during the years of reaction (1907–1915), when radical Jewish politics were in retreat and decline. While he was a committed Bundist in his youth, he expended most of his energies in other areas. He obtained a first-class university education between one revolution and the next, as a student of the Historical-Philological Faculty of St. Petersburg University from 1913 to 1917.

This was followed by a brief spurt of Bundist activity in 1917–1919, in St. Petersburg, Minsk, and Vilna. He then left the tumultuous political chaos of eastern Europe for the relative serenity of early Weimar Germany, to study German philology at Marburg University from 1919 to 1923, when he received his doctorate.

WEINREICH AND THE JEWISH SCIENTIFIC IDEAL

Weinreich's university education and professional training had a major impact on his scholarly work and on his ideas about the needs and goals of Jewish scholarship.

All the founding fathers of YIVO embraced the nineteenth-century view that scientific scholarship was the highest rung of modern culture. As Jewish nationalists, they considered the creation of modern Jewish scholarship to be an integral part of the Jewish national renaissance. And as Yiddishists, they were committed to producing a body of advanced scholarly literature in Yiddish. But in questions of methodology, all of them, with the exception of Weinreich, operated with rudimentary conceptions. From the outset, Weinreich's writings stressed methodology. This meant, first of all, thoroughness and discipline— traits he drew from his German training. Second, he stressed the need to employ theoretical and comparative perspectives when studying the Yiddish language, literature, and cultural history.

These themes are already evident in Weinreich's youthful study "What We Have and What We Lack," published in his first book, *Shtaplen: Fir etyudn tsu der yidisher shprakh-visnshaft un literaturgeskhikhte* (Rungs: Four studies in Yiddish linguistics and literary history), published in 1923. The article was a critical overview of Yiddish philology, which compared the state of the field with that of the philological sciences at large and with Germanic philology in particular. Not surprisingly, Weinreich found the Yiddish field sorely lacking. The main shortcoming was not that so little had been done, but rather that the existing body of Yiddish grammars, dictionaries, bibliographies, literary histories, and dialectological and linguistic studies was marred by methodological sloppiness and an ignorance of general philology. He was merciless in his criticism of amateurish work. ("This is a book which induces melancholy, if one stops to think that people call this scholarship." "[The author] had one virtue—he had the courage to conduct this study without knowing any Yiddish, any Hebrew-Aramaic, or any Slavic languages.") As a trained Germanist, he also criticized his Yiddishist colleagues, whose work he respected, for their lack of knowledge of German philology. In an oblique barb at Shtiff, Rejzen, and others, he stated categorically that "anyone who wishes to study Yiddish, let alone the history of Yiddish, needs to know the history of German." Yiddish scholarship required a comparative and contextual approach, not just knowledge of facts.[5]

During his later years in Vilna (1923–1939, with interruptions), during which he was secretary of YIVO's philological research division and a member of YIVO's executive committee, Weinreich, more than any other scholar affiliated with YIVO, maintained an interest in the research literature on European history, folklore, philology, and the social sciences. More than half of the fifteen reviews he published in *Yivo Bleter* between 1931 and 1940 were of books not in Jewish studies but in general fields. As his intellectual interests expanded to the newer fields of psychology, sociology, anthropology, and the social sciences, Weinreich argued that Jewish scholarship had much to learn from them—and much to contribute to them. This ideal of integrating Jewish and general scholarship, which became one of Weinreich's basic principles, was a product of his broad higher education and his professional training in German philology in particular.[6]

BETWEEN GERMAN 'WISSENSCHAFT' AND RUSSIAN POPULISM

Weinreich's scholarly activity—his research and publications, as well as his role in forging and leading YIVO—reflected, both consciously and unconsciously, a personal synthesis of German and Russian cultures. He drew on the strict *wissenschaftlichkeit* acquired in Germany and on the social and political engagement he grew up with in Russia. Weinreich combined the aristocratic elitism of a German professor with the romantic populism of a Russian *narodnik*. There was tremendous internal tension within him between these contrasting tendencies. His synthesis between them was complex, subtle, and fructifying.

It was Weinreich's goal to introduce the German conception of *Wissenschaft* into Jewish public consciousness in eastern Europe. German *Wissenschaft* was not only a method of thought based on the disciplined, thorough analysis of information and concepts; it was the *appreciation* of disciplined, methodical thinking as a value and ideal of the highest order. Weinreich found these features to be severely lacking in the Jewish community of post–World War I Poland. He criticized the excessive politicization of Jewish public discourse, in which the repetition of pat party slogans substituted for thought, and argued that to understand Jewish life one needed to investigate it—not merely rely on impressions or presumptions.

The first step toward this larger goal was the creation of an autonomous institutional and social sphere dedicated to scholarly inquiry and relieved of overt pressure to serve the objectives of the political parties—an environment similar to the universities in Marburg and Berlin, where he had studied. This was to be YIVO. From the outset, Weinreich opposed all efforts to politicize YIVO, whether they were calls for YIVO to study the Jewish experience from the perspective of class struggle (by Raphael Mahler) or calls for YIVO to become actively involved in Jewish political struggles and adopt protest resolutions (by the Bundist leader Yosef Lestschinsky). At YIVO's conference in celebration of its fifth anniversary, held in 1929, Weinreich retorted, "Leaders of our Institute may engage in any public activity they desire. But the Institute itself as an institution must stand aside from the realm of political struggle. The Institute's only path is that of concrete scholarly work. If one wishes to criticize the Institute's activity to date for the publication of poor articles and the preparation of faulty questionnaires, that is appropriate. But whoever demands resolutions which have not been passed is not speaking to the point." This was a bold affirmation of academic autonomy from politics, and a position that, at least initially, had few supporters among the friends of YIVO.[7]

But as a product of the Russian Jewish intelligentsia at the beginning of the century, Weinreich did not, and could not, conceive of YIVO as an isolated ivory tower. Rather, he considered it an institution deeply rooted in Jewish society and oriented toward its welfare. It was Weinreich who argued in 1925 that YIVO should not be established by a group of scholars acting alone, no matter how prominent they might be, but that its establishment needed to be sanctioned by the highest existing Yiddish cultural organizations.[8] Otherwise, the institute would be cut off from society, to the detriment of both. Upon receiving Shtiff's memorandum "Concerning a Yiddish Academic Institute," he brought it to a joint meeting of TsBK and the Vilna Society for Jewish Education (Vilbig) to obtain their endorsement of the idea. These two Vilna-based educational organizations subsequently introduced a resolution in support of the planned institute at the second conference of Yiddish schools in Poland, conducted by TsISHO (Warsaw, April 19–22, 1925). Through these steps, Weinreich sought to ensure that YIVO would have a communal foundation.

After its establishment, Weinreich continued to work on maintaining and cultivating a vibrant social base of "friends of YIVO," consisting of *zamlers*, supporters, and admirers. This effort had larger designs than the purely utilitarian goals of securing financial support for YIVO and enriching its collections. Through its manifold web of relationships with Jewish society, Weinreich hoped that YIVO would influence Jewish public life by elevating its intellectual level, thus serving the most profound cultural need of the Jewish community. Weinreich articulated this overarching goal in 1936: "Our contribution to the struggle of the Jewish masses, to their struggle for cultural emancipation, can be expressed succinctly: We want to understand Jewish life using the methods of modern science, and we want to bring these attainments of modern science back to the Jewish masses."[9]

This approach was infused with the spirit of Russian and Russian Jewish populism, according to which the intelligentsia was responsible for and duty bound toward the masses. YIVO was, in the final analysis, dedicated not to scholarship alone but to the "cultural emancipation of the Jewish masses," by which he meant the elevation of their autonomous culture and social life to a higher intellectual level.

But when it came to determining who belonged to the "we" of YIVO, who were to engage in this task, Weinreich was an avowed elitist. Friends, supporters, and *zamlers* were not to interfere in the institute's scholarship or try to set the direction of its research. "The members [of the research divisions], who will judge the scholarly work done by themselves and others, must only be people who have themselves already done qualified scholarly work." Weinreich added, "We must insure that the committees in charge of the research divisions have the necessary scholarly authority."[10]

Given the overarching influence of the political parties and movements on Jewish institutional life in interwar Poland, this was a difficult position to maintain, since it meant the exclusion of movement leaders from YIVO's academic decision making. It was also difficult to maintain such academic elitism when there were no clear criteria for qualification to serve on the research division committees—since most members of YIVO's research divisions did not have doctorates. There arose unavoidable tensions between Weinreich and political/communal leaders who complained of his snobbery.

DEFINING THE NEW JEWISH SCHOLARSHIP

Weinreich was much concerned, especially during the interwar years, with defining the difference between the new Jewish scholarship of YIVO and the old nineteenth-century scholarship of German *Wissenschaft des Judenthums*. His formulations on this question varied over the years. At times he stressed the divergent social goals of these two scholarly movements. YIVO served the cultural needs of a living Jewish national organism, while German *Wissenschaft* evolved as part of the era of assimilation and struggle for political emancipation. *Wissenschaft* was therefore characterized by apologetics and the denial of Jewish nationality, whereas the new Jewish scholarship was part of a proud and vibrant Jewish national culture. At times, Weinreich connected this contrast with the question of language. *Wissenschaft* was written in German and exhibited a contemptuous, or at best antiquarian, attitude toward Yiddish. YIVO conducted its scholarship in Yiddish and was thereby elevating the prestige of the Yiddish language and strengthening its future.

In the 1930s, Weinreich went a step further and argued that German *Wissenschaft* and east European Jewish scholarship differed not only in language and social orientation but also in the content of their research agendas. "For us, the present is no less important than the past; for us, the distant past isn't more respected than the recent past.

For us, perhaps the entire study of the past is primarily a means to better understand the present. . . . The here and now are the cornerstones of YIVO."[11]

In the thirties, Weinreich proposed a new paradigm: YIVO was, and needed to develop as, an institute of Jewish social science. As part of this agenda, he tried to spark his colleagues' interest in contemporary topics that could employ the methods of sociology, psychology, economics, and political science. He criticized the "bookishness" and "remoteness from life" that characterized many of YIVO's own publications and attributed these characteristics to the residual influence of German *Wissenschaft*. At the decennial conference of YIVO, in 1935, he enumerated a whole list of contemporary topics that should be investigated by YIVO: the relations between concrete groups of Jews and Christians in everyday life, recent trends in diet and personal hygiene among Jews, changes in the names given by Jewish parents to their newborn babies, the household budgets of Jews (both in large cities and smaller towns), the growth or decline of religious observance in various social environments, changes in the content of the Yiddish press in recent times, and so on and so forth.[12]

This shift was a product of Weinreich's own evolving research interest in the application of social science methods to Jewish studies. He founded and led a new commission on youth research at YIVO and composed a pioneering study on the social psychology of Jewish youth in Poland, *Der veg tsu undzer yugnt* (The path to our youth). As the director of YIVO's graduate training program *(aspirantur)*, founded in 1936, he attempted to develop a cadre of young scholars in the social sciences. The results were quite impressive. Whereas YIVO's overall publications were heavily weighted toward philology and history, more than a third of the students enrolled in the first three cadres of the graduate program (nineteen out of fifty-three students) wrote theses in the fields of Jewish economics, sociology, social psychology, and pedagogy.[13]

POSTWAR METAMORPHOSIS

After the Second World War, as research director of the reconstituted YIVO in New York, Weinreich's fervor for contemporary social science as the centerpiece of YIVO subsided. The living Jewish communities of Warsaw and Vilna had been decimated and now belonged to history, and the study of postwar American Jewry (and of other communities, including the new state of Israel) was somehow less pressing or compelling to him. While YIVO's new English-language journal, launched at Weinreich's initiative, was entitled *YIVO Annual of Jewish Social Science*, the study of the Jewish present was only moderately represented in it. In the journal's first five volumes (1946–1950), which were published under Weinreich's editorial supervision, only twelve of its sixty articles were in the fields of Jewish sociology, economics, and education.

At first, Weinreich held fast to the position he had articulated in the 1930s, contending that YIVO offered analyses of the past that "tend to contribute to an understanding of the present" and that "only by making full use of the achievements of general social science can we come nearer to an adequate understanding of Jewish social realities." But by 1950, his pronouncement shifted the center of YIVO's gravity back to the eastern European past. "The basic idea underlying YIVO's research is that the social scientist should see Jewish life in the United States in the light of antecedents and cross-influences in the old homes."[14]

In his older years, Weinreich reformulated YIVO's mission as being the study and preservation of the cultural and historical legacy of east European Jewry. In light of the Holocaust, he reoriented YIVO's research agenda toward the past. He offered a moving articulation of the reasons for this shift in his address to the fortieth-anniversary conference of YIVO in 1965.

> The Jewish people has never needed YIVO as much as today. Forty years ago, east European Jewry was alive, and carried within it the Ashkenazic version of eternal Judaism in traditional, renewed and new forms. Today, Jewish Europe is destroyed, and Jewish America is not yet fully formed.
>
> We must first and foremost preserve the memory of Jewish Europe. How is one to do this? The routine way is through museum exhibits, and we do what we can in that regard. But how can one embody into museum objects the spirit of Rabenu Gershom, Rabbi Meir of Rothenberg, the Rema and the Vilna Gaon? How does one exhibit the endless, patient struggle of the Haskalah, the vision of the return to Zion, the revolution-

ary heroism of the labor movement, the enthusiasm of the *halutzim* [pioneers], the self-sacrifice of Jewish teachers, the quiet resistance of millions of Jews under the German annihilator, and the armed combat in the forests and ghettos?

We want the spirit of Jewish Eastern Europe to live on in future generations of Jews everywhere. YIVO has a great research task in this regard, because it is a scholarly tool of the Jewish collective. It is no exaggeration to say, that the fate of world Jewry depends on the extent to which Jews in Jerusalem, Moscow, Buenos Aires, and most of all in New York, will absorb the spirit of Vilna.[15]

Weinreich's emotional turn to the past, to its commemoration and perpetuation, was in a sense a continuation of his prewar vision of Jewish scholarship in service of the welfare of the Jewish people. But now, in the aftermath of the destruction, and facing the challenges of an open society, what American Jewry needed first and foremost was memory, much as east European Jewry had needed intellectual rigor in the 1920s. Perpetuating the "spirit of Vilna" through scholarship was paramount among the needs of Jewish existence.

While shifting his focus from the present to the past, Weinreich remained committed to the use of social science methods. He dedicated a full half of his postwar magnum opus, *Geshikhte fun der yidisher shprakh* (History of the Yiddish language; 1969), to the cultural anthropology of Ashkenazic Jewry, the sociology of Jewish languages, and the social psychology of Yiddish. Linguistic history proper (the history of lexical elements, phonology, grammar, and dialects) occupied less than half of the work. Weinreich's *Geshikhte* was the culmination of his lifelong quest to introduce rigorous interdisciplinary methods into Jewish scholarship. Communal engagement and academic research remained in close, dialectical tension, as they had from the outset of Weinreich's career.

EMBERS PLUCKED
FROM THE FIRE

THE RESCUE OF JEWISH CULTURAL
TREASURES IN VILNA

The effort to collect and preserve Jewish historical documents and cultural treasures in eastern Europe was launched with an impassioned public appeal by Simon Dubnov in 1891, it was institutionalized and broadened into a social movement with the founding of YIVO in 1925, and it reached its heroic culmination with the rescue activities of Abraham Sutzkever, Shmerke Kaczerginski, and others in Vilna between 1942 and 1946. The final reverberations of that movement were felt in 1996, when surviving remnants of YIVO's Vilna archives were shipped from Lithuania to New York. That shipment was the epilogue to the story of the Vilna ghetto's Paper Brigade.

BETWEEN DUBNOV AND SUTZKEVER

Dubnov issued his appeal to save the Jewish past from oblivion at age twenty-nine, in a Russian-language pamphlet called *Ob izuchenii istorii ruskikh evreev* (On the study of Russian Jewish history) and in an adapted Hebrew version of that pamphlet called *Nahpesa venahkora* (Let us search and inquire). He opened by citing the words of Cicero that "not to know history means to remain forever a child," and declared that this maxim applies to nations as well as to individuals.

The measure of a people's spiritual development was its level of historical consciousness. From that perspective, the Jews of Russia and Poland were still immature children—despite the fact that they belonged to one of the most ancient peoples on earth. They had neither knowledge nor consciousness of their eight-hundred-year historical experience in eastern Europe. There was virtually no scholarship on Russian Jewish history, and its absence posed a serious threat to Jewish continuity, since in the modern era, shared historical consciousness was destined to replace religious faith as the glue of Jewish group cohesion.

Most shameful of all, from Dubnov's perspective, was the neglect of Jewish historical documents, especially of the record books *(pinkasim)* of communities and voluntary associations *(hevrot)*, which he called "the natural resources of our history." These irreplaceable materials, Dubnov wrote, "are lying in attics, in piles of trash, or in equally unpleasant and filthy rooms, among broken household items and rags. These manuscripts are rotting away, they are being eaten by mice, and are being used by ignorant servants and children who tear off page after page for all sorts of purposes. In other words: year by year they are disappearing and being lost to history."[1]

Dubnov concluded that the collection of such materials required an "archeological expedition," organized preferably by a central institution for the study of Russian Jewish history. The institution could appoint local representatives to acquire materials and would work on classifying, cataloging, copying, and publishing the documents in its possession.[2]

In the Hebrew version of his essay, Dubnov urged his readers to join him in the great task of documentary collection and preservation and appended detailed instructions on how to go about their work.

> I appeal to all educated readers, regardless of their party: to the pious and to the enlightened, to the old and to the young, to traditional rabbis and to Crown Rabbis. . . . I call out to all of you; come and join the camp of the builders of history! Not every learned or literate person can be a great writer or historian. But every one of you can be a collector of material, and aid in the building of our history. . . . Let us work, gather our dispersed from their places of exile, arrange them, publish them, and

build upon their foundation the temple of our history. Come, let us search and inquire![3]

The ideas expressed in Dubnov's appeal became the credo of three generations of east European Jewish intellectuals, beginning with his contemporaries S. An-sky and Saul Ginsburg, continuing with the generation of Elias Tcherikower and Max Weinreich, and culminating with the interwar generation of Emanuel Ringelblum and Abraham Sutzkever. A virtual cult of documentary collection existed in Jewish eastern Europe between 1925 and 1939, with the Vilna YIVO as its temple. Groups of volunteer *zamlers* in scores of cities and towns in Poland, Lithuania, Romania, and across the globe inundated YIVO with a mass of historical, literary, artistic, and ethnographic materials. Their work became the subject of poetic odes, short stories, and feuilletons, the stuff of folklore and legend.[4]

With the advent of the Second World War and its aftermath, with the German and Soviet occupations of eastern Europe, Jewish documents and treasures faced a new threat, infinitely more sinister than the one Dubnov had portrayed in 1891. They were at the mercies of political regimes that were intent on destroying them or locking them away. A determined group of Jewish intellectuals, driven by the Dubnovian imperative, risked their lives to rescue Jewish books, documents, and artifacts.

EINSATZSTAB ROSENBERG IN VILNA

It was the task of the Special Detail of Reich-Administrator (Einsatzstab des Reichsleiter) Alfred Rosenberg to ransack and round up Judaica collections throughout Europe and arrange for their shipment to Germany, to the Institut Zur Erforschung der Judenfrage (Institute for the Study of the Jewish Question) in Frankfurt. Rosenberg, Nazi Germany's chief ideologue, was the institute's rector and titular head of the Einsatzstab. On a day-to-day basis, however, the work of the Rosenberg detail was directed by one of the institute's senior staff members, Dr. Johannes Pohl, who had studied Judaica at the Hebrew University in Jerusalem from 1934 to 1936. Pohl was the author of a book on the Talmud, a regular contributor to *Der Sturmer*, and a spokesman for what he called *Judenforschung ohne Juden* (Jewish studies without Jews).[5]

A week after the Germans captured Vilna (on June 24, 1941), a representative of the Rosenberg detail, Dr. Gotthardt, arrived in the city. He began by collecting information—paying visits to various museums, libraries, and synagogues and asking questions about the state of Jewish collections and the whereabouts of various Jewish scholars. In late July, he instructed the Gestapo to arrest three such scholars: Noyekh Prilutski, the Yiddish folklorist and linguist who had been YIVO's director during the brief period of Soviet rule in Vilna in 1940–1941; Elijah Jacob Goldschmidt, a veteran Yiddish journalist and director of the An-sky Jewish Ethnographic Museum; and Chaikl Lunski, the fabled head of the Strashun Library, Vilna's Jewish communal library. The arrested scholars were transported daily from their prison cell to the Strashun Library, where they were ordered to compile lists of incunabula and rare books. In late August, Gotthardt left for Germany with lists and materials in hand. Shortly after his departure, Prilutski and Goldschmidt were murdered by the Gestapo. Lunski was released.[6]

The Germans apparently learned from this first attempt to seize Jewish cultural treasures from Vilna that the city housed too many rare Jewish books, manuscripts, and artifacts to seize all of them in a single raid, using one or two arrested Jewish scholars. This tactic had been employed elsewhere by the Rosenberg detail with success, but in Vilna, a long-term work group was needed to sift through tens of thousands of items. When Dr. Pohl himself visited the city in February 1942, accompanied by three *Judenforschung* specialists from Berlin, he arranged for the establishment of such a group. He ordered the ghetto to provide him with twelve workers to sort, pack, and ship materials and put two prominent Jewish intellectuals in charge of the operation: Herman Kruk, a Bundist refugee from Warsaw who was head of the Vilna ghetto library, and Zelig Kalmanovitch, a disciple of Dubnov who had been one of the directors of prewar YIVO. Chaikl Lunski was appointed as bibliographic consultant. The group was given spacious work facilities in a building belonging to the Vilna University library (located at Universitetska 3), an indication of the high priority that Pohl, as head of the Rosenberg detail, assigned to its work.[7]

The entire Strashun Library, some forty thousand volumes, was to be transported to Universitetska 3, where it was to undergo a *selektsia* between materials to be shipped to the Frankfurt institute and materials destined for destruction. The latter were to be shipped to nearby paper mills for recycling. Kruk and Kalmanovitch were to describe and catalog the items of greater value. From the first day, they looked for opportunities to take some of the books back into the ghetto, either legally—by having them reconsigned to the ghetto library—or secretly. At first, Kruk reacted to his job assignment with wistful ambivalence. "Kalmanovitch and I don't know whether we are gravediggers or saviors," he wrote in his diary. "If we'll manage to keep these treasures in Vilna, it may be to our great merit. But if the library will be sent out, we will have been accomplices. I'm trying to insure it in either case." By the end of February, the entire Strashun Library was at Universitetska 3, as were the *sforim* (religious books) from various synagogues, including the Vilna Gaon's *kloyz*. The YIVO library was rumored to be on its way.[8]

But instead of transferring YIVO's collections to Universitetska 3, the Germans decided to expand the operation of the Rosenberg detail and established a second work site in the YIVO building at Wiwulskiego 18. The Jewish work group was expanded to forty people, and its scholarly staff was increased as well. In March 1942, the Yiddish poets Abraham Sutzkever and Shmerke Kaczerginski, who had been leaders of the prewar literary group Yung Vilne, and several other members of the Jewish intelligentsia, were recruited by Kruk.[9]

The YIVO building was located outside the confines of the ghetto, and prior to its transfer to the Rosenberg detail, it had been used by the Germans as a military barracks. When Kruk and others first entered this former cultural shrine, they found it in disarray. In the majestic entry hall, where a Yiddish map of the world had once hung, with the inscription *Der yivo un zayne farbindungen iber der velt* (YIVO and its affiliates across the globe), a German eagle and swastika now hung, with a new inscription: *Deutschland wird leben und deshalb wird*

Deutschland siegen (Germany will live, and therefore Germany will prevail). The collections and catalogs were thrown into the basement or were strewn across the floor.[10]

YIVO soon became the depot and processing center for a variety of libraries and collections—Jewish, Polish, and Russian—from Vilna, Kovna, and neighboring towns. Sutzkever noted the parallels between the operations of the Gestapo and the Rosenberg detail. Just as the former raided houses in search of Jews in hiding, the latter conducted aggressive searches for collections of Jewish books. (In the course of the search of the library of Vilna University, the floor of the reading room was torn open to check for Jewish books.) Once books were seized, they were subjected to a process of *selektsia*—between life and death. Just as the Germans sent many non-Jews to their deaths along with the Jews, the Rosenberg detail destroyed non-Jewish libraries as well. The collections of the Polish Museum, the Society of Friends of Science (Towarzistwo Przyacziol Nauk), the Thomas Zohn Library, the library of the Evangelical Church, and others were seized and sent for processing in the YIVO building. And as with the extermination of the Jews, the destruction of Jewish books was meticulously recorded, with biweekly statistical reports on the numbers of books sent to Germany and the number sent to the paper mills, with breakdowns according to language and century of publication.[11]

A quota of 70 percent was set as the proportion of books to be disposed of as trash. Since the German *Judenforschung* officials in charge, Willy Scheffer and Sporket, knew virtually nothing about Jewish culture, they often decided the fate of a book based on the attractiveness of its binding. Books with impressive bindings were sent to Frankfurt, while poorly bound items went to the paper mills. In June 1942, Kruk wrote, "The Jewish porters occupied with the task are literally in tears; it is heartbreaking to see this happening." In early July he added, "YIVO is dying; its mass grave is the paper mill."[12]

THE PAPER BRIGADE

The members of the work group at YIVO mastered a variety of tactics to save books and documents from destruction. The first, and simplest, was to drag out the work process as much as possible. When the

German officers left the building in the hands of a Polish guard, the staff would often turn to other activities, mainly to reading books. Sutzkever would read and recite to others the works of his favorite Yiddish poets: H. Leivick, Aaron Leyeles, Yehoash, and Jacob Glatstein. He and Kaczerginski wrote most of their ghetto poetry inside the walls of the YIVO building at Wiwulskiego 18. But there were limits and risks to foot dragging. Members of the work group soon began smuggling materials into the ghetto, in the belief that they would be safer there.[13]

At the end of the work day, they would stuff materials inside their clothing, to prevent their detection by the guards at the ghetto gate. If, when they arrived at the gate, it was manned by the Jewish ghetto police, there would be no problem. The latter would let them pass with only a cursory inspection, knowing full well that all they were carrying was paper. The ghetto police called them mockingly Di Papir Brigade (the Paper Brigade), and the nickname spread throughout the ghetto. But if German SS, Gestapo, or military were stationed at the gate, anxiety rose among the members of the work group. If word reached them ahead of time that the Germans were at the gate, they would take a circuitous route back from work and drop off the materials temporarily with non-Jewish friends. But there were instances when the group had to pass through German inspection. When books and papers were found on their bodies, they were beaten and warned of severe consequences.[14]

Between March 1942 and September 1943, thousands of books and tens of thousands of documents made their way back into the Vilna ghetto thanks to the smuggling activity of the Paper Brigade. The group of smugglers consisted of Kruk, Kalmanovitch, Sutzkever, Kaczerginski, Dr. Daniel Feinstein, Dr. Yaakov Gordon, Naomi Markeles, Uma Olkenicki, Ruzhka Korczak, and Rokhl Pupko-Krinsky. Kaczerginski later recalled, "Jews looked at us as if we were lunatics. *They* were smuggling foodstuffs into the ghetto, in their clothes and boots. *We* were smuggling books, pieces of paper, occasionally a *Sefer Torah* or mezuzahs." To those who criticized the group for occupying themselves with the fates of papers in a time of life-and-death crisis, Kalmanovitch replied emphatically that "books don't grow on trees."[15]

Sutzkever was the most active and ingenious rescuer of materials in the group. He once obtained a written permit from one of the Germans to take some wastepaper into the ghetto, for use in his household oven, and then used the permit to take in letters and manuscripts by Tolstoy, Gorky, Sholem Aleichem, and Bialik; one of Herzl's diaries; drawings by Chagall; and a unique manuscript by the Vilna Gaon. With the help of some well-connected friends, he even managed to smuggle sculptures by Mark Antokolky and paintings by Repin and Levitan out of the YIVO building and into the ghetto.[16]

But once the materials were inside the ghetto, the question was where to hide them. Many were handed over to Kruk for concealment in the building of the ghetto library (located at Straszuna 6). Sutzkever divided his materials among ten hiding places, including the walls and floor of his own apartment (at Straszuna 1). The safest spot of all was a bunker built more than sixty feet underground by a young construction engineer named Gershon Abramovitsh. The bunker was brought to Sutzkever's attention by one of the commanders of the ghetto's United Partisan Organization (Fareynikter Partizaner Organizatsye, FPO). It featured a ventilation system of its own, electricity drawn from wires outside the ghetto, and a tunnel leading to a well on the Aryan side. Abramovitsh had constructed it as a hiding place for his paralyzed mother and agreed to keep the YIVO treasures together with her.[17]

Not all books smuggled into the ghetto were buried in hiding places. Textbooks and children's literature were delivered to the clandestine schools in the ghetto, and a Soviet munitions manual, with instructions on how to make Molotov cocktails and land mines, was handed over to the commanders of the FPO. It enabled the ghetto's partisans to produce their first arsenal. On the other hand, some rare books and documents were not smuggled into the ghetto. Sutzkever and Kaczerginski handed them over to Polish and Lithuanian friends, who paid visits to Wiwulskiego 18 during the lunch break, when the German officers were away. The Lithuanian poet Kazis Borutas and librarian Anna Shimaite were among those non-Jews who received packets of materials for safekeeping. Sutzkever also used lunchtime encounters to deliver valuable Polish books and materials to members of the Polish underground, including a document signed by Polish freedom fighter Tadeusz Kosciuszko.[18]

Unknown to Kruk and Kalmanovitch, several members of the Paper Brigade, beginning with Sutzkever and Kaczerginski, were also members of the FPO. One of their lunchtime visitors, Kaczerginski's Lithuanian friend Julian Jankauskas, used their meetings to deliver arms. At first he brought tiny pistols, then larger ones, and then one day Jankauskas appeared unexpectedly with a machine gun hidden inside a viola case. Kaczerginski and the others quickly disassembled its parts and hid them in different rooms of the YIVO building. A moment later, the German officer Scheffer returned with high-ranking visitors from Berlin, and began to show off "his" treasures, room by room. Scheffer was about to lift up the Chagall painting that covered the barrel of the machine gun, when a last-second diversion by Rokhl Pupko-Krinsky saved the day. She ran over to show the Germans a rare book from the seventeenth century.[19]

As the shipments to the paper mills intensified, it became clear that the Paper Brigade was winning small battles but losing its war. Only a tiny fraction of the treasures was being rescued. That is when Sutzkever thought of a new tactic: to create a hiding place, a *malina*, inside the YIVO building itself. Upon examining the building's architecture, he found large cavities underneath the beams and girders in the attic. All that was needed was to distract the Polish guard, Virblis, so that Sutzkever and others could whisk the materials up to the attic. Luckily, Virblis had ambitions of being more than just a guard some day and regretted that the war had interrupted his formal education. So two members of the work group, Drs. Feinstein and Gordon, offered to teach him mathematics, Latin, and German during the lunch break. As the teachers and their student were engrossed in study, the transfer of the materials to the attic proceeded.[20]

The work at Wiwulskiego 18 continued until shortly before the final liquidation of the Vilna ghetto on September 23, 1943. Kalmanovitch wrote in one of his last entries in his diary, on August 23, "Our work is reaching its conclusion. Thousands of books are being dumped as trash, and the Jewish books will be liquidated. Whatever part we can rescue will be saved, with God's help. We will find it when we return as free human beings."[21]

But this prediction was not to come true. Most of the members of

the Paper Brigade perished at Ponar, the mass-murder site outside of
Vilna, or in labor camps in Estonia. Among them were the heads of the
work group, Kruk and Kalmanovitch. But the FPO members in the
group—Sutzkever, Kaczerginski, and Korczak—managed to flee to
the forests before the ghetto's final liquidation and to join up with various partisan units.

AFTER THE WAR

Sutzkever and Kaczerginski returned to Vilna in 1944, along with
the Soviet army, and helped liberate the city as members of the Jewish
partisan brigade Nekome-nemer (Avengers). Most surviving Jews who
emerged from their hiding places or returned from evacuation to Vilna
were concerned, first and foremost, with locating friends and relatives,
including the children who had been left behind with Christians. But
Sutzkever and Kaczerginski had an additional agenda: to dig up the
Jewish books, documents, and treasures they had hidden.

Their preliminary survey of the territory yielded painful results: the
YIVO building at Wiwulskiego 18 was a pile of rubble, having been hit
by artillery shells. Its attic was burnt to a crisp. Kruk's hiding place inside the ghetto library at Straszuna 6 had been discovered just days before the liberation, and all of its materials had been incinerated in the
courtyard. On the other hand, Gershon Abramovitsh's underground
bunker was intact, as were other hiding places. An organized salvage
operation was needed to retrieve the materials.

On July 26, 1944—just thirteen days after the liberation of Vilna—
Sutzkever and Kaczerginski established the Museum of Jewish Art and
Culture, affiliated with the Ministry of Culture of the Lithuanian Soviet
Socialist Republic. The museum, which was initially located in their
private apartment on 15 Gediminas Street, was the first Jewish institution to be established in Vilna after the war. It became the prime Jewish address in the city, the place where Jewish soldiers, partisans, and
survivors gathered; where the short-lived Jewish school was founded;
and where all letters addressed to surviving Jews in Vilna were for-
warded. In mid-August, the museum moved into the only Jewish
communal building not yet expropriated by the Soviet authorities:

Straszuna Street 6, which had been the site of the ghetto library, various administrative offices, and the ghetto prison. The only part of the
building that was in usable condition was the prison. The staff of the
Jewish Museum worked in the prison cells where Jewish inmates had
been tortured by the Gestapo.[22]

With Sutzkever serving as director, and an unpaid staff of six (including the commander of the ghetto's partisans, Abba Kovner), the
salvage work in the hiding places proceeded. Strewn across Gershon
Abramovitsh's bunker were the pages to Herman Kruk's ghetto diary,
letters by Sholem Aleichem, manuscripts by Bialik, Gorky, and
Mendele. Buried in the ground beneath the bunker were paintings and
sculptures—Ilya Ginzburg's bust of Tolstoy, Mark Antokolsky's statue
of King David, and others. In digging out the sculptures, Sutzkever un-
covered an outstretched arm, and upon grabbing it realized that it was
not made of clay, but was human. Gershon Abramovitsh explained that
one of the Jews who had hidden in the bunker died there shortly before the liberation and was buried alongside Antokolsky's David.[23]

Meanwhile, unanticipated troves of material surfaced. Twenty tons
of YIVO papers were found at a local paper mill, not yet destroyed.
Thirty tons were in the courtyard of the Trash Administration (Soyuzu-
til). Various Jews and Christians started delivering potato sacks filled
with books and papers to the museum.

But there was no support coming from the Lithuanian Soviet authorities—no furniture or supplies (Kaczerginski rejoiced when someone brought him envelopes and erasers), no vehicles to transport the
vast volume of material to the museum, no salaries for the staff. Appeals to Communist Party officials in Vilnius and to Soviet authorities
in Moscow were ignored. Some Lithuanian officials responded by asking why the Jews insisted on having a separate Jewish museum, a separate Jewish school. Aren't we all Soviet citizens? Henryk Ziman, a
Jewish member of the Communist Party leadership in Lithuania, urged
patience; Jewish cultural needs would be met once Soviet rule was
consolidated. But Sutzkever was unconvinced. He returned to Moscow
in September 1944, with Kruk's diary and other materials in his bags.
He sensed that Soviet Vilnius, as the city was now called, was not a safe

place for Jewish treasures. With the help of a foreign correspondent, he sent off his first package of materials to YIVO in New York.[24]

It took Kaczerginski, who succeeded Sutzkever as director of the museum, almost a year to reach the same conclusion. A communist sympathizer before the war, Kaczerginski traveled to Moscow in March 1945 to complain to Soviet officials about the obstructionist and hostile attitude of the Lithuanian authorities toward the museum and other Jewish institutions. After receiving a sympathetic hearing in the offices of the Central Committee of the Communist Party, he returned to Vilna, stepping off the train only to learn that the Trash Administration had just transported the thirty tons of YIVO materials in its courtyard to the train depot, for shipment to a paper mill. He dashed to the shipping platform and started pulling items out of the piles—a script of a Yiddish drama, a *sefer* (religious book) from Chaikl Lunski's library, an autobiography from the YIVO autobiography competition. He then rushed from one bureau to another to prevent the shipment—first to the Rail Administration, then to the Trash Administration, then to Ziman. But by the time he returned to the train depot the next day, the mountains of paper were gone.[25]

The bad news continued: in mid-1945, the authorities officially registered the museum as the Jewish Museum of Vilna, but allocated for it a total of three paid staff positions. With a staff of three, the work of collecting and cataloging its vast holdings was effectively doomed. Then agents of the KGB began to pay repeated visits to Kaczerginski at the museum. Among other things, they reminded him that no books were to be made available to the public without their prior review by Soviet censors. Volumes that were sent to the censors were never returned. Kaczerginski later recalled, "That is when we, the group of museum activists, had a bizarre realization—we must save our treasures *again*, and get them out of here. Otherwise they will perish. In the best of cases they will survive, but will never see the light of day in the Jewish world."[26]

One by one, the museum activists began to emigrate, and smuggle out parts of the collection, in an operation that was as dangerous as the smuggling of materials into the ghetto under the Nazis. Abba Kovner,

Ruzhka Korczak, Dr. Amarant—each of them took what they could. Meanwhile, Kaczerginski put up a front of being a loyal Communist operative. He published a proud report of the museum's activities in the Moscow Yiddish newspaper *Eynikayt* (Unity) on October 2, 1945. He surveyed its collections: twenty-five thousand Yiddish and Hebrew books, ten thousand volumes of Judaica in European languages, six hundred sacks full of documentary materials from the YIVO archives, the extraordinary archives of the Vilna and Kovna ghettos. The museum's plans for the future were no less impressive: renovating the museum building, mounting a large permanent exhibit, and erecting a monument in the courtyard to Jews who fell in battle against the Nazis.[27]

None of this was ever to be, and Kaczerginski himself knew it full well. As he wrote his article, he was already making plans to emigrate and arranging the smuggling of materials abroad. In November 1945, he submitted his resignation. By July 1946 both he and Sutzkever were in Poland, with museum materials in their bags. From there, they proceeded to Paris. From both destinations, they sent packages to Max Weinreich, YIVO's research director in New York.[28]

As Sutzkever and Kaczerginski intuited, the fate that awaited the multitude of materials that remained in Vilnius was not a happy one. In 1948, word reached the West that the Jewish Museum had been liquidated and ransacked by the KGB. One Vilna émigré and former volunteer in the museum, Leyzer Ran, recorded the news in his diary: "The 'visitors' have come to the ghetto again. This time, they came in new Soviet trucks. They dumped all of the museum's materials—artifacts, books, archives—into the trucks and took them to Szniadecki Street, to the Church of St. Yuri, which is now the Bikher-palate [Book Chamber]. Materials are kept there in excellent condition. Except for the Jewish materials, which were dumped in the basement."[29]

The Jewish documents remained in the inner recesses of the Lithuanian Book Chamber, housed in a former church, for the next forty years. During the years of Stalinist terror, between 1949 and 1953, they were hidden there by the Book Chamber's director, Dr. Antanas Ulpis, who quietly disobeyed the orders of his superiors to have them destroyed. In the period of de-Stalinization, Ulpis arranged for thousands of the Jewish books in his repository to be cataloged, but the existence of the bundles of Jewish documents remained a secret that Ulpis kept to himself—until his retirement. Their existence first became public knowledge in 1988. A second batch was unexpectedly discovered during a cleanup of the Book Chamber's facilities in 1993. The materials were shipped to YIVO in 1995 and 1996.[30]

GRAINS OF WHEAT

In his memoirs, written after his emigration to the West, Kaczerginski gave voice to his bitterness and disillusionment about what happened to the treasures he had rescued. In the final analysis, he writes, geopolitics had deceived and defeated him and his colleagues. Who among the members of the Paper Brigade could have imagined that the free, liberated Vilna after the war would itself turn out to be a Soviet prison camp? Unfortunately, he writes, much of their labor had been in vain.

But Kaczerginski was, thankfully, wrong. The final word on the subject belongs to Sutzkever. In a poem entitled "Kerndlekh veyts" (Grains of wheat), written in March 1943, he expressed his faith in the eventual victory of the Paper Brigade and its enterprise. He portrayed himself running through the streets of the ghetto with "the Jewish word" in his arms, and caressing it like a child, the pieces of parchment and poetry crying out to him, "hide me in your labyrinth." Once, while burying the materials in the ground, he was overcome with despair. He then recalled an ancient parable: One of the Egyptian pharaohs built a pyramid for himself, and ordered his servants to place some grains of wheat in his coffin at the time of his burial. Nine thousand years passed, the coffin was opened, the grains were discovered and planted, and a beautiful bed of stalks blossomed forth from them. Someday, Sutzkever wrote, the grains he had planted in the soil of the Vilna ghetto would also bear fruit.

> Efsher oykh veln di verter
> dervartn zikh ven af dem likht—
> veln in sho'en basherter
> tseblien zikh oykh umgerikht

un vi der uralter kern
vos hot zikh farvandlt in zang—
veln di verter oykh nern,
veln di verter gehern
dem folk, in zayn eybikn gang.

Perhaps these words will endure,
And live to see the light loom—
And in the destined hour
Will unexpectedly bloom?

And like the primeval grain
That turned into a stalk—
The words will nourish,
The words will belong
To the people in its eternal walk.[31]

In 1996, YIVO celebrated the victory of Sutzkever's vision and spirit. Now that these materials are at long last reunited with their spiritual home and with the Jewish people, we can proclaim, *Di verter veln nern, di verter veln gehern, dem folk in zayn eybikn gang*—these words will nourish, these words will belong to the people, on its eternal walk.

Notes

Chapter 1: The Rise of Modern Yiddish Culture

1. Many of the topics in this chapter are addressed from somewhat different perspectives by Avraham Nowersztern in *Ha-sifrut veha-hayim: tsmikhata shel sifrut yidish ha-hadasha*, unit 2 of *Le'an: zeramim hadashim bekerev yehude mizrah-eropa* (Tel Aviv: Open University of Israel, 2000), and by Joshua A. Fishman, *Never Say Die: A Thousand Years of Yiddish in Jewish Life and Letters* (The Hague and New York: Mouton, 1981). See also Dovid Katz, *Words on Fire: The Unfinished Story of Yiddish* (New York: Basic Books, 2004).

2. On Yiddish language and literature in premodern Ashkenazic Jewry, see Max Weinreich, *History of the Yiddish Language*, trans. Shlomo Noble (with the assistance of Joshua A. Fishman) (Chicago: University of Chicago Press, 1980), which is a translation of the first two volumes of *Geshikhte fun der yidisher shprakh*, 4 vols. (New York: YIVO, 1973); Israel Zinberg, *History of Jewish Literature*, ed. and trans. Bernard Martin, vol. 6, *Old Yiddish Literature from Its Origins to the Haskalah Period* (Cincinnati, OH: Hebrew Union College Press, 1978), which is a translation of *Geshikhte fun der literatur bay yidn*, 2nd ed., 8 vols. (New York: Morris S. Sklarsky, 1943); Chone Shmeruk, *Sifrut yiddish: Prakim le-toldoteha* (Tel Aviv: Porter Institute for Poetics and Semiotics, Tel Aviv University, 1978).

3. On the Haskalah and Yiddish, see Dan Miron, *A Traveler Disguised: The Rise of Modern Yiddish Fiction in the 19th Century*, 2nd ed. (Syracuse, NY: Syracuse University Press, 1996). On Dik, see David G. Roskies, *A Bridge of Longing: The Lost Art of Yiddish Storytelling* (Cambridge, MA: Harvard University Press, 1995), chap. 3. On the Russian Haskalah more generally, including its attitude toward Yiddish, see David E. Fishman, *Russia's First Modern Jews: The Jews of Shklov* (New York: New York University Press, 1995); Michael S. Stanislawsky, *Tsar Nicholas I and the Jews* (Philadelphia: Jewish Publication Society of America, 1983).

4. The Yiddish mother-tongue figures are drawn from B. Goldberg, "O rodnom yazike v evreev rosii," *Evreiskaia Zhizn* 2, no. 4 (April 1905): 70–80. On the Jews of St. Petersburg, see Benjamin Nathans, *Beyond the Pale* (Berkeley and Los Angeles: University of California Press, 2002). On Jewish university students, see Gennady Estraikh, "Languages of Yehupets Students," *East European Jewish Affairs* 22, no. 1 (Summer 1992): 63–71.

5. On the Jewish and Yiddish press in nineteenth-century Russia, see Alexander Orbach, *New Voices of Russian Jewry: A Study of the Russian Jewish Press in the Era of the Great Reforms* (Leiden, Netherlands: E. J. Brill, 1980); S. L. Zitron, *Di geshikhte fun der yidisher prese* (Warsaw: Ahiasaf, 1923).

6. On Goldfaden and Yiddish theater, see Nahma Sandrow, *Vagabond Stars:*

A World History of Yiddish Theatre (Syracuse, NY: Syracuse University Press, 1996); Joel Berkowitz, ed., *Yiddish Theatre: New Approaches* (Oxford, UK, and Portland, OR: Littman Library of Jewish Civilization, 2003). Among older studies, the most important are Jacob Shatzky, ed., *Arkhiv far der geshikhte fun yidishn teater un drame* (Vilna and New York: YIVO, 1930); N. Oyslender, *Yidisher teater 1887–1917* (Moscow: Der Emes, 1940); Zalmen Zylbercweig, *Leksikon fun yidishn teater*, 6 vols. (New York: Elisheva, 1931–69).

7. This topic is considered in depth in chapter 2.

8. On *Di yidishe folksbibliotek* and the almanacs of the 1890s, see Miron, *A Traveler Disguised*; Ruth Wisse, *I. L. Peretz and the Rise of Modern Jewish Culture* (Seattle and London: University of Washington Press, 1991). On the reactions by Ravnitsky and other Hebrew writers, see G. Kressel, "A historishe polemii vegn der yidisher literature," *Di Goldene Keyt* 20 (1954): 338–55. On Dubnov's reaction, see Elissa Bemporad, "Da Letteratura del Popolo a Istoria del Popolo: Simon Dubnov e l'origine Della Storiografia Russo-Ebraica," *Annali Di Storia Dell' Esegesi* 18, no. 2 (2001): 533–57.

9. On *Der Yid*, see Ruth Wisse, "Not the 'Pintele Yid' But the Full-Fledged Jew," *Prooftexts* 15 (1995): 33–61. On *Der Fraynd*, see Saul Ginsburg, "Di ershte yidishe teglekhe tsaytung in rusland 'der fraynd,'" in *Amolike peterburg* (New York: CYCO, 1944), 184–236. On socialist literature, see J. S. Hertz, "Di umlegale prese un literatur fun 'Bund,'" in *Pinkes far der forshung fun der yidisher literatur un prese*, ed. Hyman Bass, 2:294–366 (New York: Congress for Jewish Culture, 1972).

10. Solomon Esbikher (pseudonym for Sholem Aleichem), "A reester iber ale zhargonishe verk vos zenen opgedrukt gevorn inem yor 5648 [~1888], in *Di yidishe folksbibliotek* (Kiev: Sheftel, 1888): 469–73; M. Shalit, "Statistik fun yidishn bikhermark in yor 1912," in *Der pinkes: Yorbukh far der geshikhte fun der yidisher literatur un shprakh, ar folklor, kritik un bibliografye*, ed. S. Niger, 277–306 (Vilna: B. Kletskin, 1913); Avrom Kirzhnits, *Di yidishe prese in der gevezener ruslendisher imperye* (Moscow: Tsentraler Felker-Farlag fun FSSR, 1930), 10, 44–48.

11. *Yidisher Folksblat* figures from Zitron, *Geshikhte fun der yidisher prese*, 132; 1905 figure for *Der Fraynd* from H. D. Hurwitz, "Undzer ershte teglekhe tsaytung," in Niger, *Der pinkes*, 246; *Haynt* and *Moment* circulations for 1912 taken from Zalmen Rejzen, *Leksikon fun yidisher literatur un prese* (Warsaw: Tsentral, 1914), 679, 711.

12. On Gruenbaum, see Ezra Mendelsohn, *Zionism in Poland: The Formative Years, 1915–1926* (New Haven, CT: Yale University Press, 1981), passim. On Prylucki, see Keith Weiser, *The Politics of Yiddish: Noyekh Prilutski and the Folkspartey in Poland, 1900–1926* (PhD diss., Columbia University, 2001).

13. See Kenneth Moss, "Jewish Culture between Renaissance and Decadence: *Di Literarishe Monatshriftn* and its Critical Reception," *Jewish Social Studies*, New Series, 8, no. 1 (2001): 153–98; Elias Schulman, "Di tsaytshrift, 'Di yidishe velt,'" in *Pinkes far der forshung fun der yidisher literatur un prese*, ed. Sholyme Bikl, 1:122–70 (New York: Congress for Jewish Culture, 1965).

14. On the theater, see Michael Steinlauf, "Fear of Purim: Y. L. Peretz and the Canonization of Yiddish Theatre," *Jewish Social Studies*, New Series, 1, no. 3 (1995): 44–65; Sandrow, *Vagabond Stars;* Berkowitz, *Yiddish Theatre;* Shatzky,

Arkhiv far der geshikhte; Oyslender, *Yidisher teater;* Zylbercweig, *Leksikon fun yidishn teater.*

15. Saul Ginsburg, "Gezelshaft far yiddisher folks-muzik," in *Amolike peter-burg,* 239–46.

16. The year 1905 as an ideological turning point is considered in chapter 3.

17. On the aspiration for Jewish national autonomy, see chapter 5. On the Czernovitz conference and its leading figures, see Emanuel Goldsmith, *Architects of Yiddishism at the Beginning of the Twentieth Century* (Rutherford, NJ: Fairleigh Dickenson University Press, 1976); the articles in part 4 of Joshua A. Fishman, *Yiddish: Turning to Life* (Philadelphia: John Benjamins, 1991).

18. See Ahad Ha'am, "Riv ha-leshonot," in *Al parashat derakhim,* 4:116–23 (Berlin: Juedischer Verlag, 1921); Ber Borokhov, *Shprakh-forshung un literatur-kritik,* ed. Nachmen Meisl (Tel Aviv: I. L. Peretz Farlag, 1966). For Yiddishist pronouncement and resolutions at the third conference of the Russian Poale Zion, see M. Mintz, ed., *Ha-ve'idah ha-shlishit shel poale-tziyon be-rusiyah, 1917* (Tel Aviv: Tel Aviv University, 1976), 41, 43, 71.

19. On Jewish Socialist movements, see Jonathan Frankel, *Prophecy and Politics: Socialism, Nationalism and the Russian Jews, 1862–1917* (Cambridge: Cambridge University Press, 1981). On the Bund's post-1905 brand of Yiddishism, see chapter 4.

20. On the Jewish Literary Society, see Simon Dubnov, *Kniga zhizni: Vospominania i razmyshlenia* (Riga: Jaunatas Granata, 1935), vol. 2, chap. 48 (in Yiddish: *Dos bukh fun mayn lebn,* trans. Y. Rapaport [Buenos Aires: Congress for Jewish Culture, 1962], 2:85–94); "Evreiskoe literaturnoe obshchestvo," in *Evreiskaia entsiklopediia* (St. Petersburg: Brokhaus-Efron, 1913), 7:450.

Chapter 2. The Politics of Yiddish

1. Statistics on language are available in Solomon M. Schwartz, *The Jews in the Soviet Union* (Syracuse, NY: Syracuse University Press, 1951), 12–13.

2. Chaim Zhitlovsky may have been the first to use the coinage *yidishe kul-tur* to refer to Yiddish culture in his "Tsionism oder sotsialism" (originally published in 1898), in *Gezamlte shriftn,* 5:72 (New York: Zhitlovsky Jubilee Committee, 1917).

3. This is the impression conveyed by Mark Zborowski and Elizabeth Herzog in *Life is With People* (New York: International Universities Press, 1952). Avrom Menes' erudite and evocative study "Di mizrekh eyropeishe tkufe in der yidisher geshikhte," in *Algemeyne entsiklopedye—Yidn,* 4:275–430 (New York: Jewish Encyclopedic Handbooks, 1950) suffers from the same misconception.

4. Steven Zipperstein, "Haskalah, Cultural Change and 19th Century Russian Jewry: A Reassessment," *Journal of Jewish Studies* 34, no. 2 (1983): 191–207; Steven Zipperstein, *The Jews of Odessa: A Cultural History* (Stanford, CA: Stanford University Press, 1985); Jacob Shatzky, *Geshikhte fun yidn in varshe,* vol. 3 (New York: YIVO, 1953).

5. Shmeruk's *Sifrut yiddish* creates this impression.

6. I. J. Linetski and Y. M. Lifshits were writers who insisted on Yiddish as the sole valuable vehicle of enlightenment and mockingly disparaged the use of Hebrew. On Margulis, see Peter Shaw, *The Jewish Community of Odessa: A So-*

cial and Institutional History (PhD diss., Hebrew University, 1988). On changing attitudes, see Emanuel S. Goldsmith, *Modern Yiddish Culture: The Story of the Yiddish Language Movement* (New York: Fordham University Press, 1987), 45–70. On the polemic generated by the publication of Sholem Aleichem's *Di yidishes folksbibliotek* in 1888, see G. Kressel, "A historishe polemik vegn der yidisher literatur," *Di Goldene Keyt*, no. 20 (1954): 338–55.

7. S. L. Zitron, *Di geshikhte fun der yidisher prese*, 9, 63; see also Zitron's chapter on Zederbaum in his *Dray literarishe doyres* (Vilna: S. Srebernik, 1928), 3:96–129.

8. Zitron, *Geshikhte*, 117; Simon Dubnov, "Dos yudishe folksblat in peterburg," in *Fun zhargon tsu yidish*, 10–16 (Vilna: B. Kletskin, 1929).

9. Shmeruk, *Sifrut yiddish*, 289–90.

10. Zitron, *Geshikhte*, 89–116.

11. K. Marmor, ed., *A. liberman's briv* (New York: YIVO, 1951), 141.

12. Ginsburg, "Di ershte yidishe teglekhe, 185; Dovid Druk, *Tsu der geshikhte fun der yudisher prese (in rusland un poyln)* (Warsaw: n.p., 1927), 9–10. Forty issues of the Bundist *Arbeter Shtime* appeared in Russia between 1897 and 1905; see Hertz, "Di umlegale prese, 294–366.

13. Druk, *Tsu der geshikhte*, 14–15, 20, 21, 23; S. Niger, *Yitskhok leybush perets* (Buenos Aires: Congress for Jewish Culture, 1952), 228–29.

14. Druk, *Tsu der geshikhte*, 23–30; after half a year of publication, Ravnitsky was replaced as editor by Dr. Yosef Luria, a resident of Warsaw, thus simplifying the complicated logistics involved in the newspaper's publication.

15. Druk, *Tsu der geshikhte*, 15; on *Der Fraynd*, see Ginsburg, "Di ershte yidishe." On the subsequent explosion of newspapers, see the comprehensive listing in Kirzhnits, *Di yidishe prese*.

16. Volf Tambur, *Yidish-prese in rumenye* (Bucharest, Romania: Kriterion, 1977). Tsarist laxity toward Hebrew is noted by Ginsburg, "Di ershte yidishe," 185; and Druk, *Tsu der geshikhte*, 9.

17. The three volumes of Peretz's literary almanac *Di yidishe bibliotek* (two in 1891, one in 1895) were likewise considered by the censors as separate books.

18. Niger, *Yitskhok leybush perets*, 229–46. Linetski published a series of eleven pamphlets on a monthly basis, each under a different title, in 1887; Zalmen Rejzen, "Yitskhok Joel Linetski," in *Leksikon fun der yidisher literatur, prese, un filologye*, 2:171 (Vilna: B. Kletskin, 1930).

19. For a recent treatment of this topic that is based on Russian archival sources, see Dmitry A. Elyashevich, *Pravitel'stvennaia politika i evreiskaia pechat' v rossii*, 1797–1917 (St. Petersburg and Jerusalem: Gesharim, 1999), 341–76 and 435–56.

20. Y. Riminik, "Redifes kegn yidishn teater in rusland in di 8oer un 9oer yorn," In *Teater-bukh: Zamlung tsum fuftsik-yorikn yubilei fun yidishin teater* (Kiev: Kultur-Lige, 1927), 87; Saul Ginsburg, "Der farbot fun yidishn teater," in *Historishe verk*, 1:167 (New York: Saul Ginsburg Jubilee Committee), 1937.

21. The former hypothesis is pursued by Riminik in "Redifes"; the latter is mentioned by Sandrow in *Vagabond Stars*, 62.

22. Ginsburg, "Der farbot," 170; Riminik, "Redifes," 88.

23. B. Gorin, *Di geshikhte fun yidishn teater* (New York: Max N. Meizl, 1918),

1:204–56; B. Vaynshteyn, "Di ershte yorn fun yidishn teater in ades un nyu york," in Shatzky, *Arkhiv far der geshikhte*, 243–54; Zalmen Zylbercweig, "Avrom Goldfaden," in *Leksikon fun yidishn teater*, 1:302–12.

24. Gorin, *Di geshikhte*, vol. 2, chap. 10; Jacob Shatzky, "Goldfaden in varshe," in *Hundert yor goldfaden*, ed. Jacob Shatzky, 1–16 (New York: YIVO, 1940).

25. Fishzon's memoirs are an important source on Yiddish theater in Russia after the ban; "Fuftsik yor yidish teater (zikhroynes)" appeared in serialization in the *Morgn Zhurnal* on Fridays, from October 10, 1924, to May 1, 1925, October 23, 1925, to November 13, 1925, and on December 11, 1925, and January 15 and 22, 1926. See in particular the installments of October 23, 1925, and November 13, 1925. See also Yankev Dinezon, "Dos yidishe teater," in *Zikhroynes un bilder*, 222 (Warsaw: Ahisefer, 1927); Noyekh Prilutski, "Di rekhtlekhe lage fun yidishn teater," in *Yidish teater*, 73–77 (Bialistok: A. Albek, 1921).

26. Fishzon, "Fuftsik," October 23, 1925, November 13, 1925, and January 15, 1926; Prilutski, "Di rekhtlekhe lage"; Y. Lubomirsky, "Der yidisher teater in tsarishn rusland," *Teater-bukh*, 95–98.

27. Ginsburg, "Der farbot," 170–72; B. Gorin, *Geshikhte*, 2:190–97; Oyslender, *Yidisher teater*, 7–52, 315; Elyashevich, *Pravitel'stvennaia politika*, 473–80.

28. Oyslender, *Yidisher teater;* Zalmen Zylbercweig, "Avrom Yitskhok Kaminski," in Zylbercweig, *Leksikon fun yidishn teater*, 6:5254–81; "Hirshbeyn trupe," 1:612–13.

29. Orshanskii's memorandum is mentioned in Avrom Golomb's "Di yidish-veltlekhe shul (algemeyner iberzikht)," in *Shul almanakh*, 19–20 (Philadelphia: Central Committee of the Workmen's Circle Schools, 1935). I have not found a reference to this memorandum in the histories of Hevrat Mefitse Haskalah.

30. Piotr S. Wandycz, *The Lands of Partitioned Poland* (Seattle: University of Washington Press, 1974), 196, 243.

31. Zvi Scharstein, *Toldot ha-hinukh be-yisrael ba-dorot ha-ahronim* (New York: Histadrut Ivrit of America, 1945), 1:320–21; Sabina Levin, "Toldot bate se-fer ha-yehudi'im ha-hiloni'im be-polin be-arbai'm ha-shanim ha-ahronot shel ha-meah ha-19," *Gal-ed* 9 (1986): 77–90; H. S. Kazhdan, *Fun kheyder un shkoles biz tsisho* (Buenos Aires: Shloyme Mendelson Fund, 1956), 194–202.

32. Hirsh Abramowicz, "S. Gozhansky," in *Farshvundene geshtaltn* (Buenos Aires: Central Union of Polish Jews, 1956), 33–34. The late Dina Abramowicz, research librarian at the YIVO Institute, drew my attention to this reference.

33. Scharfstein, *Toldot ha-hinukh*, 305–6, 377–410; Rahel Elboim-Dror, *Ha-hinukh ha-ivri be-eretz yisrael 1854–1914* (Jerusalem: Yad Yitzhak Ben Tzvi, 1986), 11–57. Elboim-Dror's contention that there were 774 *hadarim metukanim* in tsarist Russia in the early twentieth century seems to be exaggerated.

34. Kazhdan, *Fun kheyder un shkoles*, 178–84; S. Niger, *In kamf far a nayer dertsiung* (New York: Workmen's Circle, 1943), chap. 1.

35. Kazhdan, *Fun kheyder un shkoles*, 186–93.

36. Police also suppressed the use of Yiddish at public meetings, disrupting, for instance, the meetings of legal trade unions in 1906 conducted in Yiddish, and ordered that Russian be spoken; Gregor Aronson et al., eds., *Di geshikhte fun bund* (New York: Unser Tsait, 1962), 2:426, 433.

37. YIVO, *Di ershte yidishe shprakh-konferents* (Vilna: YIVO, 1933), 108. For the text of the Russian Helsingfors platform, and its demands concerning the rights of the "national language" (Hebrew) and the "spoken language" (Yiddish), see Yehuda Reinhartz and Paul Mendes-Flohr, *The Jew in the Modern World* (Oxford: Oxford University Press, 1980), 343-44.

38. Wandycz, *Lands of Partitioned Poland*, 253-64, 267; George Y. Shevelov, "The Language Question in the Ukraine in the Twentieth Century (1900–1941)," *Harvard Ukrainian Studies* 10, no. 1–2 (1986): 70–171.

Chapter 3: Language and Revolution

1. On the history of the society, see L. Rosenthal, *Toldot hevrat marbe haskalah be-yisrael be-eretz rusiya mi-shnat 1863 ad 1885*, 2 vols. (St. Petersburg: Y. Rozenthal, 1885 and 1890); E. Tcherikower, *Istoriia OPE 1863–1913* (St. Petersburg: OPE, 1913); "OPE," *Evreiskaia entsiklopedia*, 13:59–62; Nathans, *Beyond the Pale.*

2. On the clash between nationalists and "assimilationists" in the Odessa branch of OPE in 1901, see Simon Dubnov, *Pisma o starom i novom evreistve* (St. Petersburg: Obshchestvennaia pol'za, 1907), 113–51 (in Yiddish: *Briv vegn altn un nayem yidntum*, trans. Moyshe and Shaul Ferdman [Mexico City: Shloye Mendelson Fund, 1959], 137–56, 418–48); Simon Dubnov, *Kniga zhizni*, 1:371–90 (in Yiddish: *Dos bukh*, 1:344–62); Steven Zipperstein, *Elusive Prophet: Ahad Ha'am and the Origins of Zionism* (Berkely and Los Angeles: University of California Press, 1993), 182–87.

3. *Otchet OPE za 1905 i 1906 goda* (St. Petersburg: OPE, 1908).

4. Abraham Ascher, *The Revolution of 1905: Russia in Disarray* (Palo Alto, CA: Stanford University Press, 1988); Frankel, *Prophecy and Politics*, 134–70. On the atmosphere in Russian Jewry at the time, see Shlomo Lombroza, "The Pogroms of 1903–1906," in *Pogroms: Anti-Jewish Violence in Modern Russian History*, ed. John Klier and Shlomo Lambroza, 195–247 (Cambridge: Cambridge University Press, 1992).

5. "Ekstrennoe sobranie 'obschestvo rasprostranenie prosveschenie,'" *Voskhod* (weekly), no. 9, March 4, 1905, 10–14. The lone dissenting voice on the Executive Committee was Maxim Vinaver.

6. "Obschee sobranie chlenov obschestvo rasprostranenie prosveschenie mezhdu evream," *Voskhod* (weekly), no. 47–48, December 1, 1905, 36–38.

7. The full text of Kreinin's speech was published in a Zionist weekly: "Doklad revizionoi kommissi po otchetu obschestva rasprostranenie prosveschenia mezhdu evreami za 1904 god," *Khronika Evreiskoi Zhizni*, December 23, 1905, 48–55. Reports on the OPE meeting were also published in the Yiddish daily *Dos Lebn* (the temporary substitute for *Der Fraynd*, which had been suspended by the authorities) and the liberal *Voskhod;* see "Di algemeyne farzamlung fun der 'bildungs-gezelshaft' in Peterburg," *Dos Lebn*, December 19, 1905, 3; "Obschee sobranie 'obschestvo rasp. prosv. mezhdu evreami," *Voskhod* (weekly), December 16, 1905, 37–38. The language debates at OPE between 1905 and 1917 are surveyed by Kazhdan, *Fun kheyder un shkoles*, 367–407.

8. "Obschoe sobranie OPE," *Khronika Evreiskoi Zhizni*, December 23, 1905, 56–59.

9. Ibid., 57–58; quotation from *Dos Lebn*, December 19, 1905, 3.

10. *Voskhod* (weekly), December 16, 1905, 39–41; *Khronika Evreiskoi Zhizni*, 58–59. A scathing report on the meeting, and on the Executive Committee's behavior in particular, was published by the Bundist journalist Ben-Tziyon Hoffman (Tsivyon), "Di 'kramole' in der peterburger bildungs gezelshaft," *Der Veker*, January 11, 1906, 3.

11. "Obschee sobranie OPE," *Khronika Evreiskoi Zhizni*, January 31, 1906, 32–33.

12. On Luria and *Der Yid*, see Rejzen, *Leksikon*, 2:101–5; Kazhdan, *Fun kheyder un shkoles*, 242–49; Wisse, "Not the 'Pintele Yid,'" 33–62.

13. "Zelbst bashtimung," *Dos Lebn*, December 20–27, 1905, reprinted as "Yidish—ir natsyonaler vert," in *Der Fraynd Yubileum Baylage*, suppl. 48 (December 28, 1912): 3–8, suppl. 49 (1912): 7–8. Luria was answered by Zalman Epshtein, in "Undzer zelbst-bashtimung un hebreyish," *Dos Lebn*, January 10, 1906, February 15, 1906, February 18, 1906, February 20, 1906. Luria had the final word in the exchange, in "Tsu der zhargon frage," *Dos Lebn*, February 26, 1906, February 27, 1906.

14. Reports of the meeting: *Khronika Evreiskoi Zhizni*, 1906, 32–34; *Voskhod*, February 3, 1906, 19–23; *Dos Lebn*, February 14, 1906, 3.

15. Ratner's views were most clearly reported in *Dos Lebn*, while the other newspapers muted his radical rhetoric.

16. See *Khronika Evreiskoi Zhizni*, 1906, 32–34; *Voskhod*, February 3, 1906, 19–23; *Dos Lebn*, February 14, 1906, 3; see also the Bundist *Der Veker*, February 2, 1906.

17. "Zasedanie OPE," *Voskhod*, April 8, 1906, 30–34; "Di algemeyne farzamlung fun der peterburger yidisher bildungs khevre," *Dos Lebn*, April 2, 1906, 1–2. Katzenelson published a Hebrew translation of his speech, "Ivrit vezhargon" in *Ha-lashon ve-ha-hinukh* (Cracow: n.p., 1907), 29–39.

Chapter 4: The Bund's Contribution

1. Cited in Kazhdan, *Fun kheyder un shkoles*, 269, and in Samuel Portnoy, trans. and ed., *The Life and Soul of a Legendary Jewish Socialist: The Memoirs of Vladimir Medem* (New York: Ktav, 1979), 475–76.

2. For Bundist perspectives, see Max Weinreich's 1917 article "Der Bund un di yidishe shprakh," reprinted in *Finf-un-tsvantsik yor, 1897–1922* (Warsaw: Di Welt, 1922), 55–57; A. Litvak, "Afn feld fun kultur," in *Vos geven: Etyudn un zikhroynes* (Vilna: B. Kletskin, 1925), 148–65; J. S. Hertz, "Di umlegale prese un literatur fun 'Bund,'" in *Pinkes far der forshung fun der yidisher literatur un prese*, ed. Hyman Bass, 2:294–366 (New York: Congress for Jewish Culture, 1972). This perspective resonates in Goldsmith, *Architects of Yiddishism*, esp. 83–84; and Benjamin Harshav, *Language in a Time of Revolution* (Los Angeles: University of California Press), 1993.

3. For a discussion of these events, see Goldsmith, *Architects of Yiddishism;* Joshua A. Fishman, *Yiddish: Turning to Life* (Philadelphia: John Benjamins, 1991), 239–83.

4. See Henry Tobias, *The Jewish Bund in Russia* (Palo Alto, CA: Stanford Uni-

versity Press, 1972), chap. 3, 4, esp. 31–34; Ezra Mendelsohn, *Class Struggle in the Pale* (Cambridge: Cambridge University Press, 1970), 45–62.

5. Gozhansky's brochure, which circulated in manuscript, was published in Yiddish translation as "A briv tsu di agitatorn" in Elias Tcherikower et. al., eds., *YIVO historishe shriftn*, 3:626–48, esp. 647 (Vilna and Paris: YIVO, 1939). On the Social Democrats and the Bund, see Tcherikower, "Di onheybn fun der umlegaler literatur in yidish," in *YIVO historishe shriftn*, 3:577–603, esp. 579–94; Hertz, "Di umlegale prese," 2:331–41.

6. On Kremer's knowledge of Yiddish, see A. Litvak, "Di zhargonishe komitetn," in *Vos geven*, 98. On Medem, see Portnoy, *Memoirs of Vladimir Medem*, 177–78, 412. On the others, see Ben-Tziyon Hoffman (Tsivyon), *Far fuftsik yor* (New York: Elias Laub, 1948), 144.

7. On Kaplinsky, whose role as editor of the Bund's first underground newspaper has been suppressed in official Bundist historiography because of his later activity as an informer, see A. N., "Vozniknovenie 'arbeiterstimme,'" *Perezhitoe* 1 (1908): 264–78. The cultural gap between the Russified upper echelon and the Yiddish-speaking second tier of the Bund led to tensions between them. The Yiddish poet Avrom Liessin, himself a "half intellectual" active in the movement before he emigrated to America, complained to Arkady Kremer in 1906 that talented individuals such as Litvak and B. Charney-Vladek were not being advanced to the top ranks of the Bund "because they were orators only in Yiddish, who had come over from the world of the yeshiva, and had never worn the brass buttons of a Russian gymnasium student." Avrom Liessin, *Zikhroynes un bilder* (New York: CYCO, 1954), 296.

8. The Bundist perspectives by the young Weinreich, Litvak, and Hertz (see note 2), who claim that the modernization of Yiddish style began in the Bund, contrast with the more balanced assessment of the older Max Weinreich in his *Geshikhte fun der yidisher shprakh*, 1:295–97.

9. Aronson et al., *Geshikhte fun Bund*, 2:363, 576.

10. The calculation is based on Y. S. Hertz, "Di umlegale presse un literatur fun Bund," in *Pinkes far der forshung*, 337–41, 347–51.

11. See Mendelsohn, *Class Struggle*, 116–25. On the *zhargonishe komitetn*, which founded the Yiddish workers' libraries, see A. Litvsk's memoirs in *Vos geven*, 69–115, but note the cautionary remarks by Tcherikower, *YIVO Historishe shriftn*, 3:596–97.

12. See A. Litvak's moving essay, "Dos yidishe arbeter lid," in *Vos geven*, 226–43.

13. Litvak, "Di zhargonishe komitetn," 98.

14. See Litvak, "Di zhargonishe komitetn," esp. 80–85; Chone Shmeruk, "Yiddish Literature in the USSR," in *The Jews in Soviet Russia since 1917*, ed. Lionel Kochan, (Oxford: Oxford University Press, 1978), 245; Chone Shmeruk, *Peretz's yiyesh vizye* (New York: YIVO, 1971), 200–205.

15. See the editorial introduction to *Literarishe Monatshriftn* no. 1 (1908).

16. M. L-R (pseudonym of Mark Liber), *Di naye tsayt* no. 3 (1908): 92–96; Litvak, *Vos geven*, 256–58, B. Brokhes (pseudonym of B. Charney-Vladek), "Vegn undzer kultur-problem," *Di naye tsayt*, no. 4 (Vilna, 1909).

17. See *Materialy k istorii evreiskogo rabochego dvizhenii* (St. Petersburg: Tribuna, 1906), 74–75, 112.

18. "Di diskusye vegn der natsionaler frage afn 5tn tsuzamenfor fun Bund, Yuni 1903, Zurich," *Undzer Tsayt* 1, no. 2 (November 1927): 90, 95.

19. Vladimir Medem, *Sotsiademokratiia i natsionalnii vopros* (St. Petersburg: Tribuna, 1906), esp. 50–57 (in Yiddish, in *Vladimir medem tsum tsvantsikstn yortsayt* [New York: American Representation of the General Jewish Workers' Union of Poland, 1943], esp. 212–19).

20. M. Rafes, *Ocherki po istorii 'Bunda'* (Moscow: Moskovskii Rabochii, 1923), 394–95. For an elaborate program of implementation, see Esther Frumkin, "Glaykhbarekhtikung fun shprakhn," *Tsaytfragen* 5 (1911): 1–30.

21. See chapters 2 and 3.

22. On the Bundist press, see Hertz, "Di umlegale prese." The circulation figure for the *Folkstsaytung* is based on Litvak, *Vos geven*, 274.

23. On the Vilna school, see Gershon Pludermakher, "Di ovntshul afn nomen fun Y. L. Peretz," in *Shul-pinkes*, ed. M. Shur, 223–38 (Vilna: Jewish Central Education Committee, 1924); Kazhdan, *Fun kheyder un shkoles*, 173–76. *Dos yidishe vort* went through its fifth edition in 1919; its compiler, Olgin, went on to become the editor-in-chief of the Communist daily *Morgn Frayhayt*, in New York, and a leader of the American Communist Party. On the Warsaw courses, see *Geshikhte fun Bund*, 2:433–36.

24. Gershon Pludermakher, "Folks-shul afn nomen dvoyre kupershteyn," in Shur, *Shul-pinkes*, 167–76; Kazhdan, *Fun kheyder un shkoles*, 191–93. A third Yiddish elementary school, in Kiev, was run by Socialist Territorialists and Sejmists; ibid., 187–91.

25. The early history of Yiddish education is surveyed in Kazhdan, *Fun kheyder un shkoles*.

26. On the Jewish Literary Society, see "Evreiskoe literaturnoe obschestvo," in *Evreiskaia entsiklopediia*, 7:450; report on the society's activities, *Lebn un Visnshaft* no. 1–4 (1911): 122–42.

27. See YIVO, *Di ershte yidishe shprakh-konferents*, 89–91, 118–20.

28. The growth of Yiddish literary societies can be followed in *Lebn un Visnshaft*, no. 2 (June 1909): 180–85; no. 3 (July 1909): 155–59; no. 4 (n.d., 1909): 148–51; no. 5 (September 1909): 147–52. On the change in the Bund's position, see the editorial of the Bundist publication *Di shtime fun Bund*, cited in *Geshikhte fun Bund* 2:554–55. The resolution on joining cultural societies passed at the October 1910 eighth conference of the Bund; Rafes, *Ocherki po istorii 'Bunda,'* 392. On Peretz's ouster, see *Geshikhte fun bund*, 2:554–58; Dovid Mayer, "Yidishe literarishe gezelshaft in varshe," *Undzer Tsayt* 17, no. 11–12 (November–December 1957): 104–5. On the liquidation of the society, see *Der Fraynd* 9, no. 21 (January 21/February 6, 1912), no. 70 (March 25/April 4, 1912).

29. On the Bund resolution, see *Materialy k istorii evreiskogo*, 127. On *Der Yid*, see Wisse, "Not the 'Pintele Yid,'" 63–88.

30. On Zhitlovsky, see Goldsmith, *Architects of Yiddishism*, 161–82.

31. See the biographies of these individuals in Zalmen Rejzen, *Leksikon fun der yidisher literatur, prese, un filologye*, 4 vols. (Vilna: B. Kletskin, 1926–29). On Luria's Yiddishism, see chapter 3. On the Grünbaum affair, see Arye Tsentsiper, "Ve'idot artsiyot shel tsiyone rusiya," in *Katsir: kovets le-korot* (Tel Aviv: Tarbut Ve-hinukh, 1972), 2:254–55.

32. On Helsingfors, see David Vital, *Zionism: The Formative Years* (Oxford, UK: Clarendon, 1988), 467–78.

33. YIVO, *Di ershte yidishe shprakh-konferents*, 106.

34. Ibid., 84, 90.

35. See chapter 3.

36. See Kazhdan, *Fun kheyder un shkoles*, 383–86; also in A. Kirzhnitz, ed., *Der yidisher arbeter*, 3:54–57 (Moscow: Tsentraler Felker-Farlag fun FSSR, 1928).

Chapter 5: Reinventing Community

1. On Zhitlovsky, see Goldsmith, *Architects of Yiddishism*, esp. 161–82, and chapter 6 in this book. A minority position held by Dubnov, stressed the centrality of historical consciousness in national identity and the importance of building institutions in the Diaspora that would perpetuate that consciousness, regardless of language.

2. Simon Dubnov, "Avtonomia kak osnova natsionalnoi programy," in *Pisma o starom*, 110–11 (in Yiddish: *Briv*, 134–35). The essay was originally published in *Voskhod* 21, no. 12 (December 1901): 3–40.

3. See the stenographic report of the Kovno conference, *Soveschanie evreiskikh obshchestvenikh deiateli v g. Kovne* (St. Petersburg: Ekateringofskoe Pechatroe Delo, 1910), as well as the reports and critical evaluations in the contemporary Jewish press, including A. Perlman, "Kovenskii s'iezd," *Evreiskii Mir*, November–December 1909, 1–9, 32–61; A. Litvak, "Der kovner tsuzamenfor," *Tsaytfragen* 1 (1909): 1–14. For a brief overview of *Vestnik evreiskoi obschini*, see Yehuda Slutsky, *Ha'itonut ha-yehudit rusit be-reshit ha-me'ah ha-'esrim* (Tel Aviv: Tel Aviv University Diaspora Research Institute, 1978), 468–70.

4. This is the basic argument of Dubnov's fourth letter; *Pisma o starom*, 74–112, *Briv*, 93–136. In English, see Koppel S. Pinson, ed., *Nationalism and History: Letters on Old and New Judaism* (New York: Atheneum, 1970), 131–42. Pinson's translation of the "Letters" is based on the 1937 authorized abbreviated Hebrew edition, *Mikhtavim 'al ha-yahadut ha-yeshana ve-hakhadasha* (Tel Aviv: Ha-Khoker, 1937). With a Palestinian Jewish readership in mind and an eye to posterity, Dubnov deleted from the Hebrew version extensive sections he considered to be of mere historical value three decades after the book's original publication. These included his polemical excursuses against Zionism, a topic on which his position had changed, and the details of his proposed system of Jewish national autonomy in the Diaspora. See A. Levinson, "Beyn ha-mehaber le-metargemo," in *Sefer shimon dubnov*, ed. Shimon Rawidowicz, 184–200 (Waltham, MA, and Jerusalem: Ararat, 1954). The recent French translation by Renee Poznanzki, *Lettres sur le Judaism ancien et nouveau* (Paris: Cerf, 1989) is from the original edition, as is Ferdman and Ferdman's Yiddish translation, *Briv*.

5. See Dubnov's historical treatment of the *kahal* system in his *History of the Jews in Russia and Poland*, 2nd ed. (New York: Ktav, 1975), 1:103–13, 188–98, 274–83, 371, 379; 2:19–25, 59–62, 112.

6. See Richard Wortman, *The Crisis of Russian Populism* (Cambridge: Cambridge University Press, 1967).

7. See Eli Lederhendler, *The Road to Modern Jewish Politics* (New York: Oxford University Press, 1989).

8. See the fourth letter, in *Pisma o starom*, esp. 85–86, 90–91, 102–104; *Briv*, 106–7, 112–13, 125–26. The corresponding sections are not included in the English edition.

9. On Renner's theory, see Oscar Janowsky, *Nationalities and National Minorities (with Special Reference to East Central Europe)* (New York: MacMillan, 1945); Robert S. Wistrich, *Socialism and the Jews: The Dilemmas of Assimilation in Germany and Austria-Hungary* (London and East Brunswick, NJ: Associated University Presses, 1982), 299–349. Dubnov acknowledged his indebtedness to Renner in a note in the book version of his "Letters"; see *Pisma o starom*, 86–87; *Briv*, 107–8.

10. "Internal and External Organization," part 4 of the twelfth letter, "The Moral of the Terrible Days," originally published in *Voskhod* (weekly), no. 50, 1905. *Pisma o starom*, 311–20; *Briv*, 337–45. The corresponding section is not included in the English edition.

11. At the deliberations of the second conference of the Union for the Attainment of Full Equal Rights for the Jews in Russia, St. Petersburg, November 22–25, 1905, Dubnov and Zionists were allied. See *Voskhod*, December 16, 1905, 20–38. On Jhabotinsky's embrace of autonomy, see his article, "K voprosu o nashei politicheskoi platforme," *Evreiskaia Zhizn*, November, 1905, 39–80; Joseph Schechtman, *The Vladimir Jabotinsky Story* (New York: T. Koseloff, 1956), 1:110–25. On Helsingfors, see Vital, *Zionism*, 467–78, and the literature cited there. The full proceedings of the Helsingfors conference were published in *Evreiskii Narod*, December 2, 1906, with the resolutions of Jewish national autonomy on pp. 52–53. The subject of Russian Zionism's attitude toward national autonomy in the Diaspora still awaits comprehensive treatment.

12. On the traditional *kahal*, see Jacob Katz, *Tradition and Crisis: Jewish Society at the End of the Middle Ages*, 2nd ed. (New York: New York University Press, 1993); Salo W. Baron, *The Jewish Community*, 3 vols. (Phildelphia: Jewish Publication Society of America, 1943). On the nineteenth century German religious community, the *kultus-gemeinde*, see "Gemeinde," *Encyclopaedia Judaica* (Berlin: Eschkol, 1931), 5:213–18. The question of whether the *kehile* (and by extension Jewish communal life) should be voluntary or compulsory became a major line of demarcation between Diaspora Nationalists and Russian Jewish liberals.

13. "Programma evreiskoi natsionalnoi grupy (Folkspartei)," *Evreiskii Narod*, December 8, 1906, 11–13; point 5, and the full text of the party program, published as a separate brochure, with an introductory essay by Dubnov: *Volkspartei: Evreiskaia narodnaia partiia* (St. Petersburg: Evreiskaia Narodnia Partiia, 1907), 27.

14. On the debates within the Folkspartei, see Dubnov's memoirs, *Kniga zhizni*, 2:64; *Dos bukh*, 2:68–69. The rise of conversions at the turn of the century is referred to by memoirists and historians alike. See, for instance, Saul Ginsburg, *Meshumodim in tsarishn rusland* (New York: CYCO, 1946), 204–6; Grigorii Aronson, *Rusish-yidishe inteligents* (Buenos Aires: Yidbukh, 1962), 83–91. Much debate was sparked by the converted member of the first Russian

Duma, Mikhail Gertsenshteyn, who in filling out a Duma questionnaire, recorded his religion as Russian Orthodox and his nationality as Jewish.

15. Medem first called upon Bundists to turn their attention to the *kehiles* question in an article in *Otkliki Bunda*, March 1909. The Bund passed a resolution in favor of the creation of secular and democratic *kehilahs* at its eighth party conference, in October 1910. For the text of the resolution, see M. Rafes, *Ocherki po istorii 'Bunda,'* 394. Vladimir Medem, "Di yidishe kehile," *Tsaytfragen* 2 (1910), 24–37. On the membership issue, see p. 30.

16. For Medem's life story, see his autobiography, *Fun mayn lebn*, 2 vols. (New York: n.p., 1923) (in English: *The Life and Soul of a Legendary Jewish Socialist*, trans. Samuel A. Portnoy [New York: Ktav, 1979]).

17. Medem, "Di yidishe kehile"; Vladimir Medem, "Po voprosam obshchinoi programmi," *Evreiskii Mir*, April 1, 1910, 5–9.

18. A. Litvak, "Fragn fun der yidisher kehile," *Tsaytfragen*, August 1910, 47–59, quote from pp. 51–52. On Litvak, see H. S. Kazhdan, "Der lebnsveg fun A. Litvak," in *Gedlibene shriftn* (New York: Educational Committee of the Workmen's Circle, 1945), 11–157.

19. Litvak, "Fragn fun der Yidisher kehile," 52–53.

20. Dubnov, *Pisma o starom*, 314, *Briv*, 341 (not in English edition).

21. *Volkspartei*, point 9 of national program, 27–28.

22. Ibid., 12; Dubnov's introduction to the party platform was also published as the fourteenth letter, "On the Tasks of the Folkspartey," *Pisma o starom*, 346; *Briv*, 374; *Nationalism and History*, 229.

23. Medem, *Sotsialdemokratia*, esp. 50–57 (in Yiddish: *Vladimir medem*, 173–219, esp. 212–19). A similar postion was express by V. Kossovskii, *Voprosi natsionalnosti* (Vilna: n.p., 1906), 105–6.

24. "Our National Ideal and Our National Movement," in *Vozrozhdenie (evreiskii proletariat i natsionalnaia problema): Sbornik stateii*, esp. 56–57 (St. Petersburg: n.p., 1905). The articles in this collection were published anonymously; Zilberfarb revealed their authorship and other bibliographic details in "Di grupe vozrozhdenie," *Royter pinkes*, vol. 1 (Warsaw: Kultur-Lige, 1921), 126–27.

25. "Proiekt programi evreiskoi sotsialisticheskoi rabochei Partii *SERP*," *SERP* 1 (1907): 271–72. Zilberfarb advocated national ministries in *Vozrozhdenie*, 58. On the Ukraine, see Jonathan Frankel, "The Dilemmas of Jewish Autonomism: The Case of Ukraine 1917–1920," in *Ukrainian-Jewish Relations in Historical Perspective*, ed. Peter J. Potychnyi and Howard Aster, 263–80 (Edmonton: Canadian Institute of Ukrainian Studies, 1988).

26. Medem, "Di yidishe kehile," 27; Litvak, "Fragn," 49.

27. On Zilberfarb, see *Vozrozhdenie*, 67. On the Bundists, see Litvak, "Fragn," 53–54.

28. Litvak, "Fragn," 53–54.

29. Simon Dubnov, "K sporu o tipe evreiskoi obshchini," *Evreiskii Mir*, January 28, 1910, 1–6.

30. *Volkspartei*, point 20 of national program, 28.

31. See *Vozrozhdenie*, 69; Medem, "Di yidishe kehile," 31. Replacing the *korobka* was a major point debated at the Kovno conference. See the literature cited in note 3.

32. Medem, "Di yidishe kehile," 31–33.

33. Litvak, "Fragen," 57.

34. Moyshe Zilberfarb, "Neotlozhnie zadachi evreiskoi obshchini," *Evreiskii Mir*, vol. 1, July 1909, 1–14.

35. Ibid., 10.

36. The last sections of their respective articles are entitled "Our Tasks Today" and "What To Do Now?"

37. "Nashi zadachi," *Vestnik Evreiskoi Obschini*, August 1913, 3.

Chapter 6: New Trends in Interwar Yiddish Culture

1. Zosa Szajkowski, "The Struggle for Yiddish during World War I: The Attitude of German Jewry," in Fishman, *Never Say Die*, 565–90; Kenneth Moss, "A Time to Tear Down and a Time to Build UP: Recasting Jewish Culture in Eastern Europe, 1917–1921," (PhD diss., Stanford University, 2003); on the Kultur-Lige, see the observations by Kazhdan in *Fun kheyder un shkoles*, 432–40.

2. On Soviet Yiddish culture, see the introductions by Chone Shmeruk and Yehuda Slutsky to *Pirsumim yehudiim be-vrit ha-mo'atsot, 1917–1960*, ed. Chone Shmeruk (Jerusalem: Israel Historical Society, 1961), 19–131; Elias Schulman, *A History of Jewish Education in the Soviet Union* (New York: Ktav, 1971); Jeffrey Veidlinger, *The Moscow State Yiddish Theatre* (Bloomington: Indiana University Press, 2000); Mordechai Altshuler, ed., *Ha-teatron ha-yehudi be-vrit ha-mo'atsot* (Jerusalem: Center for Research and Documentation of East European Jewry, 1996); more generally, see Zvi Gitelman, *Jewish Nationality and Soviet Politics: The Jewish Sections of the CPSU, 1917–1930* (Princeton, NJ: Princeton University Press, 1972). The figures cited for cultural institutions are from Shmeruk, *Pirsumim*, 66, 86; Schulman, *History of Jewish Education*, 93; Altshuler, *Ha-teatron*, 3.

3. Mordechai Altshuler, *Soviet Jewry on the Eve of the Holocaust* (Jerusalem: The Center for Research on East European Jewry and Yad Vashem, 1998), 90–92.

4. Chone Shmeruk, "Hebrew-Yiddish-Polish: A Trilingual Jewish Culture," in *The Jews of Poland between Two World Wars*, ed. Yisrael Gutman, Ezra Mendelsohn, Jehuda Reinharz, and Chone Shmeruk, 285–311 (Hanover, NH, and London: University Press of New England, 1989); Ezra Mendelsohn, *The Jews of East Central Europe between the Two World Wars* (Bloomington: Indiana University Press, 1983), 11–84.

5. The publication figures are from Menakhem Linder, "Dos yidishe drukvezn in poyln in di yorn 1933–1934," *Yivo Bleter* 10 (1936): 303–12. On the Orthodox, see Beatrice Lang Caplan, "Orthodox Yiddish Literature in Interwar Poland" (PhD diss., Columbia University, 2004).

6. Book-borrowing figures from Sh. Vinter, "Vegn eynike bibliotek-tsifern," *Bikhervelt* (new series) 1, no. 6 (1928): 62–64.

7. See Nathan Cohen, *Sefer, sofer, ve-'iton: Merkaz ha-tarbut ha-yehudit be-varsha, 1918–1942* (Jerusalem: Magnes, 2003); M. V. Bernshteyn, "Di organizat-sye fun di yidishe artistn, 1916–1939," in *Yiddisher teater in Eyrope tsvishn beyde velt-milkhomes*, ed. Itzik Manger, 1:339–436 (New York: Congress for Jewish Culture, 1968).

8. See the articles on *Haynt* by Chaim Finkelstein, Yitzhak Gruenbaum, and Dr. Asriel Karlebach in *Fun Noentn over*, vol. 2, *Yidishe prese in varshe*, ed. Jacob Pat (New York: Congress for Jewish Culture, 1956), 69–213.

9. On Kultur-Lige and *Literarishe Bleter*, see the memoirs of Nachman Mayzel, *Geven amol a lebn* (Buenos Aires: Central Union of Polish Jews, 1951).

10. Nathan Cohen, "'Shund' and the Tabloids: Jewish Popular Reading in Inter-War Poland," *Polin* 16 (2003): 189–211; Seth Wolitz, "Di Khalyastre: The Yiddish Modernist Movement in Poland," *Yiddish* 4, no. 3 (1981): 5–19; Justine Cammy, "Tsevorfene Bleter: The Emergence of Yung Vilne," *Polin* 14 (2001): 170–91. On the Yiddish art theaters, see Manger, *Yiddisher teater.*

11. Issakhar Fater, *Yidishe muzik in poyln tsvishn beyde velt-milkhomes* (Tel Aviv: World Federation of Polish Jews, 1970). On drama circles, and more generally, Yiddish theater culture in interwar Poland, see the memoirs of Zigmund Turkow, *Di ibergerisene tekufe* (Buenos Aires: Central Union of Polish Jews, 1961).

12. Book figures from Nachman Mayzel, "Dos yidishe bukh in 1923," *Bikhervelt* 2, no. 6 (1923): 509–16. See Mayzel, *Geven amol a lebn*, and Turkow, *Di ibergerisene tekufe.*

13. On the Yiddish PEN club, see Zalmen Rejzen, "Der yiddisher pen-klub in vilne," in *Vilner almanakh*, ed. A. I. Grodzenski, 95–108 (Vilna: Ovnt Kurier, 1939; repr. New York: n.p., 1992); Cohen, *Sefer, sofer.*

14. See the biographies of Rejzen, Kacyzna, and Kazhdan in *Leksikon fun der nayer yidisher literatur*, ed. Berl Kagan, Israel Knox, and Elias Schulman, vol. 8 (New York: Congress for Jewish Culture, 1981), 478–82, 117–18, 36–38.

15. H. S. Kazhdan, *Geshikhte fun yidishn shulvezn in umpohengikn poyln* (Mexico City: Shul un Hilf, 1947).

16. On Yiddish education in Vilna before World War I, see chapter 4. On the growth of Yiddishism in Vilna during World War I, see Samuel Kassow, "Jewish Community Politics in Transition: The Vilna *kehile*, 1919–1920," *Yivo Annual* 20 (1991): 61–92. On Yiddish in interwar Vilna, see the memoirs of Lucy Dawidowicz, *From That Place and Time: A Memoir 1938–1947* (New York: Norton, 1989).

17. On this question, see chapter 7 and chapter 8.

18. Enrollment figures from Kazhdan, *Geshikhte*, 550; Moshe Shalit, ed., *Oyf di khurves fun milkhomes un mehumes: Pinkes fun gegnt-komitet EKOPO* (Vilna: EKOPO, 1931).

19. On ORT in Poland, see Leon Shapiro, *The History of ORT* (New York: Schocken, 1980). Most of the Yiddish-language professional schools were based in Vilna and are surveyed in Grodzenski, *Vilner almanakh.*

20. YIVO's institutional idealogy and postion in Polish Jewish life are examined in chapter 9. See Cecille Kuznitz, "The Origins of Yiddish Scholarship and the YIVO Institute for Jewish Research" (PhD diss., Stanford University, 2000).

21. On the folklore commission, see Itzik Gottesman, *Defining the Yiddish Nation: The Jewish Folklorists of Poland* (Detroit: Wayne State University Press, 2003). On modern Yiddish spelling and the YIVO system, see Mordkhe Schaechter, "Fun folkshprakh tsu kulturshprakh: An iberblik fun der historye funem eynhaytlekhn yidish oysleyg," in *Der eynhaytlekher yidisher oysleyg*, 1–113 (New York: YIVO and League for Yiddish, 1999).

22. See Isaiah Trunk, "Yivo un di yidishe historishe visnshaft," *Yivo Bleter* 46 (1980): 242–54; Lucian Dobrodzycki, "Yivo in Inter-War Poland: Work in the Historical Sciences," in Gutman, *Jews of Poland*, 494–518.

Chapter 7: The Judaism of Secular Yiddishists

1. YIVO, *Di ershte yidishe shprakh-konferents*, 74–77; also in Nachman Mayzel, ed., *Briv un redes fun Y. L. Perets* (New York: n.p., 1944), 369–74.

2. Stanley Nash, *In Search of Hebraism: Shai Hurwitz and His Polemic in the Hebrew Press* (Leiden, Netherlands: E. J. Brill, 1980).

3. For the similar rhetoric of Russian populism in the 1870s, see Wortman, *Crisis of Russian Populism.*

4. Mark Kiel, "A Twice Lost Legacy: Ideology, Culture and the Pursuit of Jewish Folklore in Russia until Stalinization" (PhD diss., Jewish Theological Seminary of America, 1991).

5. See Chaim Zhitlovsky, "Yid un mentsh," 2:103–86, "Di yidishe shprakh-bavegung un di tshernovitser konferents," 4:111–21, "Di yidishe sahprakh un di yidishe kultur," 4:165–83, "Religye un natsye," 4:187–200, in *Gezamlte shriftn* (New York: Zhitlowsky Jubilee Committee, 1912). In English, see "What is Jewish Secular Culture," in *The Faith of Secular Jews*, ed. Saul Goodman, 49–56 (New York: Ktav, 1976).

6. See I. L. Peretz, "Vos felt undzer literatur," "Tsu di tsurikkumendike geyrim," 11:53–64, 10–25, in *Ale verk* (Vilna: B. Kletskin, 1925). In English, see "What Our Literature Needs," in *Voices from the Yiddish*, ed. Irving Howe and Eliezer Greenberg (New York: Schocken, 1972), 25–31.

7. YIVO, *Di ershte yidishe shprakh konferents*, 80–81; volume 13 of the Vilna edition of Peretz's works consists of his biblical and liturgical translations, in several different versions.

8. Zhitlovsky himself penned an essay that deviated from his basic ideas and adopted the national-romantic approach to Judaism: "Der natsyonial-poetisher vidergeburt fun der yidisher religye," in *Gezamlte shriftn*, 4:221–78.

9. E-R (pseudonym of Esther Frumkin), "Vegn natsionaler ertsiung," *Tsayt-fragen* 1 (November 1909): 15–30, and "Nokh amol vegn natsionaler ertsiung," *Tsaytfragen* 5 (September 1910): 85–91. This position was already taken by Frumkin in her pioneering book *Tsu der frage fun der yidisher folkshul* (Vilna: Di Velt, 1909).

10. E-R, "Nokh amol," 88.

11. B. B-Bski (pseudonym of Boris Levinson), "Eynike bamerkungen tsum artikl fun E-R vegn natsionaler ertsiung," *Tsaytfragen* 2 (March 1910): 55–60.

12. "Lernplan far di folkshuln," *Shul un Lebn* 1, no. 1 (1921): 45–47.

13. *Shul-pinkes: finf yor arbet fun tsentraln bildungs-komitet* (Vilna: TSBK, 1924): 64–65.

14. According to the thorough bibliographical study by I. Anilovich and M. Yofe, "Yiddishe lernbikher un pedagogik (1900–1930)," in *YIVO shriftn far psikhologye un pedagogik* (YIVO: 1933), 1:465–528, eighty-two Yiddish text-books of Yiddish literature and Jewish history were published in the territory of the Polish republic between 1900 and 1930.

15. The book was intended initially for young adults studying in Vilna's Yiddish evening school and was later used for instruction in grades 6 to 8 in the TsBK schools.

16. A similar anthology published after World War I is Sh. Bastomski and M. Chaimson's *Dos naye vort: Khrestomatye far di hekhere klasn fun der folks-shul*, 4 vols. (Vilna: Naye Yidishe Folkshul, 1923–26). Volume 1, subtitled *Epics*, includes biblical epic narrative and poetry and rabbinic Agadah; volume 2, subtitled *Lyrical Poetry*, includes selections from the Psalms and Judah Ha-Levi.

17. There are two known editions of volume 1 and seven known editions of volume 2.

18. E-R, "Nokh amol," 87; Esther Rozental-Schneiderman, *Oyf vegn un umvegn* (Tel Aviv: Ha-Menorah, 1978), 2:83. When Schneiderman related this story at a conference of Soviet Yiddish educators, she was resoundingly denounced for poisoning children's minds through the celebration of a religious holiday.

19. Personal communication by former students in TsISHO/TsBK Schools, Esther Hautzig (Vilna) and Shloyme Krystal (Warsaw), May 28, 1999.

20. Esther Rabinovitch, "Yontoyvim in kinder-heym," *Di Naye Shul* (April–June 1927): 124.

21. See Zhitlovsky, "Der natsyonal poetisher," 256–58. See Avrom Golomb, *A halber yorhundert yidishe dertsiung* (Rio de Janeiro: Monte Scopus, 1957), 156. Weinreich led a demonstrative walkout from the lecture at which the TsISHO representative made these remarks. Golomb and the seminary's leadership followed up with a letter of protest to Warsaw.

22. Golomb, *A halber yorhundert*, 133–34.

23. See Sh. Liev, "A yor geshikhte in der ferter opteylung," *Di Naye Shul* 4 (January–February 1923): 96–100. The quote is from Y. Rubin, "Vos iz der iker," *Di Naye Shul* 2, no. 1 (1921): 53–54.

24. See the numerous rabbinic Aggadot included in volume 1 of Bastomski and Chaimson, *Dos naye vort;* see also, for example, Sh. Bastomski, *Yidishe folks-mayses un legendes: legendes vegn besht* (Vilna: Naye Yidishe Folkshul, 1925); Sh. Bastomski, *Yidishe legendes* (Vilna: Naye Yidishe Folkshul, 1926).

25. Pludermakher, "Der moderner yidisher shul vezn, in Vilne," in *Shul almanakh*, 239.

26. Israel Rubin, "Vos iz der iker," *Di Naye Shul* 2, no. 1 (1921): 50–54; Avrom Golomb, "Di metodn un program fun hebreyish-limed in undzer shul," *Di Naye Shul* 9 (October 1928): 75–83. Theirs was the dominant view among Hebrew teachers in the TsISHO schools; see "Hebreyish konferents in vilne (10–11 Oktober, 1922)," appendix to *Di Naye Shul* 3 (November–December, 1922).

27. M. Gutman, "Tsi darf men lernen Hebreyish in folks-shul?" *Shul un Lebn* 3 (September 1921): 19–24.

28. Kh. Sh. Kazhdan, "Di vegn fun undzer shul shafung," *Shul un Lebn* 1, no. 5 (October 1921): 8–12; H. S. Kazhdan, "Der sistem fun yidishe limudim un dertsiyung in undzer shul," *Di Naye Shul* 4 (January–June 1924): 43–47. This view was also expressed by Avrom Golomb, "Vegn hebreyish," *Di Naye Shul* 5 (January–June, 1924): 85–89. Kazhdan shifted to a much more culturally radical position after joining the Bund in 1928.

29. Kazhdan, "Di vegn," 8–9.

30. Shimshon Britmacher in *Shul-vegn* 2 (February–March, 1935): 159–65.

31. Avrom Golomb, "Nokh a mol vegn religyezer dertsiyung," *Di Naye Shul* (September–October 1922): 41–43.

Chapter 8: Commemoration and Cultural Conflict

1. Zalman Eptsein, "Ezrat sofrim: le-zekher aliyat eliyahu," *Ha-melitz*, September 28, 1897, 1; advertisements for the portrait of the gaon were placed in the September 14 and October 5, 1897, editions of *Ha-melitz.* On the nineteenth-century biographies of the gaon, see Shaul Stampfer, "The Gaon, Yeshivot, the Printing Press, and the Jewish Community—A Complicated Relationship between a Scholar and Society," in *The Gaon of Vilnius and the Annals of Jewish Culture*, ed. Izraelis Lempertas, 257–82 (Vilnius: Vilnius University Publishing House, 1998).

2. On Vilna Jewry during this period, see Samuel Kassow, "Jewish Communal Politics in Transition: The Vilna Kehile," *Yivo Annual* 20 (1991): 61–92; and more generally, Hirsz Abramowicz, *Profiles of a Lost World: Memoirs of East European Jewish Life before World War II*, trans. Eva Zeitlin Dobkin (Detroit: Wayne State University Press, 1999). On the Vilna Gaon, see I. Etkes, *The Gaon of Vilna: The Man and His Image*, trans. Jeffrey M. Green (Berkeley: University of California Press, 2002).

3. "Nemen far di gasn," *Der Tog*, January 8, 1920; an identical communiqué news item was published in the rival newspaper *Yidishe Tsaytung.*

4. Y. A. Trivush, "Ha-Gaon Ha-Vilnai: Le-yovel ha-ma'atayim le-ledato," *Ha-hayim*, June 11, 1920, 4.

5. *Der Tog*, Sunday April 18.

6. Trivush, "Ha-Gaon Ha-Vilnai."

7. The Vilna community abolished the position of chief rabbi *(av bet din)* in the late eighteenth century, and the preacher was therefore recognized as the highest local rabbinic officiary.

8. The chronicle of events in the *American Jewish Yearbook* includes the following entries from Vilna. February 20, 1920: gendarmes search the offices of the Jewish community and arrest several employees; March 19, 1920: Polish troops renew attacks and beatings of Jews, searching the residence of Dr. Shabad, president of the community; March 26, 1920: gendarmes search the offices of Tseire Tsion and arrest all persons present; *American Jewish Yearbook* 22 (1920–21): 274–75.

9. *Der Tog*, Sunday, April 11, 1920.

10. Kassow, "Jewish Communal Politics."

11. Quote from "Kol kore le-adat ir vilna ha-kdosha, ve-lekhol bnei yisrael be-khol mekomot moshvotehem," Nisan 5620 (March–April 1920), YIVO Archives, New York, Vilna *kehile* collection, RG 10.

12. "Kol kore."

13. On the failure of the campaign, see "Di anshtaltn oyfn nomen fun vilner goen zats'al," *Yidishe Tsaytung* (Vilna), April 23, 1920. M. Nokhumzohn, "Vilner briv: 'Historishe teg,'" *Moment*, April 30, 1920.

14. Chaikl Lunski, "Eynike notitsn tsum 200stn yorikn geburtstog fun vilner goen," *Lebn*, no. 2 (April 1920): 32–33. A prepublication press release on this is-

sue of *Lebn*, printed in *Tog*, March 26, 1920, cited the entire table of contents but not Lunski's note.

15. Joseph Regensburg, "Rabeinu ha-goen ha-khosid mi-vilna," *Yidishe Tsaytung*, April 23, 1920. I would like to thank Dr. Israel Lempert of Vilnius for locating this rare periodical for me in the Lithuanian National Library.

16. Ibid.

17. Ibid.

18. Chaikl Lunski, "Eynike legendes vegn vilner goen, geklibn fun mentshn un sforim," *Yidishe Tsaytung*, April 23, 1920.

19. Chaikl Lunski, *Legendes vegn vilner goen* (Vilna: Naye Yidishe Folkshul, 1924; first published in the youth journal of the Yiddish schools, *Der Khaver* 3, no. 5 [17] (May 1922), 172–92.

20. Sh. Bastomski, "Legendes vegn vilner goen," *Grininke Beymelekh* 2, no. 9 (1928): 385–92; Sh. Bastomski, "Der vilner goen un der dubner magid," *Grininke Beymelekh* 12, no. 15–16 (1938): 459–62; Bastomski, *Yidishe legendes*. Lunski himself later composed yet another collection of legends on the Vilna Gaon for the Orthodox weekly *Dos Vort*. Chaikl Lunski, "Der vilner goen: Faktn un mesoyres, agodes un dertseylungen, vegn zayn lebn virkn un shafn," *Dos Vort*, September 6 to December 28, 1934. It was preceded by a series, "Geonim un gedoylim fun noentn over" (with portraits of the gaon's disciples Chaim of Volozhin and Israel of Shklov), *Dos Vort*, December 1933 through July 1934, and was followed by a series, "Di talmidim un mekurovim fun vilner goen," *Di Vokh*, March–August 1935.

Chapter 9: Max Weinreich and the Development of YIVO

1. On the early history of YIVO, see Z. Szajkowski, "Der yivo un zayne grinders," *Yivo Bleter* 46 (1980): 22–77; *Barikht fun der konferents fun yivo opgehaltn in vilne fun 24stn bizn 27stn oktober 1929* (Vilna: YIVO, 1930), 31–32.

2. The calculation is based on *Yivo-bibliografye: 1925–1941* (New York: YIVO, 1943).

3. Zalmen Rejzen's biography differs from this paradigm, in that he did not distinguish himself as a political activist. However, he too did not receive a systematic higher education.

4. See their biographies in Rejzen, *Leksikon*, 1:331–39, 1207–10, 2:281–88.

5. Max Weinreich, *Shtaplen: Fir etyudn tsu der yidisher shprakh-visnshaft un literatur-geskhikhte* (Berlin: Vostok, 1923), 9, 18, 53. On Yiddish philologists' ignorance of German philology, see also his comments on pp. 13, 35–36.

6. On Weinrich's research in Jewish social psychology, see Barbara Kirshenblatt-Gimblett, "Coming of Age in the Thirties: Max Weinreich, Edward Sapir, and Jewish Social Science," *YIVO Annual* 23 (1996): 1–104.

7. *Barikht fun der konferents*, 35; see also 22–24, 84.

8. The term *sanctioned* is found in several documents from the early history of YIVO; see, for instance, *Tsvey yor arbet far dem yidishn visnshaftlekhn institut* (Vilna: YIVO, 1927), 8.

9. *Der alveltlekher tsuzamenfor fun yidishn visnshaftlekhn institut, tsum tsen yorikn yoyvl fun yivo* (Vilna: YIVO, 1936), 26.

10. *Barikht fun der konferents*, 33.

11. *Der alveltlekher tsuzamenfor*, 26.

12. Ibid., 64–66

13. *Der veg tsu undzer yugnt: yesoydes, metodn, problemen fun der yidisher yugnt-forshung* (Vilna: YIVO, 1935); see Max Weinreich, "Undzer aspirantur un ire perspektivn," *Yivo Bleter* 12 (1937): 559–64; Max Weinreich, "Di untershte shure funem ershtn yor aspirantur," *Yivo Bleter* 10 (1936): 99–102.

14. First quote, preface to vol. 2–3, *YIVO Anuual of Jewish Social Science* (New York: YIVO, 1947), ii. Second quote, foreword to vol. 5, *YIVO Annual of Jewish Social Science* (New York: YIVO, 1950), ii.

15. Max Weinreich, "Der yivo in zayn finftn tsendling," *Yediyes fun Yivo* 98 (1965): 6.

Chapter 10: Embers Plucked from the Fire

1. Dubnov, *Ob izuchenii*, 51.

2. Ibid., 76–77.

3. Simon M. Dubnov, *Nahpesa ve-nahkora: Kol kore el ha-nevonim ba-'am ha-mitnadvim le-'esof homer le-binyan toldot bene yisrael be-polin ve-rusiya* (Odessa: Ha-Pardes, 1892), 23–24.

4. On the *zamlers*, see the jubilee volume of *Yivo Bleter* 46 (1980): 49–57, 321–25. There were 163 registered circles of YIVO collectors in 1929. Literary portrayals of the collectors' work include Abraham Reisen's poem "Mir zamlen," first published in the *Forverts* in 1930 and reprinted in *Der yivo nokh draytsn yor arbet* (Vilna: YIVO, 1938), 23, and Abraham Karpinowitz's story "Der folklorist," in *Baym vilner durkh-hoyf* (Tel Aviv: I. L. Peretz, 1967), 69–82.

5. See "Einsatzstab Rosenberg," in *Encyclopedia of the Holocaust*, ed. Israel Gutman, 2:439–41 (New York: Macmillan, 1990); Max Weinreich, *Hitler's Professors* (New York: YIVO, 1946), 279; Herman Kruk, *Togbukh fun vilner geto*, ed. Mordecai W. Bernstein (New York: YIVO, 1961), 240.

6. Abraham Sutzkever, *Vilner geto*, 2nd ed. (Paris: Association of Vilna Jews in France, 1946), 108; Shmerke Kaczerginski, *Partizaner geyen!* 2nd ed. (Buenos Aires: Central Union of Polish Jews, 1947), 65–66. In the instances when Sutzkever's and Kaczerginski's accounts conflict regarding historical details, I have followed the former.

7. Kruk, *Togbukh*, 162–63, 178–79; Sutzkever, *Vilner geto*, 109.

8. Kruk, *Togbukh*, 178–79, 188.

9. Ibid., 200, 211. Staff figures are taken from Sutzkever, *Vilner geto*, 109, and Kaczerginski, *Partizaner geyen*, 66. Work at Universitetska 3 continued until at least May 1942, and the books of the Strashun Library were still kept there a year later, in April 1943. See Zelig Kalmanovitch, *Yoman be-geto vilna ve-ketavim min ha-'izavon she-nimtsa ba-harisot* (Tel Aviv: Moreshet-Sifriat Poalim, 1977), 101, 103.

10. Kruk, *Togbukh*, 272; Rokhl Pupko-Krinsky, "Mayn arbet in yivo unter di daytshn," *Yivo Bleter* 30 (1947): 214–23.

11. Sutzkever, *Vilner geto*, 110–11.

12. Kaczerginski, *Partizaner geyen*, 68; Kruk, *Togbukh*, 282, 300.

13. Pupko-Krinsky, "Mayn arbet," 217–19; Abraham Sutzkever, "A vort

tsum zekhtsikstn yoivl fun yivo," in *Baym leyenen penimer*, 206–7 (Jerusalem: Magnes, 1993).

14. Pupko-Krinsky, "Mayn arbet," 217–19; Shmerke Kaczerginski, *Ikh bin geven a partizan* (Bueno Aires: n.p., 1952), 53–57; Kalmanovitch, *Yoman*, 89, 94, 112.

15. Kaczerginski, *Partizaner geyen*, 69; Kaczerginski, *Ikh bin geven a partizan*, 41–42; Ruzhka Korczak, *Lehavot ba-'efer*, 2nd ed. (Tel Aviv: Ha-kibutz Ha-artzi, 1946), 110.

16. Sutzkever, *Vilner geto*, 111–12.

17. Ibid., 122–25, 229. Kruk wrote in his diary on July 9, 1942, "During the last two weeks alone I've obtained documents from the Ukrainian Ministry of Jewish Affairs, materials from the archives of Simon Dubnov, Ber Borochov, Noyekh Prilutski, a file of materials about Isaac Meir Dik, a file of Yiddish idioms, letters and manuscripts by Sholem Aleichem; manuscripts by David Einhorn, David Pinsky, S. L. Zitron, materials from Dr. Alfred Landau's [Yiddish] dictionary, photographs from YIVO's Yiddish theater museum, letters by Moyshe Kulbak, Sh. Niger, D. Charney, Chaim Zhitlovsky, Joseph Opatoshu, A. Leyeles, Zalmen Rejzen, Leon Kobrin, Moyshe Nadir, Marc Chagall, H. Leivik, Dr. Nathan Birnbaum, Yaakov Fichman, and Dr. Isidore Eliashev (Bal Makhshoves). This is only a small fraction of the material handed over. I'm recording it only to give a slight idea of our rescue-efforts. The risk undertaken when smuggling a piece of paper is enormous; every piece of paper can endanger one's life. But nonetheless, there are idealists who do the job skillfully. I'll mention these people at an appropriate time and record their names for future generations." Kruk, *Togbukh*, 300–301. On September 24, 1942, he added, "Smuggling work has recently intensified; the brigade of smugglers has grown by several times." Ibid., 351.

18. Korczak, *Lehavot ba-'efer*, 110; Sutzkever, *Vilner geto*, 112.

19. There are three versions of this incident, with slight variations: Sutzkever, *Vilner geto*, 220; Kaczerginski, *Partizaner geyen*, 71–72; Kaczerginski, *Ikh bin geven a partizan*, 45–52 (a fuller description); Pupko-Krinsky, "Mayn arbet," 220–21. See also Korczak, *Lehavot ba-'efer*, 109–11.

20. A first batch of YIVO documents was removed for shipment to Germany on October 25, 1942, and fifty crates of books were shipped to Frankfurt on November 17, 1942. Kalmanovich, *Yoman*, 73, 78, 85, 91. A second shipment of 9,403 books left for Germany on February 13, 1943. Kruk, *Togbukh*, 457. These materials were discovered in Germany after the war and returned by the U.S. government to YIVO in New York. See Davidowicz, *From That Place*. Kalmanovitch's diary includes numerous anguished entries on the destruction of valuable materials and their shipment to the paper mills in 1943. See *Yoman*, 75, 93, 100, 101, 110, 126. On distracting the guard, see Rokhl Pupko-Krinsky, "Mayn arbet," 219–20.

21. Kalmanovitch, *Yoman*, 126.

22. This account is based on Sutzkever, *Vilner geto*, 229–30; Abraham Sutzkever, "Vos mir hobn geratevet in vilne," *Eynikayt* (Moscow), October 12, 1944, reprinted as "Vi mir hobn geratevet dem yivo in vilne," *Eynikayt* (New York), February 1945; Shmerke Kaczerginski, *Tsvishn hamer un serp*, 2nd ed. (Buenos Aires: Der Emes, 1950), 37–45.

23. Sutzkever, "Vos mir hobn geratevet"; Kruk, *Togbukh*, xxviii–xxix.

24. Kaczerginski, *Tsvishn hamer un serp*, 45–51; Sutzkever, "A vort," 208–10.

25. Kaczerginski, *Tsvishn hamer un serp*, 97–102.

26. Ibid., 107–8, 110–12.

27. M. [sic] Kaczeginski, "A yor arbet funem yidishn muzey in Vilne," *Eynikayt* (Moscow), October 2, 1945. For an earlier survey of the museum's holdings, see A. Ayzen (Eisen), "Vilniuser yidisher muzey," *Eynikayt*, March 22, 1945.

28. Kaczerginski, *Tsvishn hamer un serp*, 112–13. By the time the Yiddish cultural activist Leyzer Ran returned to Vilna, in November 1945, Sutzkever and Kaczerginski were both gone, and the museum director was Yankl Gutkovicz. See Leyzer Ran, *Ash fun yerusholayim de-lite* (New York: Vilner Farlag, 1959), 174–75. On Sutzkever's and Kaczerginski's shipments of materials to New York through various intermediaries, see "Briv fun maks vaynraykh tsu avrom sutzkever," *Di Goldene Keyt* no. 95–96 (1978): 171–83. These materials have been preserved as a unit, as the Sutzkever-Kaczerginski collection of the YIVO Archives (RG 223).

29. Ran, *Ash fun yerushalayim de-lite*, 196. Ran's report is not completely accurate. The Jewish Museum's materials were transfered to several different Lithuanian archives and museums. The books, newspapers, and a small fraction of the documents were taken to the Book Chamber of the Lithuanian Soviet Republic. The Jewish Museum's final liquidation took place in July 1949. See Alexander Rindzuinski, "Vilna le-ahar ha-milhama (1944–1959)," *Yalkut Moreshet* 39 (May 1985): 55–84, esp. 59, 64–70.

30. On the history of the Jewish collections in the Book Chamber during the Soviet years, see *Yivo Bleter*, New Series, 1 (1991): 293–98.

31. Abraham Sutzkever, "Kerndlekh veyts," in *Yidishe gas* (New York: Matones, 1947), 32–33; English translation: "Grains of Wheat," in *A. Stuzkever: Selected Poetry and Prose*, trans. Barbara and Benjamin Harshav (Berkeley and Los Angeles: University of California Press, 1991), 156–58.

Selected Bibliography

Abramowicz, Hirsz. *Farshvundene geshtaltn*. Buenos Aires: Central Union of Polish Jews, 1956.

——. *Profiles of a Lost World: Memoirs of East European Jewish Life before World War II*. Detroit: Wayne State University Press, 1999.

Altshuler, Mordechai, ed. *Ha-teatron ha-yehudi be-vrit ha-mo'atsot*. Jerusalem: Center for Research and Documentation of East European Jewry, 1996.

——. *Soviet Jewry on the Eve of the Holocaust*. Jerusalem: Center for Research on East European Jewry and Yad Vashem, 1998.

Aronson, Gregor. *Rusish-yidishe inteligents*. Buenos Aires: Yidbukh, 1962.

Ascher, Abraham. *The Revolution of 1905: Russia in Disarray*. Palo Alto, CA: Stanford University Press, 1988.

Baron, Salo W. *The Jewish Community*. 3 vols. Philadelphia: Jewish Publication Society of America, 1943.

Bemporad, Elissa. "Da Letteratura del Popolo a Istoria del Popolo: Simon Dubnov e l'origine Della Storiografia Russo-Ebraica." *Annali Di Storia Dell' Esegesi* 18, no. 2 (2001): 533–57.

Berkowitz, Joel, ed. *Yiddish Theatre: New Approaches*. Oxford, UK, and Portland, OR: Littman Library of Jewish Civilization, 2003.

Borokhov, Ber. *Shprakh-Forshung un literatur-kritik*. Edited by Nachman Mayzel. Tel Aviv: I. L. Peretz, 1966.

Cammy, Justine. "Tsevorfene Bleter: The Emergence of Yung Vilne." *Polin* 14 (2001): 170–91.

Cohen, Nathan. *Sefer, sofer, ve-'iton: merkaz ha-tarbut ha-yehudit bevarsha, 1918–1942*. Jerusalem: Magnes, 2003.

——. "'Shund' and the Tabloids: Jewish Popular Reading in Inter-War Poland." *Polin* 16 (2003): 189–211.

Congress for Jewish Culture. *Fun noentn over: Monografyes un memuarn*. Vol. 2, *Yidishe prese in varshe*. New York: Congress for Jewish Culture, 1956.

Dawidowicz, Lucy. *From That Place and Time: A Memoir 1938–1947*. New York: W. W. Norton, 1989.

Dineson, Yankev. "Dos yidishe teater." In *Zikhroynes un bilder*. Warsaw: Ahisefer, 1927.

Dobrodzycki, Lucian. "Yivo in Inter-War Poland: Work in the Historical Sciences." In *The Jews of Poland between Two World Wars*, edited by Yisrael Gutman, 494–518. Hanover, NH: published for Brandeis University Press by University Press of New England, 1989.

Druk, Dovid. *Tsu der geshikhte fun der yudisher prese (in rusland un poyln)*. Warsaw: n.p., 1927.

Dubnov, Simon. *Fun zhargon tsu yidish*. Vilna: B. Kletskin, 1929.

——. *Kniga zhizni: vospominanie i razmyshlenie*. 3 vols., Riga: Jaunatas Granata, New York: Union of Russian Jews, 1934–1940.

——. *Ob izuchenii istorii ruskikh evreev i ob uchrezhdenii istoricheskogo obschestva.* St. Petersburg: n.p., 1891.

——. *Pisma o starom i novom evreistve.* St. Petersburg: Obshchestvennaia pol'za, 1907.

Dubnow, Simon. *History of the Jews in Russia and Poland.* 2nd ed. New York: Ktav, 1975.

——. *Nationalism and History: Letters on Old and New Judaism.* Edited and translated by Koppel S. Pinson. New York: Atheneum, 1970.

Estraikh, Gennady. "Languages of Yehupets Students." *East European Jewish Affairs* 22, no. 1 (1992): 63–71.

Fater, Issakhar. *Yidishe muzik in poyln tsvishn beyde velt-milkhomes.* Tel Aviv: World Federation of Polish Jews, 1970.

Fishman, David E. *Russia's First Modern Jews: The Jews of Shklov.* New York: New York University Press, 1995.

Fishman, Joshua A., ed. *Never Say Die: A Thousand Years of Yiddish in Jewish Life and Letters,* New York: Mouton, 1981.

——. *Yiddish: Turning to Life.* Philadelphia: John Benjamins, 1991.

——. *Yoivl band XLVI lekoved fuftsik yor yivo 1925–1975.* Special issue, *Yivo Bleter* 46 (1980).

Frankel, Jonathan. "The Dilemmas of Jewish Autonomism: The Case of Ukraine 1917–1920." In *Ukrainian-Jewish Relations in Historical Perspective,* edited by Peter J. Potychnyi and Howard Aster, 263–80. Edmonton: Canadian Institute of Ukrainian Studies, 1988.

——. *Prophecy and Politics: Socialism, Nationalism and the Russian Jews, 1862–1917.* Cambridge: Cambridge University Press, 1981.

Ginsburg, Saul. *Amolike peterburg.* New York: CYCO, 1944.

——. *Historishe verk.* 3 vols., New York: Saul Ginsburg Jubilee Committee, 1937.

Gitelman, Zvi. *Jewish Nationality and Soviet Politics: The Jewish Sections of the CPSU, 1917–1930.* Princeton, NJ: Princeton University Press, 1972.

Goldsmith, Emanuel. *Architects of Yiddishism at the Beginning of the Twentieth Century.* Rutherford, NJ: Farleigh Dickenson University Press, 1976. Reprinted as *Modern Yiddish Culture: The Story of the Yiddish Language Movement.* New York: Fordham University Press, 1987.

Golomb, A. *A halber yorhundert yidishe dertsiung.* Rio de Janeiro: Monte Scopus, 1957.

——. "Nokh a mol vegn religyezer dertsiyung." *Di Naye Shul,* September–October, 1922, 41–43.

——. "Di yidish-veltlekhe shul (algemeyner iberzikht)." In *Shul almanakh,* edited by H. Novak. Philadelphia: Central Committee of the Workmen's Circle Schools, 1935.

Gorin, B. *Di geshikhte fun yidishn teater.* New York: Max N. Meizl, 1918.

Gottesman, Itzik. *Defining the Yiddish Nation: The Jewish Folklorists of Poland.* Detroit: Wayne State University Press, 2003.

Gutman, M. "Tsi darf men lernen Hebreyish in folks-shul?" *Shul un Lebn* 3 (September 1921): 19–24.

Ha'am, Ahad. "Riv ha-leshonot." In *Al parashat derakhim,* vol. 4. Berlin: Juedischer Verlag, 1921.

Harshav, Benjamin. *Language in Time of Revolution.* Los Angeles: University of California Press, 1993.

Hertz, J. S. "Di umlegale prese un literatur fun 'Bund.'" In *Pinkes far der for-*

shung fun der yidisher literature un prese, vol. 2, edited by Hyman Bass, 294–366. New York: Congress for Jewish Culture, 1972.

Hoffman, Ben-Tziyon (Tsivyon). *Far fuftsik yor*. New York: Elias Laub, 1948.

Howe, Irving, and Eliezer Greenberg, eds. *Voices from the Yiddish: Essays, Memoirs, Diaries*. New York: Schocken, 1975.

Hurwitz, H. D. "Undzer ershte teglekhe tsaytung." In *Der pinkes: Yorbukh far der geshikhte fun der yidisher literatur un shprakh, far folklor, kritik un bibliografye*, edited by S. Niger. Vilna: B. Kletskin, 1913.

Janowsky, Oscar. *Nationalities and National Minorities (with Special Reference to East Central Europe)*. New York: MacMillan, 1945.

Kaczerginski, Shmerke. *Partizaner geyen!* 2nd ed. Buenos Aires: Central Union of Polish Jews, 1947.

———. *Ikh bin geven a partisan*. Buenos Aires: n.p., 1952.

Kassow, Samuel. "Jewish Community Politics in Transition: The Vilna *Kehile*, 1919–1920." *Yivo Annual* 20 (1991): 61–92.

Katz, Dovid. *Words on Fire: The Unfinished Story of Yiddish*. New York: Basic Books, 2004.

Katz, Jacob. *Tradition and Crisis: Jewish Society at the End of the Middle Ages*. 2nd ed. New York: New York University Press, 1993.

Kazhdan, H. S. *Di geshikhte fun yidishn shulvezn in umophengikn poyln*. Mexico City: Shul un Hilf, 1947.

———. "Di vegn fun undzer shul shafung." *Shul un Lebn* 2, no. 5 (October 1921): 8–12.

———. *Fun kheyder un shkoles biz tsisho*. Buenos Aires: Shloyme Mendelson Fund, 1956.

Kerler, Dov-Ber, ed. *Politics of Yiddish: Studies in Language, Literature and Society*. Walnut Creek, CA: Altamira, 1998.

Kiel, Mark. "A Twice Lost Legacy: Ideology, Culture and the Pursuit of Jewish Folklore in Russia until Stalinization." PhD diss., Jewish Theological Seminary of America, 1991.

Kirzhnits, Avrom, ed. *Der yidisher arbeter*. 4 vols. Moscow: Tsentraler Felker-Farlag fun FSSR, 1925–28.

———. *Di yidishe prese in der gevezener ruslendisher imperye*. Moscow: Tsentraler Felker-Farlag fun FSSR, 1930.

Kressel, G. "A historishe polemik vegn der yidisher literature." *Di Goldene Keyt* no. 20 (1954): 338–55.

Kultur-Lige. *Teater-bukh*. Kiev: Kultur-Lige, 1927.

Kuznitz, Cecille. "The Origins of Yiddish Scholarship and the YIVO Institute for Jewish Research." PhD diss., Stanford University, 2000.

Lederhendler, Eli. *The Road to Modern Jewish Politics*. New York: Oxford University Press, 1989.

Liessin, Avrom. *Zikhroynes un bilder*. New York: CYCO, 1954.

Linder, Menakhem. "Dos yidishe drukvezn in poyln in di yorn 1933–1934." *Yivo Bleter* 10 (1936): 303–12.

Litwak A. *Geklibene shriftn*. New York: Educational Committee of the Workmen's Circle, 1945.

———. *Vos geven: Etyudn un zikhroynes*. Vilna: B. Kletskin, 1925.

Lombroza, Shlomo. "The Pogroms of 1903–1906." In *Pogroms: Anti-Jewish Violence in Modern Russian History*, edited by John Klier and Shlomo Lambroza, 195–247. Cambridge: Cambridge University Press, 1992.

Manger, Itzik, ed. *Yidisher teater in Eyrope tsvishn beyde velt-milkhomes.* 2 vols., New York: Congress for Jewish Culture, 1968–69.

Marmor, K., ed. *A. liberman's briv.* New York: YIVO, 1951.

Mayer, Dovid. "Yidishe literarishe gezelshaft in varshe." *Undzer Tsayt* 17, no. 11–12 (1957): 104–6.

Mayzel, Nachman. "Dos yidishe bukh in 1923." *Bikher-velt* 2, no. 6 (1923): 509–16.

Medem, Vladimir. *Sotsiademokratiia i natsionalnii vopros.* St. Petersburg: Tribuna, 1906.

Mendelsohn, Ezra. *Class Struggle in the Pale.* Cambridge: Cambridge University Press, 1970.

——. *The Jews of East Central Europe between the Two World Wars.* Bloomington: Indiana University Press, 1983.

——. *Zionism in Poland: The Formative Years, 1915–1926.* New Haven, CT: Yale University Press, 1981.

Menes, Avrom. "Di mizrekh eyropeishe tkufe in der yidisher geshikhte." In *Algemeyne entsiklopedye — Yidn,* 4:275–430. New York: Jewish Encyclopedic Handbooks, 1950.

Mintz, M., ed. *Ha-ve'idah ha-shlishit shel poale-tziyon be-rusiyah, 1917.* Tel Aviv: Tel Aviv University, 1976.

Miron, Dan. *A Traveler Disguised: The Rise of Modern Yiddish Fiction in the 19th Century.* 2nd ed. Syracuse, NY: Syracuse University Press, 1996.

Moss, Kenneth. "Jewish Culture between Renaissance and Decadence: *Di Literarishe Monatshriftn* and its Critical Reception." *Jewish Social Studies* 8, no. 1 (2001): 153–98.

——. "A Time to Tear Down and a Time to Build Up: Recasting Jewish Culture in Eastern Europe, 1917–1921." PhD diss, Stanford University, 2003.

Nash, Stanley. *In Search of Hebraism: Shai Hurwitz and His Polemic in the Hebrew Press.* Leiden, Netherlands: E. J. Brill, 1980.

Nathans, Benjamin. *Beyond the Pale: The Jewish Encounter with Late Imperial Russia.* Berkeley: University of California Press, 2002.

Niger, S. *In kamf far a nayer dertsiung.* New York: Workmen's Circle, 1943.

——. *Yitskhok leybush perets.* Buenos Aires: Congress for Jewish Culture, 1952.

Nowersztern, Avraham. *Ha-sifrut veha-hayim: tsmikhata shel sifrut yidish hahadasha.* Unit 2 of *Le'an: zeramim hadashim bekerev yehude mizrah-eropa.* Tel Aviv: Open University of Israel, 2000.

Orbach, Alexander. *New Voices of Russian Jewry: A Study of the Russian Jewish Press in the Era of the Great Reforms.* Leiden, Netherlands: E. J. Brill, 1980.

Oyslender, N. *Yidisher teater 1887–1917.* Moscow: Der Emes, 1940.

Peretz, I. L. *Briv un redes,* edited by Nachman Mayzel, New York: YKUF, 1944.

Portnoy, Samuel, trans. and ed. *The Life and Soul of a Legendary Jewish Socialist: The Memoirs of Vladimir Medem.* New York: Ktav, 1979.

Prilutski, Noyekh. *Yidish teater, 1905–1912.* Bialistok: A. Albek, 1921.

Rafes, M. *Ocherki po istorii 'Bunda.'* Moscow: Moskovskii Rabochii, 1923.

Reinhartz, Yehuda, and Paul Mendes-Flohr. *The Jew in the Modern World.* Oxford: Oxford University Press, 1980.

Rejzen, Zalmen. "Der yidisher pen-klub in vilne." In *Vilner almanakh,* edited by A. I. Grodzenski. Vilna: Ovnt Kurier, 1939. Reprinted, New York: n.p., 1992.

——. *Leksikon fun der yidisher literatur, prese, un filologye.* 4 vols. Vilna: B. Kletskin, 1928–29.

Roskies, David G. *A Bridge of Longing: The Lost Art of Yiddish Storytelling.* Cambridge, MA: Harvard University Press, 1995.

Sandrow, Nahma. *Vagabond Stars: A World History of Yiddish Theatre.* 2nd ed. Syracuse, NY: Syracuse University Press, 1996.

Schaechter, Mordkhe. "Fun folkshprakh tsu kulturshprakh: An iberblik fun der historye funem eynhaytlekhn yidish oysleyg." In *Der eynhaytlekher yidisher oysleyg.* New York: YIVO and League for Yiddish, 1999.

Schulman, Elias. "Di tsaytshrift, 'Di yidishe velt.'" In *Pinkes far der forshung fun der yidisher literatur un prese*, vol. 1, edited by Sholyme Bikl, 122–70. New York: Congress for Jewish Culture, 1965.

———. *A History of Jewish Education in the Soviet Union.* New York: Ktav, 1971.

Shalit, M. "Statistik fun yidishn bikhermark in yor 1912." In *Der pinkes*, 277–306. Vilna: B. Kletskin, 1913.

Shatzky, Jacob, ed. *Arkhiv far der geshikhte fun yidishn teater un drame.* Vilna and New York: YIVO, 1930.

———. *Geshikhte fun yidn in varshe.* 3 vols. New York: YIVO, 1947–53.

———. *Hundert yor goldfaden.* New York: YIVO, 1940.

Shevelov, George Y. "The Language Question in the Ukraine in the Twentieth Century (1900–1941)." *Harvard Ukrainian Studies* 10, no. 1–2 (1986): 70–171.

Shmeruk, Chone. "Hebrew-Yiddish-Polish: A Trilingual Jewish Culture." In *The Jews of Poland between Two World Wars*, edited by Yisrael Gutman, Ezra Mendelsohn, Jehuda Reinharz, and Chone Shmeruk, 285–311. Hanover, NH: University Press of New England, 1989.

———. *Pirsumim yehudiim be-vrit ha-mo'atsot, 1917–1960.* Jerusalem: Israel Historical Society, 1961.

———. *Sifrut yiddish: Prakim le-toldoteha.* Tel Aviv: Porter Institute for Poetics and Semiotics, Tel Aviv University, 1978.

———. "Yiddish Literature in the USSR." In *The Jews in Soviet Russia Since 1917*, edited by Lionel Kochan. Oxford, London, and New York: Oxford University Press, 1978.

Slutsky, Yehuda. *Ha'itonut ha-yehudit rusit be-reshit ha-me'ah ha-'esrim.* Tel Aviv: Tel Aviv University Diaspora Research Institute, 1978.

Stanislawsky, Michael S. *Tsar Nicholas I and the Jews.* Philadelphia: Jewish Publication Society of America, 1983.

Steinlauf, Michael. "Fear of Purim: Y. L. Peretz and the Canonization of Yiddish Theatre," *Jewish Social Studies*, New Series, 1, no. 3 (1995): 44–65.

Sutzkever, Abraham. *Vilner geto.* 2nd ed. Paris: Association of Vilna Jews in France, 1946.

Szeintuch, Yechiel. *Preliminary Inventory of Yiddish Dailies and Periodicals Published in Poland between the Two World Wars.* Jerusalem: Center for Research on Polish Jewry, 1986.

Tambur, Volf. *Yidish-prese in rumenye.* Bucharest, Romania: Kriterion, 1977.

Tcherikower, Elias. "Di onheybn fun der umlegaler literatur in yidish." In *YIVO historishe shriftn*, 3: 577–603, edited by Elias Tscherikower. Vilna and Paris: YIVO, 1939.

———. *Istoria OPE 1863–1913.* St. Petersburg: OPE, 1913.

Tobias, Henry. *The Jewish Bund in Russia.* Palo Alto, CA: Stanford University Press, 1972.

Trunk, Isaiah. "Yivo un di yidishe historishe visnshaft." In *Yivo Bleter* 46 (1980): 242–54.

Turkow, Zigmund. *Di ibergerisene tekufe.* Buenos Aires: Central Union of Polish Jews, 1961.

Veidlinger, Jeffrey. *The Moscow State Yiddish Theatre.* Bloomington: Indiana University Press, 2000.

Vinter, Sh. "Vegn eynike bibliotek-tsifern." *Bikhervelt* 1, no. 6 (1928): 62–64.

Vital, David. *Zionism: The Formative Years.* Oxford, UK: Clarendon Press, 1988.

Weinreich, Max. "Der Bund un di yidishe shprakh." Reprinted in *Finf un-tsvantsik yor, 1897–1922,* 55–57. Warsaw: Di Welt, 1922.

———. *History of the Yiddish Language,* translated by Shlomo Noble (with the assistance of Joshua A. Fishman). Chicago: University of Chicago Press, 1980.

Weiser, Keith. *The Politics of Yiddish: Noyekh Prilutski and the Folkspartey in Poland, 1900–1926.* PhD diss., Columbia University, 2001.

Wisse, Ruth. *I. L. Peretz and the Rise of Modern Jewish Culture.* Seattle and London: University of Washington Press, 1991.

———. "Not the 'Pintele Yid' But the Full-Fledged Jew." *Prooftexts* 15, no. 1 (1995): 33–62.

Wolitz, Seth. "Di Khalyastre: The Yiddish Modernist Movement in Poland." *Yiddish* 4, no. 3 (1981): 5–19.

YIVO. *Di ershte yidishe shprakh-konferents.* Vilna: YIVO, 1931.

Zborowski, Mark, and Elizabeth Herzog. *Life is With People.* New York: International Universities Press, 1952.

Zhitlowsky, Chaim. *Gezamlte shriftn.* 10 vols. New York: Zhitlowsky Jubilee Committee, 1912–19.

Zilberfarb, M. "Neotlozhnie zadachi evreiskoi obshchini." *Evreiskii Mir* 1 (July 1909): 1–14.

Zinberg, Israel. *History of Jewish Literature,* edited and translated by Bernard Martin, 12 vols. Cleveland: Press of Case Western Reserve University, 1978. Translation of *Geshikhte fun der literatur bay yidn.* 2nd ed., 8 vols. New York: Morris S. Sklarsky, 1943.

Zipperstein, Steven. *Elusive prophet: Ahad Ha'am and the Origins of Zionism.* Berkeley and Los Angeles: University of California Press, Berkeley-Los Angeles, 1993.

———. "Haskalah, Cultural Change and 19th Century Russian Jewry: A Reassessment." *Journal of Jewish Studies* 34, no. 2 (1983): 191–207.

———. *The Jews of Odessa: A Cultural History.* Stanford, CA: Stanford University Press, 1985.

Zitron, S. L. *Di geshikhte fun der yidisher prese.* Warsaw: Ahiasaf, 1923.

———. *Dray literarishe doyres.* 4 vols. Vilna: S. Srebernik, 1928.

Zylbercweig, Zalmen. *Leksikon fun yidishn teater.* 6 vols. New York: Elisheva, 1931–69.

Index